HOMER

and the

DUAL MODEL *of the* TRAGIC

HOMER

and the

DUAL MODEL *of the* TRAGIC

Yoav Rinon

THE UNIVERSITY OF MICHIGAN PRESS   ANN ARBOR

Copyright © by the University of Michigan 2008
All rights reserved
Published in the United States of America by
The University of Michigan Press
Manufactured in the United States of America
ⓒ Printed on acid-free paper

2011   2010   2009   2008   4   3   2   1

A CIP catalog record for this book is available from the British Library.

Library of Congress Cataloging-in-Publication Data

Rinon, Yoav.
      Homer and the dual model of the tragic / Yoav Rinon.
         p. cm.
      Includes bibliographical references and index.
      ISBN-13: 978-0-472-11663-8 (cloth : alk. paper)
      ISBN-10: 0-472-11663-0 (cloth : alk. paper)
         1. Homer—Criticism and interpretation.   2. Tragic, The, in
literature.   3. Absurd, The, in literature.   I. Title.

PA4037.R56   2008
883'.01—dc22   2008015030

TO *Hannah Cotton*

Acknowledgments

This book originated in research initiated during a 1997 postdoctoral fellowship at Balliol College of Oxford University, with Professor Jasper Griffin as host. I am greatly indebted to Professor Griffin for his personal kindness and intellectual magnanimity during that period and much after. The humane insights of his classic text, *Homer on Life and Death* (Oxford, 1980), have profoundly influenced my own conception of the *Iliad* and the *Odyssey*, as evident in this book.

The project began in Oxford and continued in Israel, funded in 2003–5 by a very generous three-year grant from the Israel Science Foundation (ISF), founded by the Israel Academy of Sciences and Humanities. I gratefully acknowledge the ISF's contribution to the realization of this project.

While working on *Homer and the Dual Model of the Tragic*, I was supported by friends and colleagues whose encouragement was essential to its completion. I would like to thank Margalit Finkelberg and Deborah Levine Gera for their professional advice and personal interest. Nita Schechet, as always, was an endless source of inspiration, and her acute responses enabled me to better formulate my ideas and to get rid of some very long passages that were "sent before their time into this breathing world, scarce half made up." In addition, I was blessed with two generously attentive anonymous readers who gave me many excellent suggestions that greatly improved my argument. I also wish to thank Chris Hebert, Ellen Bauerle, Mary Hashman, and Alexa Ducsay of the University of Michigan Press for their highly professional and extremely efficient production of this book. All remaining mistakes are, of course, my responsibility.

Last but not least, I would like to thank my family: my parents, Shlomo and Yardena Rinon; my daughter Danielle; and my life partner, Gershon Lanzberg, for their boundless sustenance.

This book is dedicated to Hannah Cotton, my teacher, my mentor, and most of all my friend, whose constant and indefatigable support enabled me to safely cross that sea of troubles, "the tenure track."

The following chapters are based on earlier and previously published essays, for which permission is gratefully acknowledged as follows.

Chapter 1: Harvard University Press for "A Tragic Pattern in the Iliad," from *Harvard Studies in Classical Philology*, vol. 104, edited by Nino Luraghi (2008).

Chapter 3: The Johns Hopkins University Press for "The Pivotal Scene: Narration, Colonial Focalization, and Transition in *Odyssey* 9," *American Journal of Philology* 128 (2007): 301–34.

Chapter 5: Koninklijke Brill N.V. for "*Mise en abyme* and Tragic Signification in the *Odyssey:* The Three Songs of Demodocus," *Mnemosyne* 59 (2006): 208–25.

Chapter 6: *Phoenix, Journal of the Classical Association of Canada* for "Tragic Hephaestus: The Humanized God in the *Iliad* and the *Odyssey*," *Phoenix* 40 (2006): 1–20.

I would also like to thank the Museo Nacional del Prado for permission to use Velázquez's *La Fragua de Vulcano* for the jacket design.

Contents

Introduction

$\mathcal{W}$hile ancient tragic drama has drawn much theoretical attention, the notion of the tragic, whose philosophical potential is realized in Attic tragedy, has consistently been marginalized in literary discourse. The paucity of theoretical discussion of the tragic is both pervasive and enduring. Even in antiquity, where the nature and features of at least two generic realizations of the tragic (the epic and tragic drama) were a source of ongoing reflection and argumentation, there were only brief references to and little conceptualization of the tragic.[1] This is evident in the Scholia on ancient drama, where *tragikos* (τραγικός) or *tragikôs* (τραγικῶς) usually function as adjective or adverb, meaning "suitable for tragedy" or "in a way suitable for tragedy." The latter describe either a word or a phrase,[2] a dance,[3] or things associated with the production of tragic drama (*opsis tragikê*)[4] or they focus on reception and the effect of tragic drama on its spectators.[5] Aristophanes' *Frogs,* a comedy in which there is a heated debate between two leading tragedians, Aeschylus and Euripides, offers little theoretical guidance. Stephen Halliwell elucidates this thus: "The leading themes of the debate, precisely because they revolve around a generalized conception of the fine, civically useful poet, bring with them no genre-specific standards of distinctively tragic qualities, let alone a more abstract consciousness of 'the tragic' as a form of *Weltanschauung.*"[6] References to tragic poetry in Aristophanic comedies are similarly conceptually evasive.[7] Contemporary critical discourse, while rich and fertile on the subject of ancient tragedy, is surprisingly taciturn on the topic of the tragic as a distinct field of research. The meager extant theoretical discourse has its own conceptual problems. To quote Halliwell once more:

> Conceptions of tragedy that base themselves on a theory of "the tragic" (*das Tragische* or *die Tragik*) are associated especially with a line of thought that derives from German idealism and romanticism, a line that connects, in this respect, Schelling, Hegel, Schopenhauer, and Nietzsche, to name the most prominent figures in this tradition. [. . .] One commonly drawn corollary of the Germanic cast of interest in the tragic is the claim that while ancient Greece created the first and most concentrated tradition of dramatic tragedy, it lacked anything that can be classified as an explicit notion of the tragic.[8]

The absence of the notion of the tragic is a strangely persistent lacuna in critical discourse on tragic drama in Ancient Greece. This is the space engaged by this book.

I therefore begin by distinguishing between the tragic and its eponymous genre (tragedy), hoping to clarify a frequent conceptual conflation.[9] The tragic is a potential with diverse artistic realizations, and it appears in works other than those generically labeled as tragic. By concentrating on the tragic as a characteristic rather than on tragedy as a genre, a wide field of artistic representations unrestricted by generic dictates is opened. The tragic can be traced in the novel or film, while in drama it is not confined by definitions of tragedy: a component of tragicomedy, it can also be found in a history or revenge play, as well as in comedy.

I define the tragic as a worldview reflecting the precarious position of the human being in a world determined by two factors, time and the divine, over which he or she has almost no influence. Since time and the divine affect lives separately and in tandem, the tragic can be realized either through the effects of time, by means of divine intervention, or as a result of both. The model I propose for conceptualizing the artistic realization of this worldview consists of a pattern of events relating characters' behavior to these two factors, separately and in combination, and a view of characterization that sheds light on the tragic human condition. I also contend that this model generally has a didactic aspect that links the precariousness of the human with a humane perspective.

The basic duality of this model of the tragic refers to a movement on the axis of time between two poles of contrasting states of luck, good and ill. The tragic is a reflection of this movement regardless of its points of departure and termination. In other words, whether the movement opens with good luck and ends in ill luck or proceeds in the opposite direction, from ill luck to good luck, is irrelevant to this model. Both movements are equally tragic.[10] In fact, as we shall see, it is exactly this indifference to the direction of the movement that is an essential element of the notion of the tragic.

I derive the above axis of luck from Aristotle's *Poetics* (1451a12–15), a treatise whose insights and formulations are indispensable to my theoretical framework. My usage of this text in general, as well as my reasons for adopting this specific axis, will be dealt with shortly. At this point of my discussion, I wish to elucidate the two opposing poles of the axis, good and ill luck. My English translation reflects the Greek original, where both terms have a common root to which a prefix is added in order to create a dual concept. The Greek root is *tuchia,* which is derived from *tuche,* "chance" or "luck," and the prefix is either *eu,* which means "best," or *dus,* which means "bad." Thus, the two poles, *eutuchia* and *dustuchia,* are those of "good luck" and "ill luck." These words are often and judiciously translated as "prosperity" and "disaster," implying that prosperity and disaster, at least within the domain of the tragic axis of time, are outcomes of chance.[11] According to this model, it is the indifferent component of luck or chance that characterizes the two extreme poles of an individual's life. Chance is indifferent because it is arbitrary, marked by the absence of any detectable reason for the occurrence of an event or phenomenon. The tragic model teaches that one cannot explain why one's life leads either to prosperity or to disaster, concomitantly stressing the inability to pinpoint a satisfactory reason for the vector of the movement from good to ill luck or vice versa. This incapacity is a given, a fact of the human condition that one must accept.[12] The tragic therefore reflects a double helplessness regarding both itinerary and final destination. Note that while the question of whether one's life leads to good luck or to ill luck is crucial to the individual, the tragic lesson emphasizes the impossibility of acquiring this indispensable information at the right time. Moreover, when one does know one's position, it is always late. The question (and here the duality of the model is again apparent) is whether it is almost too late or already too late.[13]

In ancient Greek there is a special term for synchronization that has become a *terminus technicus* in rhetoric for the skill of identifying and utilizing the right time for one's purposes: *kairos.*[14] In a seminal paper, John E. Smith defines *kairos* in opposition to *chronos.*

Chronos expresses the fundamental conception of time as measure, the *quantity* of duration; [. . .] *kairos* points to a *qualitative* character of time, to the special position an event or action occupies in a series, to a season when something appropriately happens that cannot happen at "any" time, but only at "that time," to a time that marks opportunity which may not recur.[15]

He refines his definition of *kairos* in the following way.

Three distinct, but related, concepts are involved in the notion of *kairos*. It means, first, the "right time" for something to happen in contrast with "any time"; [. . .] Second, *kairos* means a time of tension or conflict, a time of "crisis" implying that the course of events poses a problem which calls for a decision at that time. Third, *kairos* means a time when opportunity for accomplishing some purpose has opened up as a result of the problem that led to the crisis. Thus *kairos* means *the time when* something should happen or be done, the "right" or "best" time.[16]

The essence of the tragic lies, therefore, in an individual's relation to time, marked by an ineluctably ill synchronization or a core lack in relation to *kairos*. What should be emphasized is the unavoidable nature of this ill synchronization. It is impossible to learn to be attuned to time so as never to err. This flaw, this error of interpretation regarding time that Aristotle (in a different context) termed *hamartia,* is an inherent component of human nature and an inalienable element of human destiny.[17] It is not just that *errare humanum est* but that erring in such a crucial matter as comprehension of the nature of time is actually part of what defines a human being as such. If we are lucky, we can still put this belated understanding to use; if we are not, then we will have to live with an irreparable wound caused by an irredeemable loss.[18] Note that this essential characteristic of the tragic is not associated with the divine. Poor synchronization (and, of course, an irrevocable missed opportunity) can derive from the malevolent intervention of a godly power, but it is not necessarily so. The tragic can be realized either due to the effects of time alone or because of its association with divine intervention, and both cases are valid manifestations of the tragic.

In response to the problematic of literary discourse described earlier—the tendency to conflate the tragic with only one of its realizations (tragedy)—I have constructed my tragic model on a foundation of texts that do not belong to the genre of tragic drama. My choice of the *Iliad* and the *Odyssey* to exemplify and investigate my conception of the tragic demonstrates its freedom from the confines of genre by focusing on these epics rather than tragic drama. This is not the sole reason for my selection; the two epics have other advantages. Chronologically, the *Iliad* and the *Odyssey* are the earliest surviving exemplars of the tragic in Western culture.[19] Moreover, it is these texts that have shaped and influenced subsequent representations of the tragic both in Ancient Greece (in profound and fertile ties to tragic drama) and later in the novel. As far as the notion of *kairos* is concerned, all three interpretations of *kairos* (the "right time" for something to happen, a time of tension or conflict, and a time when opportunity for accomplishing some purpose has opened up) are prevalent in the *Iliad* and the *Odyssey*, although the word itself is absent from both.[20]

I would underscore in this context that my conception of the tragic aspires to transcend the limits of concrete spaces and times. While deeply and specifically anchored in two epics realized within the limits of a particular culture, my model of the tragic is general. Characters such as Achilles, Hector, or Telemachus and events such as the Trojan War or Odysseus' late homecoming are exemplary, presented as reflections, albeit concrete and subjective, of the general unhappy human condition. This is why this book is not engaged with questions such as the origins of tragic sensibility in archaic Aegean culture or the association between the tragic and the society in which the poems were composed (or their real audience). Such queries are beyond the scope of a model whose focal point is the inevitable common unhappiness of human beings stemming directly from the fact of their humanness.[21]

I noted earlier that the relationship of the *Iliad* and the *Odyssey* to Attic tragedy is evident to writers, critics, and audiences, ancient and modern, who view these epics as the forebears of tragic drama. Plato, for one, regarded the poet of these works as "the first teacher and guide to all tragic beauty" (τῶν καλῶν ἁπάντων τούτων τῶν τραγικῶν πρῶτος διδάσκαλός τε καὶ ἡγεμών *Rep.*x 595c1–2) and considered him "the preeminent" (*akros*) poet of tragedy (*Theaet.* 152e4–5).[22] Aristotle refers to this poet's work as exemplary of the technique of tragic writing, lauding his "keen perception" in organizing the *Odyssey* around a single action (8.1451a23–30) and calling the composer "divine" (*thespesios*) in reference to his construction of events in the *Iliad* (23.1459a30–37). So do Scholia A and T who, commenting on the opening of the *Iliad*, state that the poet "invented a tragic prologue for his tragedies" (τραγῳδίαις τραγικὸν ἐξεῦρε προοίμιον).[23] Contemporary analyses of the *Iliad* follow principles similar to those of their ancient predecessors.[24]

There are two somewhat limited exceptions to the pervasive silence of ancient writers regarding the tragic. As noted briefly earlier, Plato and Aristotle offer some leads that I will occasionally follow in this book. On Plato's conception of the tragic, Halliwell's attentive analysis of the topic is exquisitely exhaustive.[25] I therefore summarize his conclusions briefly here. The tragic, according to Plato, is a conception of life, a philosophy *in embryo,* in which human lives are governed by forces either indifferent or malevolent vis-à-vis individual happiness. Thus, in the *Phaedo,* Socrates' death is conceived as an evil representative of a general phenomenon, that of the irreversible loss of something supremely treasured, which, in its turn, appallingly affects the fragile fabric of human values. In like manner, tragic heroes in the *Republic* (605d1–2) are envisaged as characters whose lot elicits grief as well as rage against divine callousness regarding the human condition. Suffering is also a major component in the Platonic conception of the tragic, and it has a distinctive character that defines it as specifically tragic.

> One obvious but far-reaching fact about tragic suffering is that it is almost always witnessed and responded to within the dramatic context of tragedy, most often by the chorus. This means that suffering is not just shown in its raw state but already to some extent *interpreted* in the immediate environment of the events. And one distinctively tragic interpretation of suffering—the interpretation which Plato has in mind both in *Republic* 10 and in other passages [. . .]—is the translation of a particular *pathos,* a particular injury to the fabric of life, into a symbol of the limits of the human condition in general.[26]

As the following will demonstrate, Halliwell's formulation of Platonic tragic suffering, though based on tragic drama, is also applicable to the epics under discussion here. In like manner, Halliwell's emphasis on irretrievable loss educing both grief and rage is also relevant to the tragic model conceptualized in this book, where both the event and the emotional states it triggers are pertinent.

As noted earlier, Aristotle's *Poetics* is also a prime source for my own tragic model. The philosopher's frequent reference to the *Iliad* and the *Odyssey* derives from his assumption that the epics delineate a "schema," or model, later utilized by the poets of tragic drama (*Poetics* 1448b36–1449a2). I shall soon discuss this passage in more detail, but first I would like to consider an essential aspect of this Aristotelian text, its prescriptive nature.

Aristotle's principles of judgment and valuation are based on his notions of the ideal function of tragic drama and the ways it can ameliorate the lives of its audience. Yet in the construction of a tragic model these principles, while impressively formulated, raise several questions. Among them is the range of works the philosopher deems relevant to his argumentation, a problem succinctly articulated by one of the *Poetics'* greatest modern admirers, Gerald F. Else.

> It so happened the knife-edge of his [Aristotle's] judgment hit square on one masterpiece, the *Oedipus* [. . .] and meanwhile masterpieces like the *Trojan Women* or the *Bacchae,* to say nothing of the *Oedipus at Colonus* or the *Agamemnon,* remain outside the range of Aristotle's formula. This is not the way one can arrive at an organic comprehension of the best of Greek drama.[27]

Margalit Finkelberg, commenting on this passage, extends Else's reservations and notes that his words are a

> harsh verdict, to be sure, but hardly undeserved. If anything, it is perhaps even too restricted, for it is not only the *Trojan Women* and the *Bacchae,* the *Oedipus at Colonus* and the *Agamemnon* that Aristotle ignores or finds objectionable. He ignores the entire genre of lyric poetry and practically the entire oeuvre of Aeschylus, and he hardly even mentions the choral odes of tragedy. His comments on the so-called Cyclic epics are negative throughout [. . .] [a]nd he strongly disapproves of episodic tragedy.[28]

Obviously, in a model that is intended to reflect a general worldview, Aristotle's restrictions limit that achievement. And yet one can extract some very useful information about ancient sources and conceptions now lost to us from his treatise. It is true that the *Poetics* offers a theory biased and bound by prescriptive rules, but it is not wholly prescriptive. The *Poetics* contains many descriptive sections, and it is to these, especially when they are either explicitly or implicitly associated with the epics, that the critic should attend.

One such passage is Aristotle's perception of the *Odyssey* as no less a paradigm of tragedy than the *Iliad,* suggesting a dual model of the tragic. While the *Odyssey* is perceived as a representation of the comic rather than as a depiction of the tragic in contemporary scholarly discourse,[29] Aristotle's statement asserts both the *Iliad* and the *Odyssey* as the paradigms of tragedy.[30] He claims that the poet of these epics "was the first to mark out the paradigm (*schema*) of comedy by putting into dramatic form not the invective but the ridiculous; for the *Margites* is analogous to comedy just as the *Iliad* and the *Odyssey* are analogous to tragedy" (*Poetics* 1448b36–1449a2).

What should be underlined in this context is the self-evident way in which Aristotle presents the *Iliad* and the *Odyssey* as on par with reference to their tragic nature. If Aristotle had deemed his perception of the *Odyssey* as a tragic epic innovative or novel, he would have emphasized and reiterated it. This is what he does, for example, in his numerous references to the notion and definition of *mythos*. The fact that he explicitly mentions the tragic aspect of both epics only once, and even then as a parenthesis to his theory of the development of genres, attests to a shared cultural perception. Apparently the audience in the fourth century B.C. agreed, and so should we, despite the current contrasting *communis opinio*.[31]

Another aspect relevant to the tragic model described in this book, which is also linked with its dual nature, finds expression in a descriptive part of the *Poetics* dealing with the sequence of events in tragedy. I refer here to the above-mentioned delineation of two possible and opposing movements on an axis whose poles are associated with luck: good (*eutuchia*) and ill (*dustuchia*). In first mentioning this axis, in chapter seven, Aristotle restricts himself to the domain of the descriptive: a character can move from either pole to the other (1451a12–15). Somewhat later Aristotle returns to this definition in two successive chapters, thirteen and fourteen, yet here the movements are incorporated in a prescriptive discussion: in chapter thirteen he prefers the movement from *eutuchia* to *dustuchia* (1453a12–15), while in chapter fourteen he prefers the movement from *dustuchia* to *eutuchia* (1454a4–9). Such a blunt contrast within such a short textual span has not escaped the critics who have tried to reconcile the two.[32] Whatever the answer to this conundrum—and it is dubious whether it can ever be definitive—all three references indicate that Aristotle discerned two possible movements on the *eutuchia-dustuchia* axis in the great mass of tragedies he had read. Both were pervasive, and both seemed potentially the best. Note that the *Poetics* presents two exemplary tragedies: *Oedipus Rex,* where the hero moves from *eutuchia* to *dustuchia,* and *Iphigenia in Tauris,* where the protagonists move from *dustuchia* to *eutuchia.* This descriptive point of his theory fits not only the Greek tragedies that have survived and reached us but also the scant knowledge we have about those tragedies that are now lost.[33] It is also a description of the two movements in the *Iliad* and the *Odyssey,* where the former represents the vector *eutuchia* to *dustuchia* and the latter its opposite. It is reasonable to conclude that both movements were conceived by ancient writers and critics as tragic, as I claim for my dual model of the tragic.[34]

There are two other tragic components that Aristotle enumerates in a descriptive part of his treatise that are relevant to my model: suffering (*pathos,* 1452b11–13), already mentioned in association with Plato's conception of the tragic; and recognition (*anagnorisis,* 1452a29–32). Suffering is defined as a "destructive or painful act,"[35] and recognition is defined as a change or transition (*metabolê*) from ignorance to knowledge that leads either to great affiliation or intimacy on the one hand, or to hatred or enmity on the other.[36] This transition is closely linked with the tragic poles of *eutuchia* and *dustuchia.* These features, as noted by Aristotle, can be traced in the *Iliad* and the *Odyssey,* and, although they appear as part of a prescriptive section of the *Poetics* (Aristotle compliments the poet on his superb handling of these components, 1459b12–15), they are also descriptive. Both suffering and recognition are recurrent motifs in the subsequent analyses of the *Iliad* and the *Odyssey,* and their various appearances and different functions will serve in the demonstration of the tragic model that is the substance of this book.

While the notion of suffering is sufficiently explained by Aristotle, my concept of recognition modifies it into three types. This calls for further clarification, especially in light of this divergence from its Aristotelian origin, *anagnorisis.* In contrast with current broad applications of the notion of *anagnorisis,* Aristotle's definition refers to a very limited aspect of recognition that takes place within the context and agency of the physical world and pertains to one's status and relationship to fellow beings. Thus, Odysseus is recognized in the *Odyssey* as Odysseus, the king of the Ithacans, the husband of Penelope, and the father of Telemachus. That this recognition is occasionally achieved by means of physical signs—either as marks on the body, for which Odysseus' scar is an emblem, or, as happens in later literature, by means of definitively associated objects—exemplifies the Aristotelian notion in the specificity of its original meaning: one's relation to the physical world is marked by and incarnated in physical signs.[37] I therefore term this type of recognition "physical recognition."

The second category of recognition, one not mentioned by Aristotle, refers to a deeper level of recognition relating to an individual's understanding of his or her actions. Such recognition, which can be cognitive or emotional or both, reflects insight into the motives and implications of one's own conduct not easily perceived due to deeply rooted psychological hindrance. An example of this type of recognition in the *Iliad* is Achilles' admission of his error in adhering to his anger, an adherence that ultimately led to the death of his beloved friend Patroclus (28.107–13). I term this "psychological recognition."

The third type of recognition coined here, and also absent from Aristotle's treatise, is termed "metaphysical recognition" and refers to an individual's relationship with the domain beyond the physical. As noted briefly earlier, this recognition can be realized in the context of one's relationship with the divine, but it can also reflect acknowledgment of the power of time and its inevitably harrowing afflictions. Metaphysical recognition is therefore a deep cognizance of one's total subjection to the gods, fate, or time, powers either indifferent or, most commonly, hostile to individual success and happiness. An example of this type is Nestor's recognition that both the nine long years of suffering by the shores of Troy and the quarrel between Agamemnon and Menelaus that followed the fall of the city (and led, in turn, to even more suffering) were contrived by Zeus (*Od.* 3.118–19, 130–34, 151–52).[38]

With my preliminary definition of the tragic and explication of choice of texts in construction of my model in mind, I now turn briefly to questions of methodology. Since the process of configuration of my model of the tragic is first and foremost a textual one, all the following chapters engaged in extensive close readings of various parts of the epics. Consequently, there are several illustrations that recount considerable parts of the poems. This somewhat conservative strategy is essential to my demonstration, for the magnificent subtlety of the texts requires intensive ferreting in anchoring the formulation and realization of the model. In addition to tracking the components mentioned earlier in order to construct an integrated model of the tragic, my methodology applies a novel narratological tool that enables me to approach the texts from diverse angles. This is Nita Schechet's concept of *fissures*, "sites of textual entry" or "openings into textual intentionality" through which the reader is activated to reflect on the text as a whole.[39] Each of the following chapters engages the texts through a different fissure or fissures, thereby shedding new light on the topics under discussion. Strongly anchored in the text, the various exegetical routes marked by these fissures finally converge in the text's tragic signification. The exact nature of these fissures will become apparent in the next chapters in the process of reading the texts in illustration of my conception of the tragic.

But before setting aside the theoretical and turning to the epics, I refer summarily to that unavoidable Gordian knot of "the Homeric Question." This sorry "question" concentrates on the problem of authorship: given the elusive nature of authorial identity within the context of the composition of oral poetry, who composed these poems or fragments that were later collated as epics? The question, to my mind, is insoluble,[40] which is why I have chosen one of the accepted methods of discussing these texts, namely, to regard each singly. During the process of reading that is the substance of the book, traces of the oral tradition will be detected and then integrated within the broader exegetical movement.[41] I share the belief of many critics that the poet of the *Odyssey*, regardless of whether he is also the poet of the *Iliad*, was well acquainted with it and that the *Odyssey* is in many respects a thoughtful commentary on the Trojan War epic.[42] There is, however, one aspect of this much discussed question that I find persuasive: the name Homer is misleading. As concluded by Graziosi in her masterful study of the topic, the name Homer does not signify a historical figure but rather the need "to link the poems to particular audiences and places; but [. . .] these links fail to establish themselves to the exclusions of others, because the poems do not make any claims about their author."[43] I therefore avoid naming the poet or poets of the epics throughout, referring merely to the *Iliad* and the *Odyssey* or "the poet of the *Iliad*" and "the poet of the *Odyssey*."

Since the dual model finds its expression in two epics, one might expect my itinerary to start with one and then move toward the other, especially since the epics are, at least with regard to the story, two consecutive texts. However, my presentation of the model follows a different organization, which I find more advantageous to my purposes.[44] In chapter 1, I begin with a discussion of a tragic pattern in the *Iliad*, using its opening frame as a fissure from which to view the narrative's tragic signification. Exposing this pattern reveals the characteristics of tragic time as well as its essential contribution in the construction of the epic as a tragic text. This chapter also depicts the function of suffering and recognition, both psychological and metaphysical, in the general tragic fabric of the *Iliad*. In chapters 2 and 3, I concentrate on the *Odyssey*. In chapter 2, I trace these same two motifs of suffering and recognition. Using them as key fissures, I claim that their ubiquity in the *Odyssey* attests to the general tragic character of the epic in a manner similar to (though not identical with) the tragic pattern in the *Iliad*. In chapter 3, I read a single seminal scene, the Cyclops episode, where I again track the motif of time and its function in the epic. The central fissure in this part is textual heteroglossia, a neologism coined by Mikhail Bakhtin to describe a double-voiced discourse that expresses two different intentions simultaneously, one embedded in Odysseus' first-person narration and the other rooted in the context of the text's framing third-person narration. This fissure leads to the mapping of an aspect of the tragic generated by the concomitant representation of two contrasting worldviews and their ineluctable contention.

Both chapters on the *Odyssey* perceive this work as an epic of survival where the notion of heroic value has gone through a considerable process of change. This reading enables me to view the motif of heroism in a new light through its representation in the epic, which seems unequivocally to epitomize it. The analysis of this theme in the *Odyssey* is followed by a turn back to the *Iliad* in chapter 4 in order to demonstrate that this text is no less subtle than the *Odyssey* in its conception of heroic valor. Three central fissures are employed here in interpreting heroism: characterization, permanent textual gaps, and the motif of flight.

Thus far, I have concentrated on the textual fissures of framing, repetition, and heteroglossia in demonstration of my tragic model. Chapters 5 and 6 utilize a different kind of fissure generated by reflexivity, that is, the strategies established and displayed by the poem as keys to its own reading. Chapter 5 uses the narratological technique of *mise en abyme* in the three songs of Demodocus in book eight of the *Odyssey* as a fissure through which it describes the poem's tragic signification. *Mise en abyme,* coined by André Gide, has become a narratological term denoting a certain part of a literary work of art that represents the work as a whole. My focus in chapter 5 is on three aspects of *mise en abyme* represented in the bard's three songs. Chapter 6, which concludes my readings of the epics and discusses both the *Iliad* and the *Odyssey,* considers another aspect of reflexivity and the tragic through the fissure of characterization in the portrayal of Hephaestus. Here I examine the function of Hephaestus' artistic creativity in the emergence of tragic signification and consider the link between art, especially poetry, and the humane. The final chapter is devoted to the description of my dual model of the tragic founded on the readings that precede it.

A final few bibliographical notes: I have translated the Greek into English for the non-Greek reader. In those instances where word choice and translation issues are central, I have also transliterated the Greek concepts or phrases and marked them in italics. In those few cases where long phrases are crucial to the discussion, and where lengthy transliteration would be tiresome for the non-Greek reader, I cite the Greek original in addition to its translation. All references and citations of the *Iliad* are to Martin L. West, ed., *Homerus: Ilias* (Stuttgart: Teubner, 1998–2000); all references and citations of the *Odyssey* are to T. W. Allen, ed., *Homeri opera*[2] (Oxford: Clarendon, 1917). I follow West's edition in using iota adscript when quoting the *Iliad* and Allen's edition in using iota subscript when quoting the *Odyssey*; all citations and references to the *Poetics* are to Lucas's edition. All citations and references to Scholia on the *Iliad* are to Erbse's edition. All translations from all languages are my own unless otherwise noted.

Let us go, now, to the texts.

I

A Tragic Pattern in the *Iliad*

Missed Kairos, *Misunderstandings, and Missing the Dead*

*I*n my introductory chapter I emphasized the importance of the notion of time in theorizing the tragic, claiming that its contribution is illuminated by a reading of the epics. The aim of this chapter is to consider the function of time in the *Iliad* and its fundamental contribution to the tragic in this text. I do this through the delineation of a pattern of events at the core of the epic that affects its general construction, as well as its signification, and in which time has a central role. The pattern is tragic in its association of three components that have already been mentioned and will continue to be explored: time, human suffering, and recognition. As I claim in my introduction, the tragic is marked by ill synchronization reflected in a missed *kairos,* a term that connotes the right time for one's purposes. Inevitably, the missed *kairos* breeds immense suffering, but what is tragic in its specific occurrence within the pattern of events traced here is its irretrievability: Unrealized in its first appearance, the *kairos* is lost forever. Worse still, the suffering thereby instigated is perpetuated until the character responsible for the loss recognizes its irrevocable nature.

The pattern is as follows: A man is obliged to relinquish something dear to him and is offered compensation in its stead.[1] Believing the renunciation not obligatory, he refuses to comply and thus unknowingly misses the chance for compensation. Somewhat later he is forced to give up what he refused to willingly relinquish and, worse yet, is compelled to add compensation for his earlier refusal. At this point there are two possibilities. If he complies, giving up and adding compensation, the tragic pattern is resumed; if he refuses either to give up or to add compensation, the tragic pattern is not resumed and the man is consequently doomed to suffer even greater loss. The tragic pattern is not limited to actions and their external consequences; it also has psychological dimensions, including emotional and cognitive aspects. The emotional aspect is rather simple since, quite expectedly, the character reacts with pain and anger at the loss, thus introducing elements of suffering and sometimes wrath. The cognitive aspect, however, is somewhat more complicated.

The dominant feature of the cognitive facet of the tragic pattern is the mental process the character must undergo. Since it is the original refusal to yield to the necessary that leads to the tragic path, acknowledgment of past error also implies relinquishing compensation in return for freedom from the vicious circle of the tragic pattern. This painful acknowledgment is the outcome of a process of learning during which the character internalizes the irrevocability of the past and accepts full responsibility for his error. Given the difficulty of the lesson, it is hardly surprising that the road leading to its attainment is replete with obstacles. The character suddenly finds himself within an agonizing situation that he does not fully understand and to which he must fully acquiesce. The immediate and obvious reaction is total negation of the inevitability of any loss, and it is here that another aspect of the cognitive dimension of the tragic pattern is manifest in explanatory discourse. The character does not simply reject the possibility of loss; he gives a forceful explanation with a variety of causes in justification of his behavior. This explication is based on profound blindness, and acknowledgment of its irrelevance is another aspect of the process of learning represented here by a shift from one kind of explanation, which I term causality, to another, which I term divine intervention.

I regard causality as an explicatory means that associates two phenomena on a cause-and-effect basis. Causality is both concrete and limited: It explains the occurrence of an event by means of a certain factor or factors, thus tracing the root or roots of this event in a way that is both well defined and comprehensible. The factor can be either internal (mental or emotional) or external (another event) or a combination of both; for example,

Achilles refuses to join the fighting alongside the Achaeans both because Agamemnon took his war prize (external factor) and due to the wrath this dispossession has aroused in his soul (internal factor).

Divine intervention is also an explanatory means, but it is a higher one than causality, associating different phenomena on a more abstract level and referring to general conduct rather than particular occurrences. Olympic intervention elicits the mechanisms of human behavior in much broader terms than causality, pointing to the more hidden strata at the roots of human conduct and to general paths leading to action. Unlike causality, this intervention entails a supernatural and superhuman agent, such as the gods or fate, perceived as the causal force behind phenomena within the boundaries of the natural and human. I shall soon discuss the implications of this for human understanding, but first I wish to exemplify divine intervention and clarify its difference from causality.

I take my example from the fourth book of the *Iliad*, where Zeus and Hera settle their quarrel over the destiny of Zeus' beloved city, Troy (4.14–68). Zeus wants Troy to survive while Hera aspires to its total devastation. The solution they reach is as follows. Zeus agrees to the annihilation of his beloved city while Hera agrees to the destruction of not one but three cities, which she loves, Argos, Sparta, and Mycenae (4.51–53). The poet of the *Iliad* therefore gives an explanation for the future fall of Mycenae that is based on divine intervention: the fall is the realization of a resolution of an earlier conflict between two gods. Of course, the existence of divine intervention does not negate or cancel the existence of human causality. After all, the end of Mycenae can be explained by means of human agents participating in a war whose end is the total ruin of this city. Yet a fundamental breach between the two explanatory means of godly intervention and causality does exist, and it is this breach, and especially its dispiriting implications for the limitations of human understanding, that link the cognitive dimension of this basic pattern of the *Iliad* with the tragic. A short example from the myth of the Trojan War will clarify my argument.

After Strife hurled three goddesses into a debate over the frivolous question of beauty, the goddesses chose a mortal, Paris, to be their judge. He had to choose, and he had to choose but one. There was no way he could avoid profoundly insulting the other two goddesses, an insult that would have catastrophic consequences.[2] Paris chose the goddess of beauty, and his prize was the most beautiful woman in the world, who was, incidentally, married. He abducted her with the help of the goddess, and his abduction ignited a war that ended in his own death and the total demolition of his city, Troy. The four main events in this story, the beauty contest, the abduction of Helen, the death of Paris, and the fall of Troy, are explained by both human causality and divine intervention. Causality links the abduction of Helen and the death of Paris while godly intervention links the beauty contest and the fall of Troy. The events are also interconnected, for it was the beauty contest that led to the abduction that caused the fall of prince and city alike. The lacuna is not between perception of events and the formulation of their causal linkage but between formulation of their causal linkage and understanding of the reasons that led to this sequence of events. The causality linking the abduction of Helen to the death of her abductor is clear, as is that linking the abduction of Helen and the fall of the abductor's city. Even the intervention that points to the judgment of Paris as the cause of his own death is comprehensible, for insult to two powerful goddesses cannot be left unavenged. But what is utterly beyond human comprehension is the reasoning associating the devastation of a whole city with a divine beauty contest. The straight line linking this example of divine frivolity with its catastrophic outcome for an entire people is incomprehensible in human terms.[3] Note that this formulation does not exclude all cooperation between divine and mortal spheres regarding causation. In fact, both the beginning of the *Iliad* and its end are examples of the convergence of divine and human causation. In the first book of the epic the insulted Achilles accosts his divine mother, the goddess Thetis, imploring her to plead with Zeus to avenge his (Achilles') wounded pride by means of the deaths of many Greeks (1.407–12). In like manner, in the last book of the *Iliad* it is the god Apollo who calls on his fellow gods to put an end to the constant abuse of Hector's corpse, grounding his summons in Hector's past pious behavior (24.33–54). Zeus' acquiescence in both cases vindicates the notion of comprehensible causality, for the divine is motivated by the human, complementing men's deeds or responding to solicitations by intervention, which leads to the outcome solicited. Causal interactions such as these between mortal and immortal spheres, though included in the text, are excluded from the domain of the tragic. The tragic is marked by a breach of causality incomprehensible to characters and audience alike.

Note, too, that there is no doubt about the validity of the causal chain in the case of the beauty contest and the end of Troy, the two extremes of a chain of events whose status is that of absolute truth. The only thing that is questionable is the human capacity to cope with this kind of truth, a truth based on causality that is both uncontested and ungraspable. To reiterate, it is here that the notion of the tragic becomes pertinent. For it is exactly this gap between divine intervention and human causality, delineating the limit of the human capacity to understand, that marks the tragic core of human existence.[4] Both perception and acceptance of this tragic core as an inalienable part of life are necessary conditions for the resumption of this tragic pattern of the epic, and many passages of the *Iliad* are devoted to the depiction of the long route to tragic recognition. Such recognition is not innate; it is an outcome of a process of learning during which one's own private experience serves as a painful lesson about human life in general. This lesson is as horrible as it is difficult to absorb, which is why very few persons, in life or fiction, are capable of internalizing it. But those who succeed in doing so, if *success* is the right term in this context, serve as a symbol of human achievement in the face of the direst aspects of reality. The *Iliad*, which is both a tragic masterpiece and a masterpiece of the tragic, utilizes the pattern just described as a means for a powerful representation of this aspect of the human condition, and its central hero, Achilles, is fashioned as an emblem of the immense difficulty, as well as of the great merit, of achieving such recognition.[5] Since my claim asserts a recurring pattern, the argumentation calls for several demonstrations of essentially one basic sequence of events. The tragic pattern is the organizing principle of the first book of the *Iliad*, and it has a central role in other books of the epic: book nine, the end of book fifteen (which is closely connected to the beginning of book sixteen), book eighteen, book nineteen, and book twenty-four. These will be discussed in their textual order.

I begin at the beginning, with the epic's *prooemium*, both because of its succinct realization of some of the basic components of the tragic pattern and its utility as a "fissure," a point of textual entry. In a chapter on textual framing, Schechet defines the fissure of narrative framing as that which "functions similarly to prefaces (in dialogic exchange with the central narrative), while constituting part of that central narrative."[6] An epic's *prooemium* is a narrative framing that facilitates interpretation of more general techniques and significations. And, indeed, the first twelve lines of the *Iliad* interweave three of the main components of the tragic pattern: wrath, which belongs to the emotional dimension; causality, which belongs to the cognitive dimension; and divine intervention. I say "interweave" and not merely "present" to emphasize that these dimensions are inseparable, though I detach them for analytic purposes. Even the opening noun, *mênin* (wrath),[7] which is an explicit reference to the emotional, has an adjective, "accursed," (*oulomenên* 1.2), which has an implicit explanatory hue (the wrath is accursed because it has probably caused terrible things) and is immediately followed by a relative clause with explicit clarification: The wrath of Achilles brought the Achaeans a multitude of woes and hurled to Hades many mighty souls of heroes whose bodies have become carrion for dogs and birds (1.2–5). The bitter end of the heroes was not merely an outcome of Achilles' wrath; it was also a fulfillment of Zeus' plan (1.5).[8] Thus, in no more than five lines the poet of the *Iliad* has presented his audience with the complex web of the emotional and the cognitive that is generated within a tragic context.[9] The wrath of mortal Achilles is an explanation belonging to the domain of causality while the plan of the god Zeus is an explanation belonging to the domain of divine intervention. These explanations reflect different aspects of the same phenomenon, namely, the terrible deaths of many warriors. This mutual explanatory illumination of the catastrophes of the *Iliad* is stressed once more immediately afterward when the poet refers to the strife between Agamemnon and Achilles that led to the situation depicted in the opening of the poem.

This time the poet starts with divine intervention, asking the identity of the god that hurled Achilles and Agamemnon into strife (1.8) and answering that it was the son of Leto and Zeus (1.9).[10] But this is only a partial answer, for the god is followed by a human being, the son of Atreus (1.12), and the two are causally connected: The son of Leto and Zeus threw Achilles and Agamemnon into strife, for (γάϱ) Achilles was enraged by Agamemnon because (οὕνεϰα) the latter disgraced his priest (1.9–12).[11] Now comes a full explanation prefaced by "for" (γάϱ) and depicting the causal sequence of events.

When the poet narrates the first link in this causal chain, Chryses' appearance before the Achaeans, he opens with a description of the priest, lingering on the objects he carries: a huge ransom and the scepter of Apollo (1.13–15). This description is not merely ornamental, for the priest's appearance is strongly associated with both causality and divine intervention, as the following will prove. Thus, although Chryses comes to plead for the release of his daughter, his request contains an implied threat; he arrives not as a private individual but as the representative of a god. Rejecting his offer will therefore be an insult by a human to a god with a consequent divine reaction. When the poet moves from indirect speech to the direct words of the priest, he retains the same mixture of pleading and threat: Chryses commences with a wish that the gods grant the Achaeans both the total destruction of Troy and a safe return home (1.17–19) but then goes on to a polite form of the imperative (λύσαιτε), asking them to release his daughter and accept the compensating ransom while reminding them of their duty of reverence to Apollo, who shoots from afar (1.21).[12] The two components of

Chryses' pleading, generous compensation and threat, are easily perceived by almost all of the Achaeans, who approve of both due respect to the priest and acceptance of the gifts (1.23). Not all of the Achaeans perceive the implied threat, however, for Agamemnon rejects the offer and ejects the priest with harsh words, threatening that if he ever returns not even the god can protect him (1.24–32). This is blunt *hubris,* and the audience of the *Iliad* is well prepared for the consequent retaliation after so many references to the religious aspect of the request. The priest prays to Apollo to punish the Achaeans (1.33–42), and the god who shoots from afar starts shooting arrows into the camp, bringing death to beasts and man alike (1.43–52).

After nine days of plague Achilles, advised by Hera, summons an assembly where he exhorts the prophet Calchas to tell the whole army the reason for the god's wrath and how the latter can be appeased (1.84–91). Calchas is asked to turn implicit godly intervention explicit by naming the exact source of this expression of divine wrath. Note that there is no dispute regarding the source of the plague; it is clear to all that it lies within the domain of divine intervention, that is to say, it originates with a god. The prophet's answer is a presentation of the situation as an outcome of a causal sequence of events: the cause of the god's wrath is the priest (ἕνεκ' ἀρητῆρος, 1.94) whom Agamemnon humiliated by not returning his daughter and by rejecting the ransom offered in exchange. This is the cause (τούνεκ') for the recent woes as well as the ground for future ones (1.96); the only way that might stop all this loss is to return the daughter to her father. This is a succinct presentation of the first stages of the tragic pattern. Chryses' daughter is the original object doomed to be lost from the beginning, and Agamemnon is the human agent who, blind to its inevitable loss, clings to the object and refuses compensation in return for renunciation. However, the situation has changed dramatically since the last opportunity to return the priest's daughter, for now not only must she be returned but she must be "returned without compensation" (1.99); what is worse, it is Apollo whose insult must now be compensated by means of a hecatomb (1.99–100). There is therefore a triple loss: Chryses' daughter, the offered and now lost compensation in exchange for Chryses' daughter, and the future compensation to Apollo.

I shall soon consider Agamemnon's reaction to the new situation, but before that I would like to point out a certain problem here, namely, the failure of reasoning to apprehend both causality and divine intervention. By depicting the priest as the god's representative and by giving the approving reaction of the army to his offers, the narrative states quite clearly that Agamemnon must part with Chryses' daughter. What is not at all clear is the reason for Agamemnon's inability to see the necessity of this loss and the ground of his refusal to give her up in exchange for such a wonderful ransom. There is something deeply flawed here, as becomes even more evident during the subsequent heated debate with Achilles.

Agamemnon adheres to a reasonable, though far from convincing, causality, explicating his clinging to the girl. He states that he prefers Chryses' daughter to Clytemnestra, his wedded wife, because (ἐπεί) she is not inferior to Clytemnestra in anything (1.114), not in figure, physical stature, the quality of her mind, or her skills (1.115). This might be true, but from a mercantile perspective his calculations still seem extremely faulty. Whatever the merits of the girl, the offerings of the father surpassed them to such an extent that their rejection seems almost irrational. But this is not all, for at this stage Agamemnon does realize he has made a mistake, and so he agrees to return the daughter to her father while articulating his wish for the army's safety (1.117), although on one condition.

> However, you must prepare me immediately a *geras* [prize of honor],
>   so that I shall not be the only one
> among the Argives without a *geras*, for (ἐπεί) this is not seemly.
> For indeed (γάρ), you all see *that,* that my *geras* is going somewhere
>   else.   (1.118–20)

So the girl is not that precious after all; in a few lines she has deteriorated from something unique and indispensable to an exchangeable *geras,* which, one may recall, was her status in the first place.[13]

The introduction of the term *geras* introduces the issue of prestige into the story,[14] and prestige becomes a recurring motif in the complications of the tragic pattern. Note that Agamemnon's willingness to accept much less than what was offered him earlier is obsolete. However great his concessions, the loss is total and utterly irretrievable. The moment of compensation is forever over since the past is irrevocable. This is actually what Achilles states in his categorical answer: at this point it is impossible to gather all the booty of the war in order to redistribute it; consequently, any compensation must wait for the unknown future after Troy has been captured and sacked (1.122–29). This solution calls for great patience and is hardly what Agamemnon could or would accept at any time and least of all now.[15] He therefore insists on getting the *geras* of one of the other prominent leaders, either Achilles or Ajax or Odysseus, in exchange for his *geras* (1.131–39). Agamemnon does not yet indicate whose *geras* he intends to take for the loss of Chryses' daughter, and he even ends his declaration in a very general statement about the predictable anger of the one who will compensate him for his loss (1.139). His insistence on compensation and the mention of anger are portentous, anticipating the next stage of the first realization of this tragic pattern. Agamemnon tries to negotiate the non-negotiable, wishing to get compensation, though it is he that must compensate for his former error. His blindness to his real situation can breed nothing but anger that, in contrast to what he believes at the moment, will cause him great loss. Agamemnon's misreading of the situation is most bluntly expressed in the comparison he makes between his situation and Achilles' regarding the *geras*.

> Do you really wish that while you yourself hold your *geras*, I will nevertheless
> be deprived of any, and you ask me to bring her back?   (1.133–34)

This is a *non sequitur*, for what does Achilles' present situation have to do with Agamemnon's past error? The latter's complaint is outrageous, and it is unsurprising that Achilles takes his words personally, responding fiercely to the implied personal threat to take his own *geras* from him.

In his answer he states that not only has he justly achieved his prize, a reward for his terrible toil in war (1.161–66), but in every distribution of spoils of war in the past his own *geras* was always much smaller than Agamemnon's despite so much labor (1.166–68). He therefore threatens to leave Troy and return to his fatherland Phthia, which is definitely much better than staying, deprived of prestige (*atimos*), merely in order to amass a fortune and wealth for Agamemnon (1.169–71).[16] In light of the opening lines of the epic, there is nothing especially unwonted in the fact that anger begins to play such a significant role in the sequence of the events comprising the tragic pattern. Nor is there anything unique in the resemblance emerging between Achilles and Agamemnon in their persistent anger, insistence on impossible compensation, and inability to acknowledge irretrievable loss. Since both leaders serve as the focal human agents at the core of the two main realizations of this tragic pattern in the *Iliad*, it is conceivable that they have similar traits that lead to similar tragic outcomes.

I have already mentioned the problem of reasoning in Agamemnon's argumentation. Achilles displays a similar characteristic when he continues his speech to Agamemnon, but his reasoning is even more conspicuously flawed than that of Agamemnon. Achilles' argumentation is based on causality that goes back to the origins of the expedition to Troy.

For (*gar*) *I* did not go here because of (*henek'*) the Trojans the spear
bearers
in order to fight, since (*epei*), as far as I am concerned, they are not
culpable (*aitioi*) in anything.   (1.152–53)

The causal nature of this contention is emphasized by four indicators: *gar,*
henek', epei, and *aitioi,*[17] and is further developed as Achilles continues his
complaint by means of *gar* (1.154) and *epei* (1.156). But if the Trojans are not
aitioi to Achilles in anything, and if, as he bitterly indicates, the purpose of
this war is not his prestige but rather that of Menelaus and Agamemnon
(1.158–59), and if, on top of it all, his *geras* is usually disproportionately
smaller than his efforts, then one starts wondering not about Achilles' threat
to return home but about his prior decision to remain in Troy to this moment. The discordant features of a seemly reasonable argumentation become more and more evident as the epic evolves; it is one of the key concepts by means of which the tragic worldview of the *Iliad* is presented.
Achilles' cogitations regarding his personal participation in a war whose
causes do not seem reasonable will serve him much later as a means of recognizing the tragic aspect of human conduct in general. According to this
metaphysical recognition, the Trojan War is just one more realization of the
miserable doom of mortals. But I anticipate. Let us return to the first book
of the *Iliad* and to Agamemnon's answer to Achilles, referring directly to this
causality.

The Greek leader first dismisses the notion that he is the cause of
Achilles' attendance, claiming that if this is so Achilles may leave instantly
(1.173–74). Agamemnon goes on, insinuating that the real motive for
Achilles' presence in Troy is Achilles' genuine attraction to strife, battles, and
wars (1.177). It is only now that Agamemnon states explicitly that he will
take Briseis, Achilles' prize of war, as *geras* for *geras,* an act that serves both as
a compensation for the loss of the daughter of Chryses and as proof of
Agamemnon's prowess and ability to command (1.182–87).[18] Thus, in addition to loss of and compensation for a concrete object, the transference of
the girl symbolizes less palpable things such as seniority and independence.
Agamemnon claims that he does not need Achilles' aid to win the battle because he is superior to Achilles, and the capture of Briseis will have proved it
before Achilles' departure.[19]

Quite expectedly, anticipated loss of a desired object is a source of great
wrath, and Achilles' first reaction to Agamemnon's words is an attempt to
kill him on the spot. Athena prevents him from doing this (1.188–210), and

so he resorts to words again, cursing Agamemnon and swearing that a day would come when he, Agamemnon, would bitterly regret the humiliation of the best of the Achaeans (1.225–44). Nestor intervenes but to no avail (1.247–84), and the two dismiss the assembly while still clashing verbally (1.304–5). It is now time for Agamemnon to return Chryses' daughter. He starts the preparations for her departure, which include purgation and sacrifice (1.306–17), and simultaneously sends heralds to bring Achilles' prize of war (1.318–26). The temporal proximity between giving up the old object and seizing the new one reinforces the strong connection between the first stage of this realization of the tragic pattern and its immediate extension: the narration of the return of Chryses' daughter and Apollo's appeasement (1.430–74) is not immediately subsequent to description of the ritual preceding the girl's departure from the Greek army. Rather, it takes place after the poet depicts Achilles' pleading with his mother to avenge his damaged prestige (1.348–430). Thus, the narration of the end of the first stage of this manifestation of the tragic pattern is split in two, and it encompasses the beginning of the second stage, which narrates Agamemnon's maltreatment of Achilles and its consequences.

And this is not all, for the two stages have other parallels between them. To begin with, there is a strong resemblance between the two focal characters of the two episodes, the offended Achilles and the abused priest of Apollo:[20] Both distance themselves physically from the camp (1.35, 349) and go to the beach (1.34, 350); both cry (1.42, 349) and pray (1.35, 351) because the son of Atreus has dishonored them (1.11–12, 355–56).[21] Both are heard by the ones to whom they prayed (1.43, 357), who come from their divine abode (1.44, 358) and sit (1.48, 1.360). In addition, Achilles' words imply a parallel between leading the first girl away to her father (1.389–90) and leading the second girl away to Agamemnon (1.391). Immediately afterward comes Achilles' direct pleading with his mother to accost Zeus and avenge his damaged prestige (1.393–95). Since Zeus is at present with the Ethiopians (1.423–24), Thetis awaits his return; she then presents her request to him (1.495–510) and he yields (1.523–27). Here another parallel appears, for her plea is formulated in the same manner as the priest's invocation to Apollo: if ever in the past I did X for you, please grant me now my wish Y (ἤ᾽ εἰ δή ποτέ τοι [. . .] τόδε μοι κρήηνον ἐέλδωρ [1.40–41], εἴ ποτε δή σε [. . .] τόδε μοι κρήηνον ἐέλδωρ [1.503–4]).[22] It is now a time of suffering, and once more the Achaeans pay dearly for their leader's mistake. Like Apollo's plague, Zeus' intervention brings death and loss, until finally, as predicted by Achilles, Agamemnon recognizes his mistake. He takes responsibility and wishes for a reconciliation with the offended Achilles so that order will be restored to the Greek army well before the capture of Troy.[23]

According to the pattern I am delineating here, when the human agent gives up both the desired object and any claims for compensation, and when he is willing, in addition, to compensate for his earlier error, the tragic pattern reaches its termination. And, indeed, at least regarding the pattern whose human agent is Agamemnon, there are no more complications. Yet as far as the *Iliad* is concerned, this is merely the first manifestation of the pattern, for now Achilles moves to the center of the next round of the pattern. The end of the first round of the pattern and the beginning of its second appearance are closely related, and their detailed description takes place in the ninth book of the epic.

The book opens with Agamemnon's acknowledgment of the disastrous situation created by Achilles' departure. Soon after Nestor recommends a closed assembly for the elders (9.70–78), and when his wish is granted he opens the council with a direct appeal to Agamemnon to compensate Achilles for the maltreatment he suffered over Briseis (9.104–13). Tactfully, he does not explicitly suggest that Agamemnon return her, but he does mention the deep insult of the girl's abduction (9.111), which implies that she should be returned cum compensation.

Agamemnon's reply consists of several points and refers both to the past and to the future. He first admits his own wrongdoing, calling it *emas atas* (9.115), and pleads guilty (*aasamên* 9.116).[24] Then he accepts Achilles' claim in the quarrel, namely, that Achilles is worth the entire Achaean army, for Zeus loves him, as proved by the defeat of the army (9.116–18).[25] He reiterates his acknowledgment of his mistake, describing it as the result of his willingness to be persuaded by his own poor judgment (*epei aasamên* 9.119), and offers "an abundance of gifts" (9.120). In these words, which formulate Agamemnon's psychological recognition regarding his motives for the erroneous action, he accepts the implied causality of Nestor's view of the present disaster, namely, that his behavior toward Achilles brought the terrible defeats to the Greeks, and expresses his willingness to remedy the situation. He enumerates the gifts he is offering and promises to return the girl Briseis (9.131–32) whom he swears he did not touch (9.132–34). In addition, he promises to give Achilles a generous part of the spoils of war after Troy has been sacked (9.135–40), to make him his son-in-law without paying any bride-price after their return home (9.146), and to present him with seven rich cities that will pay him taxes (9.149–56). He is willing to give all this in order to appease Achilles' anger (9.157). But Achilles' anger, the terrible dimensions of which serve as the starting point for the whole epic, is not to be appeased yet, as the embassy sent to him is soon to discover.

It is Nestor again, noting the generosity of the gifts (9.164), who suggests immediately appointing an envoy consisting of Phoenix, Ajax, and Odysseus with two heralds, Odios and Eurybates, to plead with Achilles (9.165–70). When they reach Achilles' place, they are greeted courteously by their former ally who prepares them a sumptuous meal (9.192–221), after which Odysseus begins his plea.[26] He starts with a description of the terrible situation of the Achaean army (9.229–46), calls for Achilles' help (9.247–51) and reminds him both of his father's maxim that fellowship (*philophrosynê*) is better than prowess (9.254–56) and of his advice to abstain from strife and evil machinations (9.257).[27] He then enumerates Agamemnon's presents (9.264–99) and adds a last comment: if Achilles hates Agamemnon so much that his gifts cannot persuade him, he should at least take pity on the army that suffers so much at the hands of Hector (9.300–305).

But the intransigent Achilles will not listen and, answering Odysseus at great length, rejects all of Agamemnon's offers. This is, no doubt, a pivotal moment in the epic,[28] and Achilles' long speech attests to the complexity of the new situation. Thus, while the tragic pattern that dictates Achilles' present behavior is essentially the same as that responsible for Agamemnon's past decisions, its realization in a new context acquires depth and resonance as well as complexity, all contributing to its far-reaching consequences.[29] Achilles restates his bitter charges against the unjust war in general and the mischievous Agamemnon in particular, linking causality with the concept of prestige (*timê*). Achilles says he does not intend to be persuaded either by Agamemnon or by the rest of the Danaoi because (*epei*) after all (*ara*) there was no *charis* (χάρις) whatsoever in going to war, forever and without pause (9.315–17), since an equal share awaits one who stays behind and one who goes to battle (9.318).[30] In other words, the same *timê* is given to everyone regardless of status (9.319).[31] Seen in this light, Achilles is constantly maltreated since (*epei*) he is always in battle and never stays behind (9.321–27); what is more, even when he wins the battle, Agamemnon, who stays behind with the swift ships, gets the major part of Achilles' spoils (9.328–33). Agamemnon's capture of Briseis in exchange for the priest's daughter is therefore a multifaceted sin against Achilles: first, the girl is Achilles' prize; second, it is a very small prize compared to the spoils given to Agamemnon; and, on top of it all, it is Agamemnon, who did not go to war himself, who takes it from Achilles, who actually earned the plunder by risking his life in battle.[32]

There is nothing particularly novel in the link made by Achilles between his obstinate refusal to be persuaded, on the one hand, and causality on the other. Like Agamemnon's former refusal to give up the daughter of Chryses without compensation, so Achilles' present refusal to accept compensation is presented as reasonable, a decision based on comprehensible logic. The novelty in his argument lies in the linkage between causality and the notion of sincerity.³³ Achilles opens his speech by contrasting his own words, which are in harmony with what he thinks, with someone who thinks one thing and says another (9.312–14). That Agamemnon is implicated in this context becomes more and more evident as Achilles continues his speech. Once again Agamemnon is portrayed as deeply deceitful, full of mischief and insincere to the core. Achilles terms the capture of Briseis an act of *hubris* (*eph'hubrizôn* 9.368),³⁴ warning that if Agamemnon ever again tries to commit such a deeply deceitful act (*exapatêsein* 9.371) the Achaeans will be angry. He goes on and says that there is no way he will participate in either councils or action with Agamemnon (9.374), for, indeed, (*gar dê*) Agamemnon deeply deceived (*ek* [. . .] *apatêse*) him and sinned against him (9.375). It will be impossible to deeply deceive (*exapaphoit'*) him again with words (9.375–76). In light of this, Agamemnon's gifts are conceived as rooted in his essential insincerity and consequently cannot serve as the basis for any reconciliation with Achilles. In other words, the deceitful nature of the donor contaminates his attempts to restore peace, and it is therefore Agamemnon that should be regarded as the source of continuation of the strife. Whatever the validity of this argument, in terms of the tragic pattern it has only one implication: The refusal of compensation must generate additional loss to the refusing party.

Let us consider the nature of Achilles' initial loss and its connection to the rejection of the gifts. At first sight one might think the real loss lies in the domain of prestige (*timê*). Yet, despite Achilles' repeated evocation of *timê* in his conversation with the different envoys,³⁵ *timê*, which is by definition retrievable, cannot explain his obstinacy. What is lost forever, at least in the eyes of Achilles, is not external but internal, something associated with self-esteem and internalized humiliation, as explicitly stated in his reference to the notion of outrageous insult (*lôbê*). Since *timê* is something measurable by external means, injury can be gauged and materially compensated; *lôbê*, however, has serious internal implications, and compensation for causing it does not lie solely in the domain of external goods. This is why Achilles states so forcefully that even if these gifts were multiplied by ten or twenty or more (9.379–86), he would not consider them compensation, for what is at stake here is humiliation (*thumalgea lôbên* 9.387).³⁶ The gifts are incapable of placating Achilles' rage because of both the flawed reliability of their donor and their essential incompatibility with appeasement of emotional distress.

At this stage, when the long harangue seems to have reached its conclusion, Achilles starts meditating on the deep meaning of participating in war and the validity of its price. Once more, as in the first book of the epic, the hero starts describing a causal chain that is both intelligible and reasonable, though extremely problematic. Achilles, the emblem of heroic values, is pondering no less than the essential worth of these same heroic values. For (*gar*), he commences, nothing is as precious as the soul (9.401); cattle and fat sheep can be taken as booty (9.406), tripods and baying horses may be acquired (9.407), but the soul of a man, after leaving the body, can neither be taken as booty nor caught (9.408–9). Again, what is so strange in these remarks is not so much their appearance in the middle of a war epic (the *Iliad* is far from being an advocate of war)[37] as their utterance by one whose commitment to these values has seemed beyond doubt. These troublesome claims have a purpose in the text. The high value of life they reflect is a crucial step in Achilles' gradual process of acquiring a humane perception of the human condition. This step is indispensable for Achilles' transformation from a slaughtering machine to a tragic hero.[38]

It is now that Achilles is answered by his old friend and tutor, Phoenix, who bases his reply on two historical cases, his own private story and that of Meleager. Both deal with anger and its consequences, and both depict a sequence of events organized according to the pattern hitherto depicted.[39] The stories therefore serve as a reflection of the situation in which their addressee is presently entangled and offer possible insight into the mechanism and future consequences of his behavior.[40] Phoenix' biographical story tells how his father repeatedly dishonored his mother and damaged her status (*atimazeske* 9.450) by means of the love he showed his concubine. The afflicted mother pleaded with her son to sleep with the concubine in order to make the father hateful to the younger woman. The son was persuaded (9.453) to do this and soon after was cursed by his father never to have children of his own, a curse that was granted by the gods (9.453–57). Phoenix ran away to Phthia where he found in Peleus a surrogate father (9.481) and in Achilles a surrogate son (9.485–95). In terms of the tragic pattern I am illustrating here, Phoenix' story is an example of a man who suffers a loss (of father and potential children) and is able both to acknowledge the irreversibility of the loss and to accept compensation for it. One who has lost a father and been deprived of future sons accepts the fatherly love of a stranger and treats the stranger's son as his own. The text is explicit concerning the compensatory role of the surrogate son (ἀλλὰ σὲ παῖδα [. . .] ποιεόμην, ἵνα μοί ποτ' ἀεικέα λοιγὸν ἀμύνῃς 9.494–95), and is therefore directly connected with Phoenix' two pleas to Achilles, first to subdue his great heart (9.496) and then to accept Agamemnon's gifts as worthy compensation for his wrath (9.515–22).[41]

The second plea does not immediately succeed the first, and the delayed transition from the first to the second reveals Phoenix' subtle understanding of the psychological complexity of the situation.[42] He opens with a general remark concerning the Prayers of Sorrow and Repentance, the *Litai,* who are Zeus' daughters (9.502), giving a minute description of their repugnant physicality: they are crippled and wrinkled and squint-eyed (9.503). They are always behind *Atê* (9.504), who is mighty and swift of foot (9.505) and therefore runs on ahead (9.506).[43] And yet appealing *Atê* is a damaging force while the disgusting *Litai,* who come behind, have a healing capacity for making amends (9.507).[44] One who treats them with awe (9.508) gains their help (9.509), but if they are rejected, they go to their father and start pleading against the rejecting agent, who falls prey to punishing *Atê* (9.512). It is only now that Phoenix mentions Agamemnon and treats his gifts as *Litai* (9.513–15), thus making the general principle relevant to the specific occasion. The abhorrent depiction of the *Litai* reflects Achilles' revulsion, and Phoenix' words thereby adopt his interlocutor's emotional focalization.[45] In doing this he manifests his understanding of the difficulty embedded in Achilles' situation while insisting on the necessity of subordinating emotion to reason: although it is much more tempting to yield to *Atê,* especially in light of the revulsion the *Litai* arouse, it is they who must nevertheless be obeyed. I postpone discussion of *Atê* and its relation to the irrational to a later stage. Meanwhile I merely wish to point out the resemblance between Phoenix' description of *Atê* and the *Litai* and the extension of the tragic pattern: the rejection of the *Litai,* like the rejection of compensation, is the source of a new round of *Atê*'s hostile intervention.[46] And it is the same theme of rejection of compensation that is at the core of Phoenix' second story, that of Meleager.[47]

The account is a narratological masterpiece, weaving into a relatively short passage as many as four analepses that establish a strong connection between past and present.[48] The merit of this temporal linkage is not limited to the domain of artistic creativity. It also has didactic implications, for the relevance of the past to the present has general validity for the *Iliad* as a whole. In fact, one can find many resemblances between the story of Meleager and the story of Achilles.[49] Like the *Iliad,* the story of Meleager opens *in medias res,* and like the *Iliad* it depicts a war in which one army, that of the Couretes, besieges a city, Calydon, belonging to another people, the Aetolians (9.529–32). Then comes the first analepsis (9.533–49), where Phoenix asserts divine intervention in depicting the origin of the war: Artemis was angered (*chôsamenê* 9.534) and enraged (*cholôsamenê* 9.538) by Oeneus, the Aetolians' ruler, who had neglected her sacrifice while remembering the rest of the gods. She therefore sent a wild boar that constantly caused devastating damage to Oeneus' orchard until it was finally killed by Meleager, Oeneus' son, who gathered many heroes to this end. Unfortunately, the end of the wild boar was not the end of the goddess's anger, and she instigated a great battle among the heroes over the wild boar's head and his shaggy pelt, a battle that, in its turn, led to the present war.

Yet the divine origin of the war, however important, is not the essential component of Phoenix' argument. The main interest of the story, which makes of it an exemplum, lies in its human agents.[50] For, while the goddess's rage is beyond the reach of human beings and its proportions transcend human understanding,[51] man's anger can be measured and restricted accordingly. The story therefore leaves the domain of divine intervention and moves to causality, where human beings serve as the source of action and conduct. Like Achilles, Meleager is full of rage (*cholos* 9.553); he is extremely angry (*chôomenos*) in his heart (9.555) and his heart-grieving rage (*cholon thumalgea* 9.565) is due to the words (here "curses") of another human being, his mother (9.566). Like Achilles, the manifestation of his anger is abstention from war (9.556–58), which also has devastating consequences for his people (9.573–74). Now comes the third analepsis, which again raises the question of divine intervention. During the description of the genealogy of Meleager's wife, Phoenix mentions an incident in which Idas, Meleager's father-in-law, lifted his bow against Apollo because of a girl, an act that led to the latter's death at the hands of Apollo (9.559–64). This story strongly alludes to Achilles' case: it tells of the fight over a girl by the strongest man of his age (9.558–59), and it mentions Apollo and his killing arrows. In addition, Apollo parallels Artemis in Phoenix' story; both are divine powers insulted by humans that avenge the insult.[52] It is also worth mentioning that in both cases divine anger lies within the limits of the comprehensible; the deeds of Artemis and Apollo are understandable in light of the human conduct that preceded them. Note that this story is literally framed in Meleager's anger, as if Phoenix wanted to emphasize the ubiquity of anger, as well as its catastrophic outcome, regardless of its origin. The fourth analepsis returns to causality and depicts the reasons for Meleager's anger against his mother. The latter, grieving over the death of her brother at her son's hand, beseeches the gods to avenge him. The outcome of her prayers is beyond the limits of Phoenix' story, but there is a reference to the fact that *Erinus*, who has an implacable heart, listens to her (9.566–72).[53]

From this point on, the story continues in chronological order, depicting the delegation of elders to Meleager and their promises (9.573–80), the rejection of his parents' and friends' supplications (9.581–87), and then the turning point, the fire at his own house and his wife's entreaty foretelling the calamities awaiting her as a prisoner of war. It is this plea that leads to Meleager's intervention and the expulsion of the enemy (9.588–98).[54] The story, however, does not end here, for Phoenix adds a last detail:

> but they did not pay him his dew gifts,
> which were many and beautiful, and he prevented the catastrophe
> even so.   (9.598–99)

Phoenix' argumentation leads to this point. He pleads with Achilles to change his mind and prevent the *daimon* from turning him toward the road chosen by Meleager (9.600–602).[55] The reason for this is connected with the gifts and their association with Achilles' *timê* (9.603–5): now the Achaeans give him *timê* equal to that of a god (9.603), but if he went to battle without the gifts, his *timê* would suffer (9.605). In other words, since Achilles, like Meleager, will eventually join the battle, the relevant question is not so much when he will do it but under what conditions: will he do it now, with the gifts and their associated *timê*, or later, without the gifts and with damage to his *timê*?[56] Phoenix' argumentation therefore does not linger on the emotional aspect of Achilles' refusal and neutralizes the association between the gifts and their donor. He concentrates on the damage to Achilles' *timê*, thus restoring compensatory power to the gifts.

It seems that Phoenix' words affect Achilles, for the latter, though still resistant to the idea of returning to battle, does not adhere to his former threat to leave Troy altogether but rather suggests a reconsideration of the departure (9.618–19). What is more, in his answer to Ajax, the last spokesman of the embassy, Achilles says that he will not intervene in the war before Hector comes and sets fire to the huts and ships of the Myrmidons (9.650–53), which means that he does intend to join the battle exactly at the time Phoenix set. It is here that one can detect the complexity of the tragic pattern, where it is revealed as not merely a structural principle but also as constructing an intricate nexus serving a variety of ends. The partial success of the embassy in pleading with Achilles (namely, their achievement in deterring Achilles from leaving Troy altogether and, what is more, departing with his implied promise to rejoin the battle at a future stage) sustains the tragic pattern and enables the poet to construct a heroic figure deserving immortal glory that is realized in his poem. For it is here that Achilles states explicitly that cessation from fighting guarantees him a happy, though inglorious, long life (9.410–16). Obviously, had he chosen to adhere to this path there would have been no *Iliad* to recount his glory and no tragic pattern to organize its sequence of events.[57] What is interesting here is how the poet utilizes the motif of friendship in this context. Although Odysseus' reference to fellowship (*philophrosunê*) did not prevail (9.254–56), Phoenix' allusion to his own enduring and close relationship with Achilles (9.485–91) and Ajax' admonition about neglecting the affectionate friendship due comrades in arms (9.630) ultimately do. Yet, paradoxically, it is this very discourse of affection and friendship that induces Achilles to perform the act that will eventually bring his own ruin, for soon this seemingly temporary postponement of retirement will be revealed as a necessary condition for the death of his most beloved friend, Patroclus.[58]

For the present, however, there is no doubt that Achilles is not relinquishing his anger, and the embassy therefore returns having failed in its mission.[59] Note that, unlike the first occurrence of the pattern, where compensation was possible only at a very specific point, here there is a whole span of time during which Achilles can change his mind. This aspect enables the poet to utilize a more developed version of the pattern, where emotional and cognitive dimensions are given detailed description, thus shedding light on the complexity of the situation and the enormous difficulties with which the human agent at its center must contend. This is the end of the first phase of the second realization of the tragic pattern. Achilles' abiding anger, his refusal to accept any compensation, and his decision not to rejoin the battle prevent the conclusion of the tragic sequence of events.

In the short term, however, Achilles' refusal to rejoin the battle seems to benefit his enraged ego. His absence leads to a crisis culminating in extreme danger for the Greek army, and by the end of book fifteen we hear that Hector, encouraged by Apollo, attacks the Argive army and comes close to its fleet. With a torch in his hand, he galvanizes his people to set fire to the ships (15.716–25), but whenever they try to do so they are frustrated by Ajax, who prevents them with his sword (15.743–45). Not for long, however, for when Ajax recognizes that it is Zeus who plans victory for the Trojans (16.121) he yields and the ship catches fire (16.122–23). Meanwhile Patroclus begs Achilles to come back to battle (16.2–35) or at least to let him, Patroclus, join the warriors (16.36–45). Achilles, still angry with Agamemnon, refuses to return to war in person, but he does let Patroclus go and aid his fellow warriors with the army of the Myrmidons (16.49–100). When Achilles sees the ship on fire he is appalled and urges Patroclus to put on armor while he rouses the army (16.124–29).

As can be seen from this rupture in the narrative sequence of the two scenes, both the progress of the war and the conversation of Achilles and Patroclus are split: the progress of the war starts in 15.716–46 and continues in 16.101–24, while the conversation starts in 16.1–100 and continues in 16.124–29. In fact, the editor responsible for the book divisions found this split so prominent that he actually marked it as the end of a book. However, this editorial break of the sequence is misleading, for the poet has constructed a single coherent episode consisting of two scenes occurring concomitantly in different places.⁶⁰ The split of each of the two scenes is therefore a conscious narratological device, marked by the recurrence of the *men . . . de . . .* construction (ὡς οἵ μέν [. . .] Πάτροκλος δέ [. . .] [16.1–2], ὡς οἵ μέν [. . .] Αἴας δέ [. . .] [16.101–2]), that strengthens the connection between the two and emphasizes their interrelationship. The split should therefore be conceived as a crucial transitional point not between two different episodes but within one. When the poet leaves the battle scene on hold and moves to the scene of Patroclus' pleading with Achilles, he stresses the fact that Achilles is still unmoved because he remains in the grip of his emotions.⁶¹ And then, quite surprisingly, a hint of a possible change of mind appears. Achilles' speech attests to at least a partial psychological recognition, admitting that he should let go and that his anger cannot last forever:

> But let us let alone the past. For indeed it is impossible
> to be furiously angry in my heart.   (16.60–61)⁶²

However, it is not due time yet for such a change, and so Achilles sticks to his words and his anger, insisting on not joining the battle until fire reaches his own ships (16.60–63).⁶³ But now, when Hector has already killed many Argives and is approaching the Myrmidons' huts and ships, Achilles also realizes that it is impossible to wait until fire reaches his own ships, for then it will be too late and there will be no homecoming for them (16.80–82). The narratological device that leaves Achilles' situation in suspense is therefore a reflection of the hero's hovering between the emotional and the cognitive. Like Agamemnon before him, Achilles has achieved a partial understanding of the need to give up while still adhering emotionally to long-held convictions. Like Agamemnon, he tries to find a compromise, and his efforts will bring similarly dismal results.

Thus caught between the realization of the impossibility of his own terms and the impossibility of giving up, Achilles sends Patroclus as his surrogate.[64] Although he himself does not join the battle, his closest friend will represent him there not merely by means of his participation but also in the armor he wears and the army he leads; Patroclus is specifically asked by Achilles to wear his, Achilles', armor and lead the Myrmidons, Achilles' army, to battle (16.64–65).[65] Achilles' compromise is aimed at utilizing Patroclus' intervention on his, Achilles', behalf in a way that will both affirm his indispensability and retain his *timê* (16.83–86). This is why Patroclus is not allowed to outshine Achilles, for overprowess in war will diminish Achilles' high *timê* (16.90). He is therefore asked merely to push the Trojans back, save the ships, and return to Achilles (16.91–100). However, Achilles' attempts to come to terms with the difficult situation are doomed to failure since no compromise is really viable at this phase of the tragic pattern. His belief that he has found a solution is based on the false assumption that surrogacy is an option, that someone else can literally be in the battle in his stead, that total loss can be at least partially spared. But the tragic pattern is not negotiable; it is either all or nothing as far as giving up is concerned, and time is running out. Worse still, sending Patroclus to battle in a vain effort to escape the ineluctable will soon prove Achilles' greatest tragic error and the source of his most exacerbating suffering. It will also be the starting point for another phase of the second manifestation of the tragic pattern. To repeat, all this happens before Hector sets fire to the ship, an action narrated immediately after the scene just described. The narratological split emphasizes the importance of this specific point of time, for even at this crucial moment, on the verge of a fire on a Greek ship, Achilles does not wholly change his mind. Despite the danger close at hand, he is not willing to give up anger and rejoin the battle. It is his refusal that dooms him to his severest loss: Patroclus enters the battle and forces the Trojans back from the ships (16.257–305), but, contrary to Achilles' explicit instructions, he chases the Trojans to their city and attacks its wall (16.684–710), dying soon after (16.786–857).

One can again perceive how this tragic pattern functions on various levels, thereby contributing to the realizations of different ends. Achilles' decision to send Patroclus as his surrogate is not his own idea. Rather, it is Patroclus who comes up with this suggestion, utilizing both the arguments of Nestor, of which Achilles is not aware (16.24–27 = 11.658–62 and 16.36–45, which are very close to 11.794–803), and the rebukes of Ajax during Achilles' meeting with the envoy in book nine (16.29–35, recall 9.628–30 and 1.636–38). The allusion to Ajax' words revives the notion of friendship, and, although Achilles' opening remarks to the weeping Patroclus seem to mock the latter's sensitivity to the Achaeans' sorry lot (16.7–19), it seems reasonable to conclude from his emotive description of the battle (16.66–79) that he does feel for his former allies, despite his incandescent hatred for Agamemnon (16.76–77). As in its earlier appearance in book nine, here, too, the discourse of friendship leads to destruction: Patroclus, who speaks both for and in the name of his friends, is actually, though unwittingly (as the poet emphasizes in 16.46–47), accelerating his own death. It is worth noting in this context that a destructive potential is inherent in the concept of surrogacy, thus imbuing Patroclus' offer with the tragic hues of an unwilled catastrophe effected through the agent's ignorance of the actual significance of his words and actions.[66] And this is not all, for the complexity of this tragic pattern is enriched even more by Achilles' tacit agreement with Zeus regarding the return to battle.

When Achilles implores his mother to beg Zeus to avenge his insult by Agamemnon, he asks explicitly that the Achaeans be driven back to their ships and penned in there (1.408–10). In book nine he conditions his return to battle with Hector's arrival upon his, Achilles', ships (9.650–53), a condition he reiterates in book sixteen (61–63). After Patroclus' fall, Thetis, ignorant of this event, comes to the aid of her mourning son and asks him why he is suffering so much given Zeus' fulfillment of his wish (18.73–77). Achilles, returning to the notion of the fulfillment of his wish (18.79), adds that it is worthless now since Patroclus is dead (18.80–82). It therefore seems likely that Achilles was bound to remain by his ships until the realization of his desire and that his behest had not yet been granted at the time of his conversation with Patroclus in book sixteen. Characteristically for a tragic text, achieving a desired goal implies a terrible loss for the supplicant.

Such profound loss breeds both predictable pain and anger in Achilles; he deeply mourns the death of his friend (18.15–35) and decides to return to war and avenge him (18.97–126). Still refusing to renounce anger, Achilles is reluctant to acknowledge his total loss, and he therefore tries to compensate for it by means of revenge. This is, of course, impossible, and his behavior will merely prolong his suffering. What is unexpected in this context is Achilles' deep insight, the psychological recognition manifest in the argumentation regarding anger. Unfortunately, insight here is marred by an even deeper blindness. On the one hand, Achilles is aware of the need to renounce anger: he wishes the complete annihilation of strife and anger (ὡς ἔρις ἔκ [. . .] ἀπόλοιτο / καὶ χόλος 18.107–8) and, what is more, formulates a sagacious perception on anger in general and its devious manipulations of the human soul.

> much sweeter than trickling honey
> it diffuses in the breasts of men, like smoke.   (18.109–10)

He also makes a direct association between this general maxim and his anger toward Agamemnon (18.111) and repeats his earlier words to Patroclus concerning his personal yielding (ἀλλὰ τὰ μὲν προτετύχθαι ἐάσομεν 18.112 = 16.60), stating the need to subdue his feelings (18.113).

On the other hand, he immediately proclaims his decision to avenge his friend (18.114), which triggers another sequence of events based on anger, thus extending the course of this tragic pattern. In other words, Achilles is blind to the fact that he is heading along the same track that he has just defined as erroneous. The general principal, so succinctly expressed, is deemed applicable only to the past but not to the present; it was wrong to be angry with Agamemnon some time ago, but it is right to be angry with Hector now.[67] Note that, despite the fact that this decision is an act of free will representing a real choice,[68] Achilles conceives of it as the will of Zeus and the rest of the gods (18.116). He starts talking of doom (*kêr* 18.117) and lot (*moira* 18.119, 120) and stresses the overwhelming power of death even over Hercules (18.117), who was subdued by *moira* and the anger of Hera (18.119). Hercules, who is here an emblem of undeserved suffering instigated by divine powers, is emphatically equated with Achilles (ὣς καὶ ἐγών 18.120) who sees himself as potentially sharing the same *moira* (18.120). This is a very quick transition from an active agent about to subdue his anger to a passive recipient subdued by the anger of a goddess. Achilles deliberately ignores the starting point of the forthcoming events, namely, his own decision to rejoin the battle. No doubt this is inevitable from his personal emotional focalization, for he must avenge the death of his friend. But recourse to the discourse of glory (νῦν δὲ κλέος ἐσθλὸν ἀροίμην 18.121), which is so closely connected with stubbornness (18.126), reverberates with earlier perceptions and their bitter outcome.

Achilles' speech to his mother reflects the internal end of the quarrel with Agamemnon. Yet the formal termination of strife has not yet been accomplished, and therefore Achilles calls an assembly (19.40–53) and publicly renounces his anger (19.54–73). In like manner Agamemnon again assumes public responsibility for his past error, pleading guilty regarding his treatment of Achilles. However, there is a difference between his statements in book nine and his words on this occasion, for now he emphasizes the central role of *Atê* in his misjudgment of the situation. The notion of *atê* was already present in book nine, where Agamemnon repeatedly used it in his speech (*emas atas* 9.115, *aasamên* 9.116, *aasamên*, 9.119),[69] but here both *atê* and the goddess *Atê* start functioning as an explicating principle that transforms the entire conception and presentation of the past.[70] Agamemnon opens his *apologia* with a direct reference to causality, insisting on not being the active agent instigating the strife (19.86). Rather, these are Zeus, *Moira*, and *Erinus* (19.87). What these divine powers literally did when he took Achilles' prize of war was to throw savage *atê* into his bosom (19.88). Being a goddess herself, *Atê* is responsible for the realization of everything to termination (19.90), and it is she, the venerated daughter of Zeus, who brings *atê* to everyone (19.91). Agamemnon ends his speech stressing this notion by referring three times to either the goddess or her actions (*Atês* [. . .] *aasthên* [. . .] *aasmên* 19.136–37). The introduction of *Atê* transposes Agamemnon's explications from causality to divine intervention and from the rational to the irrational.[71] To recapitulate, Agamemnon still takes responsibility for his actions, but the forces that led him to his miserable deed are deemed external, divine, and beyond rational comprehension.[72] However revolting this might sound from the mouth of an arrogant and selfish character such as Agamemnon, his is a metaphysical recognition of the human condition, delineating the deepest and most terrible roots of human conduct.[73] *Atê*, as one may recall, was also a prominent figure in the speech of Phoenix, in which he warned Achilles of her mischievous effects on men. And if Phoenix could see *Atê* as responsible for Achilles' behavior, then so can Agamemnon, regarding her responsible for his mistake.

Agamemnon's metaphysical recognition is formulated explicitly when he continues his speech, depicting the essential nature of *Atê* and her power over gods and men alike. Agamemnon gives the etiology of *Atê*'s appearance among men, depicting her first intervention in human affairs with its doleful outcomes. In fact, the first to fall prey to *Atê*'s maneuvers was no less than the mightiest of gods, Zeus, who was once misled (*asato*) by her (19.95). The story is that of the birth of Hercules, whom Zeus, his father, intended to be the lord of all those who live around him (19.104). But Hera deceived him (*apatêsen* 19.97), and Zeus was deeply misled (*aasthê* 19.113) when Hera tricked him into pronouncing someone else the lord of all those who live around him.[74] Agamemnon stresses the fact that, despite this act of deceit (*dolophrosunêis* [19.97], *dolophroneousa* [19.106], *dolophrosunên* [19.112]), Zeus could not revoke his words. The motif of deceit echoes Achilles' words in book nine, where he objects to any reconciliation with Agamemnon, claiming that the situation is irreversible exactly on the basis of Agamemnon's deceitful nature. *Atê,* whose conduct is based on deceit, utilizes her distorted machination in order to create an irreversible situation.

In addition to explicating Agamemnon's behavior toward Achilles as nothing more than another realization among many of this deceitful and destructive potential, the etiological story of *Atê* serves another purpose. Agamemnon's tragic understanding, his ability to abstract a general perception regarding the human condition from his own personal case, can also be perceived as a guiding line not just for his internal audience, his listeners in the assembly, but also for his external audience, the addressees of the *Iliad.*[75] For if *Atê* is a force that activates human beings in general, then her concrete intervention in the fictive world of the *Iliad* is a representation of its effect on human beings in reality. The text leads to this kind of interpretation by means of Agamemnon's equation of his feeling when he saw Hector near the Argive fleet to those of the grieving Zeus over his son's labors (19.134–36). The character who last made exactly the same equation was Achilles, who not much earlier referred to his own *moira* as responsible for the realization of his future suffering and death.[76] Needless to say, Agamemnon could not be aware of Achilles' remarks, which were uttered in his absence; the narratees of the epic, however, are very aware of this striking parallelism, and they are therefore invited to make an analogy between the divine intervention informing Agamemnon's arguments concerning his deeds in the beginning of the *Iliad* and that of Achilles' recent decision to come back to battle. Both cases can be regarded as manifestations of *Atê* in the world of men, as an intervention of a divine power that brings suffering and loss to its human agents. And this is not all. Agamemnon's etiological story illuminates not just the essential difference between the human and the divine as far as the deceitful actions of *Atê* are concerned (while there is no doubt that Zeus was extremely angry, it was Hercules, not him, who suffered immensely); this story also sheds light on the roots of the sorrowful essence of the human lot in general. When gods quarrel, it is human beings who pay the full price.

As claimed earlier, the end of the dispute with Agamemnon is the beginning of another sequence of events realized within the same tragic pattern, for Achilles' revenge against Hector is an extension of the events originating in the capture of Briseis by Agamemnon. When Achilles speaks with his mother and tells her of his decision to return to war, his discourse insinuates causality based on *timê*. Achilles himself does not explicitly mention it, but his insistence on revenge and retaliation implies it (18.90–93, 114–15). What is more, when soon afterward the poet describes Hector's attempts to possess Patroclus' corpse, he says that if Hector succeeded it would be for him a source of renown that could not be formulated in words (18.165). But as the story evolves, it becomes apparent that what Achilles is really after is not honor. Just like the capture of Briseis, an act that instigated an emotional loss far greater than the mere deprivation of a war prize and which therefore could not be materially compensated, so the death of Patroclus is an act with devastating emotional implications that could not be compensated by glory and prowess in war. Achilles concentrates on revenge rather than glory, but, as in the case of Briseis, he is once more unaware of the irretrievable implications of his loss, adhering to external action as a means of coping, unsuccessfully, with his internal wound. There is no better proof of that than his behavior after the death of Hector, when Achilles, still immersed in sorrow, insists on his basic indifference to matters of war (22.385) due to his inability to forget his friend (22.386–90). And even after the burial of Patroclus, he is still crying, unable to sleep (24.3–12) and remembering his beloved friend (24.4).[77] His original wrath, merely transferred from Agamemnon to Hector, has not dissipated, which is why he constantly dishonors Hector (24.22). And it is this mistreatment of the corpse of the dead Hector that finally provokes the gods' intervention.

Apollo finds Achilles' behavior outrageous, and he reproaches the gods for denying Hector the honorary rituals of the dead (24.38). These remarks provoke the anger of Hera (*cholôsamenê* 24.55), who does not think that the same *timê* should be given to a mortal and the son of a goddess (24.56–61). This description is essential to resolving the tragic pattern, for the vocabulary of anger and *timê*, which substitutes for that of wrath and humiliation, brings feasible proportions to the debate, thus reflecting the change that is about to occur. Zeus answers Hera, saying that their *timê* would not be the same (24.66) and yet, since Hector had special status among the gods due to his reverence toward them (24.66–70), his body would be redeemed. Note that Zeus insists on direct interaction between Achilles and Priam, where compensating gifts are given in exchange for the dead body, and rejects the offer to smuggle Hector's corpse to his father's house without Achilles' notice.[78] He emphasizes this interaction both in the latter passage and when Thetis comes (24.107–9), telling her that direct contact is a means of giving Achilles renown (*kudos* 24.110). When Zeus tells Thetis to bid Achilles to return the corpse to Priam he mentions the anger of the gods (24.113) caused by Achilles' behavior and refers explicitly to his own anger (*eme* [. . .] *kecholôsthai* 24.113–14), which is a direct outcome of the wrath of Achilles (24.114). Wrath, which opened the epic, should therefore yield to the power of the gods, and Zeus finishes his speech with the word *iênêi* (ἰήνῃ) denoting the melting of Achilles' heart (24.119).

> Moreover, I shall send Iris to great-hearted Priam,
> to go to the Ships of the Achaeans and release his son,
> bringing such gifts to Achilles, that will melt his heart.   (24.117–19)

It is as if there is a direct line connecting Zeus via Iris to Priam, and then Priam to Achilles, thus making both Priam and Achilles the agents realizing Zeus' will. There is also a delicate balance between the two parts of the last phrase, where the parallelism between its two halves reflects the change in Achilles: Priam will bring the gifts to Achilles, and these gifts will melt his heart; the release of the beloved son entails the softening of the resilient soul.

So Thetis comes to her son, and after referring sympathetically to his grief (24.128–32) she relates Zeus' bidding, word for word (24.133–36). She does not, however, mention Priam's name, and in no more than two sentences Achilles yields to Zeus' will (24.139–40). The choice of the poet regarding what to omit and what to repeat is revealing both here and in the subsequent passage. The conventions of oral tradition allow the poet to repeat the words said by Zeus to Thetis when Thetis transmits them to Achilles. There is therefore nothing exceptional in this phenomenon as such; what is exceptional here is the decision of the poet to bring merely these words and to omit the rest of the conversation. Thus, although the dialogue between mother and son was apparently quite long, as can be deduced from the poet's own reference to the conversation (24.141–42), what we have in the text is very scant, nothing more than Zeus' words, with their natural conclusion that Achilles must release the body and accept ransom in exchange (24.137), in addition to Achilles' own acceptance of Zeus' will summarized succinctly in two lines (24.139–40). We hear nothing of the process leading to his final answer, which is illuminating when one recalls how persuasion, or more precisely the refusal to be persuaded, was so crucial to Achilles' behavior through all former occurrences of the pattern. This is an indication that this time there is something essentially different in the realization of the pattern. In like manner, Zeus' repetition of his words regarding the softening of Achilles (24.146–47 = 24.118–19) and their recurrence with slight modifications by Iris to Priam (24.175–76) and by Priam to his wife (24.195–96) serve as a reemphasis of the importance of the process that Achilles is about to go through. In his reply to his mother he acquiesces only in Zeus' will, for he is willing to give up the corpse solely because Zeus demands it (24.140); what remains is his acknowledgment of the importance of this act to himself.[79]

The circling of the tomb of Patroclus with Hector's corpse (24.14–18) is basically a ritualistic act of honoring the dead.[80] But it is also a reflection of Achilles' inability to start the process of mourning, the end of which is separation from the beloved. Achilles is still moving in the same emotional circle, trying to be close to his loved one who has gone down to Hades. All is in vain, for Patroclus is now forever beyond reach. It is, of course, extremely painful, but what the *Iliad* teaches is that the only possible way to cope successfully with such pain is through psychological recognition, whose initial and enormous step is acknowledging one's helplessness in the face of this absolute limit.

Achilles' powerful scene of acknowledgment is woven into the conversation with Priam, where actions get their full depth and meaning in a verbal formulation of the tragic. Full acknowledgment of the basic helplessness inherent in the human condition is as praiseworthy as it is difficult. But the ability to recognize that this doleful aspect of human life is part of an overall tragic situation shared by every human being is even harder to conceive. What is so remarkable in this episode in the *Iliad* is not so much the mere occurrence of tragic wisdom or its sophisticated formulation; rather, it is the decision of the poet to let this formulation emerge from the mouth of the once self-centered, egocentric, and implacable Achilles. This is the same Achilles who, in response to an insult, was on the verge of killing Agamemnon in the beginning of the *Iliad*; the same Achilles who, out of spite, beseeched his mother to bring many woes on his fellow Argives; and the same Achilles who refused the generous compensation offered him for this insult since nothing, absolutely nothing in the world, could compensate his wounded ego. The poet's choice in endowing such a character with a tragic voice is especially striking due to the incongruity between his former characterization and his present state of mind. Moreover, it is this incongruity, the final stage of a long process of learning, that enhances Achilles' tragic recognition with such convincing force. Achilles' humane understanding reflects a real and profound change that has gone through several phases before its final formulation in the last book of the *Iliad*. A clear path can be now traced from his previously articulated thoughts regarding the absurd nature of the war, the value of human life, and the evil implicit in wrath. What remains in order to attain tragic metaphysical recognition is consciousness of the horrible essence of the human condition due to its inextricability from malevolent divine schemes. And it is here, in the tale of Zeus' two jars, that Achilles both formulates and accepts the breach between divine intervention and human causality.

Indeed, the tale of Zeus' two jars, one full of evil and the other full of blessings (24.527–33), is a masterful representation of the tragic human lot.[81] Not only is Zeus' choice of good and evil for every human being an arbitrary one, but this choice is either a mixture of good and evil or purely evil; there is not a single human being who can be considered totally blessed, and the lengthier text given to the description of one whose lot is exclusively dismal (24.531–33) emphasizes the basic misery of the human condition. The reason for Zeus' choice of this agonizing ground for the lives of mortals is beyond the limits of human understanding, but its existence is both acknowledged and accepted as an inalienable part of every human being's life. It is this general maxim that Achilles applies to his life and that of his interlocutor, and he applies it in such a way that indicates the thoroughness of his personal change. The fact that he starts with his father and not with himself attests to the long way he has come since the beginning of the *Iliad* (24.534–42), for now he is able to fully consider the price that other people must pay for his enterprises. But the most astonishing feature of his speech is the move from his own father to Priam. No doubt, the capacity to see the pain he has caused and is still causing another is a remarkable achievement for someone who was until very recently blind to the existence of others. And yet even now this other is his closest relative, namely, his father.[82] When Achilles moves so smoothly from mention of himself bringing grief to Priam and his sons (24.542) to description of Priam's tragic reversal from prosperity to disaster (24.543), we know that the wheel has come full circle.[83] Achilles' remark concerning the grief he brings to Troy is carefully incorporated within his first self-reference in the speech: "I do not take care of my aging father since I sit here idly, away from my fatherland, bringing grief to you and your children" (24.540–42). This could be the opening sentence of a self-absorbed and self-pitying oration, but Achilles' choice is to direct his attention to the concrete other in front of him: "and of you too, old man, we hear that once you were blessed" (καὶ σέ, γέρον, τὸ πρὶν μὲν ἀκούομεν ὄλβιον εἶναι 24.543). Achilles deliberately concentrates on the "you" (σέ) rather than falling back on his own personal woe (24.543–48). His concluding remarks echo the phrases anticipating the tale of the two jars (24.522–24) and call for endurance in light of the futility of grief; the dead will never come back to life, and much pain is still ahead:

Endure, and do not mourn incessantly in your heart,
for you will act to no avail if you grieve about your son,
you shall not raise him before you suffer once more another evil.

(24.549–51)

The tragic moral of his speech could not be more transparent.[84] These words undoubtedly reflect the depth of the process that Achilles has gone through, a process culminating in the metaphysical recognition he can now articulate. Once someone so inhuman that he was compared to an object, the durable stone,[85] he has now grown into a human being moved to tears on comprehending the meaning of his humanity and accepting the lot of being human.[86] This is not to say that the situation is irreversible. What the poet unfolded at length and what asked so much of Achilles can easily deteriorate to the former state of uncontrolled anger. Even now the situation is extremely volatile, as can be seen from Achilles' angry reaction to Priam's refusal to sit down (24.559) and his implied threat (24.568–70). The long and arduous itinerary from anger to grief, which is the vehicle leading to the humane insight of Achilles, can always, and very easily, be reversed. Indomitable anger lurks constantly behind reconciliation, waiting to grip again the souls of grieving human beings in order to rekindle the fire of wrath.[87] One of the most terrible aspects of the humane insight of Achilles is the perception that it is exactly the same grief that nourished his recently acquired understanding that can be responsible for his future decline and inhumanity. This is why Achilles bids the servants to wash Hector's corpse far from the eyes of his father

[. . .] so that Priam shall not see his son,
lest he will not check the anger in his grieving heart
when he sees his child, and Achilles' heart will be stirred.

(24.583–85)

After preparing the corpse of Hector, Achilles exhorts Priam to join him in a meal.[88] As one may recall, Achilles refused to eat after he heard of Patroclus' death until he had killed Hector, and Athena had to nourish him with nectar and ambrosia (19.349–54). After Patroclus' burial, when everyone went to eat and sleep (24.1–3), Achilles did not join them, and when his mother came to him twelve days later she found him eating his heart, abstaining from food and drink (24.129–30). His proposal to Priam to remember the meal (24.601), as well as the exemplum of Niobe who remembered to eat (24.602–13) after the great loss of all her children, testify to his accept-ance of the finality of Patroclus' death.[89] Memory of the beloved friend fi-nally gives way to remembering the necessities of living, which include sleep and sex in addition to food (24.675–76).[90]

The tragic insight of Achilles, according to which extreme suffering, a horrifying yet ineluctable component of human life, cannot be avenged but merely mourned and endured, has thus terminated the recurrence of the tragic pattern. His willingness to give up his anger, as well as his awareness of the ease of its possible resurfacing, prevents another sequence of blindness and futility. And yet the price of this deep understanding of the human lot is no less than Achilles' own life. Achilles could not have reached this final per-ception without repeating the tragic pattern, including the killing of Hector. This act, an inevitable link in his process toward insight, also entails his doom.[91] Achilles had a choice, and, although he was aware of the conse-quences of his choice to kill Hector, he was blind to the full significance of this act. When blindness turns into insight, its applicability is too late for him, who has acquired it so laboriously, for his end is very near.[92] The useless-ness of Achilles' tragic wisdom is no doubt one of the most haunting aspects of this pessimistic epic, where the grueling path Achilles has to go through leads to an acknowledgment of his helplessness regarding the essence of his existence. Valor and prowess are of no avail in this context, and the newly acquired tragic depth can offer no consolation either. Yet it is exactly this use-lessness, this incapacity to put newly acquired wisdom to use, in short, this impracticality embedded in the tragic, that makes the *Iliad* such an impres-sive tragic masterpiece. For Achilles' formulation of the basic helplessness at the root of the human condition is uttered in full consciousness of its rele-vance to the speaker. Achilles may be the greatest hero of the Trojan War, but his excellence in battle cannot ameliorate his most acute pain. And it is this full acceptance of his agonizing doom that reflects the greatness of his achievement: his ability to relinquish his status as a hero in order to become a tragic hero.

To conclude: In this chapter I have limned a tragic pattern in the *Iliad* with its diverse realizations. The pattern, which traces a missed *kairos,* charts the arduous path of one who has missed his opportunity as he makes his way toward the painful psychological recognition of the irretrievable nature of his loss. In addition, the pattern both reflects and explicates the quintessential role of suffering in this tragic epic where the lives of the protagonists are con-demned to misery from the outset. This terrible lot, so vividly depicted in the tale of the two jars, is frequently an outcome of an arbitrary divine act that refutes any human effort to comprehend it by causality; while there is no doubt that this arbitrariness originates in a godly intervention, the reasons for its occurrence constantly elude rational human understanding. It is the metaphysical recognition of human helplessness in the face of the hostile divine that comprises the epic's deepest lesson, so exquisitely encapsulated in the words and characterization of its hero, Achilles.

2

Painful Remembrance of Things Past

*Passive Suffering, Agonizing Recognitions,
and Doleful Memories in the* Odyssey

*M*y introductory chapter noted that, in contrast to the *Iliad*, whose tragic nature is affirmed by ancient and modern critics alike, the status of the *Odyssey* as a tragic epic is questionable. Analysis of the tragic aspects of this work is consequently more complex than that of the *Iliad*, necessitating further clarification and textual anchoring. I have therefore split my primary discussion of the *Odyssey* and the tragic into two chapters. This chapter traces two motifs that were presented in chapter 1, suffering and recognition, and is followed by chapter 3's reading of a single seminal scene, the Cyclops episode. In this chapter I use the motifs of suffering and recognition as my key fissures, that is to say, as my central openings into textual intentionality through which I reflect on the tragic nature of the text as a whole. My claim here is that the ubiquity of these motifs in the *Odyssey* attests to the general tragic character of the epic in a manner similar to (though not identical with) the tragic pattern in the *Iliad*. The *Odyssey*, an epic with a branching episodic structure, does not share the pattern I map in my previous chapter on the *Iliad*, which is an epic revolving around a rather condensed kernel of action. Yet the *Odyssey*'s somewhat diffuse elements do converge into a unified narrative, and the tragic motifs of suffering and recognition are central to the construction of its tragic essence. Here, too, as in the *Iliad,* time plays a significant role, and its association with the tragic will again be taken up in this chapter.

To underscore once more my preliminary claim in the introduction, although suffering and recognition are necessary conditions for the tragic, they are not, in themselves, sufficient. It is their specific association with time, especially with missed or lost time, which enables the tragic to fully emerge. This is why I discuss neither Telemachus' suffering, despite its centrality in the first books of the *Odyssey,* nor his recognition of his father in spite of its considerable contribution to the last stages of the epic. This is not to diminish either the acuteness of Telemachus' suffering or the importance of his recognition; it is rather to stress the fact that Telemachus cannot be considered a tragic figure since the notion of missed *kairos* cannot be applied to him. In fact, his situation is the opposite of that of a tragic figure as regards *kairos*. The maturing Telemachus, who comes of age at the beginning of the epic, does find himself in the middle of *kairos* in its second meaning (as postulated by Smith), namely, at "a time of 'crisis' implying that the course of events poses a problem which calls for a decision at that time." But for him *kairos* has its third meaning as well: "a time when opportunity for accomplishing some purpose has opened up as a result of the problem that led to the crisis."[1] Telemachus, no longer a child, begins to pose a threat to the suitors, who consequently contrive his murder. This crisis in turn provides the opportunity to achieve the reestablishment of the house of Odysseus in Ithaca. Thus, his reunion with his father, essential for this purpose, takes place exactly at *kairos* as "the right time for something to happen,"[2] channeling the crisis to its happy resolution. Note also that, in addition to terminating the perilous period during which Telemachus' life is in jeopardy, Odysseus' homecoming also enables the son to mature successfully in his role as future ruler of his country.

For similar reasons, I refrain from discussing the recognition scene between Odysseus and his two slaves, Eumaeus and Philoetius. Although this recognition is necessary to attain their cooperation in the war against the suitors and its consequent reappropriation of the household by its former master, it cannot in itself raise these figures to the level of tragic characters. In fact, in the world of the *Odyssey* it is almost impossible for any slave, however dutiful and praiseworthy, to become a tragic figure; his time by definition dispensable, there is no meaning of the notion of "missed" *kairos* relevant to him. This is why the long absence of the master, undoubtedly an agonizing event for both staunch slaves, cannot reach the realm of the tragic for them. Since their time is devoid of the specific value that can make its loss meaningful in a tragic framework, their recognition of their master cannot imbue the long time that has elapsed with tragic signification.

One might object to my distinction between slaves and the tragic potential, claiming that slaves can be regarded as tragic figures both because of their origin, as they are not necessarily born slaves, and as human beings naturally sharing the human condition, including its tragic aspects. True, slaves can be freeborn and become slaves later in life, as in the case of Eumaeus, who was not merely freeborn but also of royal stock (15.412–14). Moreover, every freeborn woman could be enslaved after the conquest of her city, a frequent phenomenon in the world of the *Iliad* and the *Odyssey* as well as much later in the Greek city-states. In these instances, there is no doubt that a "total loss" in relation to time does exist, a loss that might be regarded as emblematic of tragic suffering; and in fact both the *Iliad* and the *Odyssey* show traces of awareness of this horrifying loss for slaves who were once free citizens. Thus, in the *Iliad,* when Briseis weeps over the corpse of Patroclus, she speaks of her past suffering when her city was destroyed and both her husband and her three brothers died (19.291–97). Similarly, in commenting on the other female mourners, the narrator adds the very subtle remark that in addition to their grief at Patroclus' death, each one wailed due to private woe (19.301–2). In like manner, Eumaeus' account of his kidnapping (15.403–84) is suffused with grief while implicit perspectives on his horrendous fate are scattered in comments throughout his narrative. And yet, even such humane epics as the *Iliad* and the *Odyssey* succeed only very partially in transcending the limits posed by a social reality in which a crudely absolute demarcation exists between slaves and free people.[3] While slaves can gain a lot of sympathy from benevolent masters, their irretrievable loss of liberty is conceived as no more than a sad occurrence; from the moment of the unchangeable reversal in their fortune, they are viewed as slaves whose time is dispensable. Note that even as sensitive a man as Odysseus not only responds somewhat indifferently to the grief of his own loyal slave (whose role as a future collaborator is essential) but, most revealing, he does so in the midst of his own ordeals back home while still disguised as a poor beggar. For what Odysseus has to say to Eumaeus on hearing his narrative of loss of freedom is that, although he, Odysseus, found the story very moving (15.486–87), Eumaeus should be grateful to Zeus for having added good fortune to his travail. In Odysseus' view, in reaching Ithaca Eumaeus has arrived at the house of a very generous man who takes care of all his needs (15.488–92).

Let us go, then, to the construction of the tragic in the *Odyssey*. My first step in tracking the fissure of suffering in all its tragic ramifications is to trace a salient aspect of this motif, namely, the passivity of the tragic character in response to his or her suffering. To put this somewhat differently, in those instances in which a tragic character is passive, the actions precipitating his or her suffering are not an outcome of the decisions of a conscious agent who willingly chooses to act in one way rather than another. On the contrary, they reflect the helplessness of a victim of circumstance subjected to powers beyond his or her reach. Take, for example, the case of Menelaus' missed *kairos*, the late return to his home that prevents him from avenging the murder of his brother Agamemnon by Aegisthus. Nestor says that if Menelaus had found Aegisthus alive on his return he would have killed him and disgraced his corpse (3.256–61), but he did not avenge his brother because Zeus had hurled his ship to distant Egypt (3.286–300), from which he returned only after many years and on the day that Orestes killed Aegisthus (3.306–12). Menelaus himself refers explicitly to this awful point in time when the two brothers were moving on two parallel axes, separated from each other at such a *kairotic* moment: while (ἦος) Menelaus was making a fortune (4.90) at the same time (τῆος) someone stealthily killed his brother (4.92–93);[4] from that time on, his fortune no longer brought him joy (4.94). The full story of the delay appears later when Menelaus recounts his negligence of the sacrifices to the gods as he tells of his adventures in Egypt (4.351–52, 471–80).

Menelaus' missed *kairos* is exemplary in illustrating the notion of tragic time. The *Odyssey* constantly addresses the tragic implications of the human inability to be ceaselessly attuned to the demands of time. Characteristically, scenes revolving around missed *kairos* are associated with a temporary lapse—of vigilance, of consciousness, of will—that leads to catastrophic results. Such is the case of the exhausted Odysseus falling asleep, a sleep that, however short, is unfortunately long enough to breed agonizing consequences. This happens twice. The first time is soon after Odysseus' visit to Aeolus, controller of the winds. The latter gives Odysseus a bag with all the winds except that blowing from the west to enable him to reach his home safely and swiftly (10.19–26). After nine days at sea, so close to the fatherland that even human beings on the shore are recognizable, the exhausted Odysseus (who has been handling the sail all that time) is overcome by sweet sleep (10.31), thus giving his crew an opportunity to open the bag, of whose contents they are ignorant (10.38–45). They soon become aware of both the contents and their calamitous mistake when the newly released winds burst free and carry them back to Aeolus' island (10.47–55). It is worth noting that, with the benefit of hindsight, the narrator Odysseus refers to this homecoming as something that was not destined to be realized, emphasizing both the crew's ignorance of the possible result of their deed[5] and the shared responsibility of leader and crew for this mistake: "for we were lost due to our own folly" (10.27). The fact that this statement is narrated as a prolepsis gives it an ominous hue,[6] stressing the metaphysical powers that contribute to the realization of this inverted homecoming. This is an inversion as it sends Odysseus and his men back to the undesired home they have just left. The association of their mistake with divine powers soon becomes even clearer in the dialogue between Odysseus and his hosts. Seeing their former and unexpected guest, the astonished family of Aeolus asks Odysseus which evil *daimon* attacked him (10.64) after they had taken such care to ensure his successful homecoming (10.65–66). Odysseus answers that his bad comrades aided by his sleep injured him (10.68–69). He therefore pleads for help, but Aeolus rejects both man and plea, claiming that Odysseus deserves reproof more than any living creature (10.72). In addition he opines that the occurrences are proof of Odysseus' status as a hated object to the gods, a statement he repeats twice in two consecutive lines (10.74, 10.75).[7] To conclude my discussion of this episode and its tragic significations: the tenth day of the journey from Aeolus' island is an exemplary instance of *kairos,* a time of crisis during which Odysseus' arrival home with all his crew safe and sound is at stake. Odysseus' temporary lapse of vigilance, his falling asleep, resolves this *kairotic* scene as a catastrophe that generates immense suffering for both his men (who will meet their deaths at sea) and himself (delaying his homecoming by many years).

The second incident of falling asleep that leads to the missing of *kairos*—with even more execrable consequences—is in Thrinacia, the island of the cattle of Helios. Warned both by Tiresias (11.106–13) and by Circe (12.127–41) of the hazardous potential of the place, Odysseus first tries to persuade his comrades to avoid disembarking and sail on (12.271–76). No doubt this is good counsel, but it is nevertheless rejected by the overextended and weary crew, who find their leader's suggestion too daunting (12.279–93). Odysseus must yield, though regarding their refusal as an evil omen planned by a *daimon* (12.295), but not before he stipulates that all must refrain from eating the cattle (12.298–302).[8] As long as they have enough food the men do not touch the forbidden meat, but trapped on an island they cannot yet leave and having consumed the provisions given them by Circe, the famished comrades find the temptation more and more difficult to resist.[9] It is during this perilous period that Odysseus sneaks away from his men in order to pray for the gods to rescue them (12.333–37). According to Odysseus it was they, the gods, who then poured sweet sleep on his eyelids (12.338), thus enabling Eurylochus to induce the rest of the crew to kill and eat some of the cattle. Odysseus repeats this version as soon as he smells the roasted beef, accosting Zeus and the rest of the gods as those who lulled him pitilessly to a sleep (12.372) that would bring him to ruin (*eis atên* 12.372). Soon afterward Helios justifiably demands retribution for the desecration (12.377–83); when the men leave the island Zeus attacks their ship, killing all but Odysseus (12.399–419). Thus, Odysseus' lapse of vigilance during *kairos,* at a time of crisis in which his crew's lives are at stake, again facilitates the wrongs of his men, their catastrophic mistake, and their consequent deaths.

In addition to exemplifying the notion of missed *kairos* and its tragic implications, these examples illustrate my earlier claim that the motif of suffering refers not merely to active agents who bring misery upon themselves but also to victims of powers that are beyond their reach and influence. There are other cases in which human beings who did not instigate or initiate an action are nevertheless forced to endure its devastating consequences. And, indeed, the *Odyssey* is so replete with the agonizing experiences of a tragic epic that one wonders how it ever became a prototype of comedy. Note that the presentation of the eponymous hero as a passive victim of suffering is a leitmotif in the *Odyssey.* Already in the fourth line of the opening book the narrator describes Odysseus as "the one who suffered so many woes at sea," and not long afterward Athena pleads with Zeus to aid Odysseus, "who indeed suffers calamities for a long time, away from his friends" (1.49). She also recounts his grievances (*kêdea*) to the rest of the gods (5.5). Human beings, too, refer constantly to Odysseus as a sufferer. In the first assembly in the epic, explaining a divine portent to his fellow people in Ithaca, the hero Halitherses refers to Odysseus as the one who "suffered many terrible woes" (2.174). Menelaus tells Telemachus that of all those who died in Troy he mourns most for Odysseus, "since none of the Achaeans suffered so much as Odysseus suffered and endured" (4.106–7). Even Alcinous, after only a brief acquaintance with Odysseus, intervenes in Odysseus' narrative of his past, calling it a story of "mournful grievances" (*kêdea lugra* 11.369). What is more, Odysseus' suffering looms large in the ultimate realization of the much desired homecoming. Thus Zeus, in a speech that is highly favorable to Odysseus, predicts his homecoming without omitting the disasters that still await the hero (5.33); thus Calypso mentions Odysseus' lot of grievances (*kêdea*) before he reaches home (5.206–7); and thus Tiresias states his prophecy of the arrival at Ithaca despite the suffering of woes (11.104). Reference to suffering is most frequent in the hero's own words, in his pleas to a total stranger such as Nausicaa (6.173), her mother Arete (7.152), or her father Alcinous (7.211–14); in the opening section of the narrative of his life story as told to the Phaeacians (9.12–13, 15); or in his stories about his fictive self, which he recounts disguised as a beggar (17.284–85, 444; 19.170).

Suffering, an essential component of the tragic, is a central motif in the *Odyssey* that is not limited to the lot of the hero of the poem. Menelaus depicts himself to Telemachus as being in a state of constant mourning due to the death of his brother (4.90–101), Nestor's son refers to the suffering of Telemachus in the absence of his father (4.164–67), and Eumaeus regards his life story as one of "wretched grievances" (*kêdesin* [. . .] *leugaleoisi* 15.399). The notion that suffering is inherent in the life of every human being is succinctly formulated by one of the characters in the epic, the herdsman Philoetius:

> but the gods plunge in misery men who wander afar
> whenever they weave woe into their lot, which they do even to
> kings.   (20.195–96)

This is a general truth, which he applies immediately to the case of Odysseus (20.199–225). And it is this misery, so deeply rooted in the tragic conception of human life that is reflected in my next topic of discussion, the recurrence of crying in the epic.

When Hermes arrives at Calypso's cave the narrator expatiates on the beauty of the place (5.59–77), stressing no less than three times how wonderful it is to behold (*thêêsaito, thêeito, thêêsato* 5.74–76). This repetition might be regarded as inelegant,[10] but it emphasizes the subsequent description of the tearful Odysseus who sits on the shore and cries (5.81–84). This description of "the most woeful man" (5.105) in tears is repeated somewhat later (5.151–58).[11] The cave is no doubt a wonder to behold, but, and here is another instance of the poet's subtlety, it is only a wonder to behold if one belongs to the immortals (5.74). Note that both the general statement regarding the beauty of the place and the specific occasion of Hermes' arrival refer to a divine gaze.[12] In contrast, the human gaze, that of Odysseus, is "full of tears" (*dakrusi* [. . .] *erechthôn* 5.83) as he looks, heartbroken and crying (*dakrua leibôn*), at the barren sea (5.84).[13] Thus, while a god might feast his eyes on the astonishing aspects of Calypso's abode and its variegated birds and trees, a mortal, who is literally absent from this beauty, sits with his back to it, perceiving nothing but the same despair-inducing, barren sea.

Crying is also frequent in Odysseus' story of his adventures. Thus, upon arrival at Aeaea, Circe's island, Odysseus confronts his comrades, asking them to listen to him "although they had definitely suffered misfortunes" (10.189).[14] When they hear his suggestion to land on the island their hearts break (10.198), and, remembering their former cannibalistic experiences (10.199–200), they start crying, "shedding heavy tears" (10.201). Later when the crew is divided in two—one part goes off to explore the new place while the rest remain—both parties cry (10.208–9). As one may recall, Circe bewitches the crew members that come to her home and turns them into animals until Odysseus arrives and forces her to dispel the charm. Yet the moment they are metamorphosed into men the comrades start crying, and this despite the fact that they look younger and more handsome than they were before (10.395–99). When Odysseus returns to the group that was left behind he finds them "shedding heavy tears" (10.408–9), and when the two parties meet at Circe's house they weep (10.453–54). These are not tears of happiness, as becomes clear in Circe's comment in response to their cries, saying she is quite aware of their past suffering (10.457–59). She also implores them to stay with her for a while until they recuperate, for now "their heart is remote from joy" (10.464–65) "since they have suffered exceedingly" (10.465).

The Hades episode is also replete with tears both before and during its actual occurrence. When Odysseus first hears from Circe that he has to go down to the realm of the dead his heart breaks (10.496) and he starts crying, wishing to die (10.497–98).[15] The hearts of the crew also break when they hear the news (10.566),[16] and they start crying and tearing their hair (10.567). When Circe arrives, just before they leave, Odysseus again uses the formulaic expression "shedding heavy tears" (10.570), and he uses it once more soon afterward (11.5).[17] In Hades, Odysseus bursts into tears the moment he sees Elpenor (11.55) and his mother (11.87). Agamemnon weeps on meeting Odysseus, "dropping heavy tears" (11.391), and Odysseus bursts into tears the moment he sees Agamemnon (11.395); at the end of their conversation both men stand in sorrow "shedding heavy tears" (11.466).[18]

As many of these examples attest, it is not so much suffering itself that makes people cry as it is the agony of resurfacing memories.[19] In other words, it is the act of recollection, with its vivification and re-presentation of past sorrows, that turns the present into such a doleful and tearful experience. The association between fretting memories and the tragic will be more thoroughly discussed in chapters 5 and 6. At this point I will focus on the hazards embedded in memory's opposite, sweet forgetfulness and its anodyne effects. I do this both to accentuate the importance of memory in this epic and to shed light on the link between choosing not to forget, choosing to live, and the tragic.

In light of the centrality of these themes, it should come as little surprise that the perils entailed in forgetfulness can already be detected in one of the first episodes to take place soon after the sacking of Troy. When Odysseus and his crew reach the land of the Lotophagi, the leader sends three heralds to scout the new land. Odysseus states explicitly that the denizens did not intend any harm to his men, but they gave the crew the lotus to taste (9.92–93). Yet the fruit, though not destructive to the body, is extremely destructive to the soul, for the three who eat from it immediately lose the will to move from the place, to say nothing of a return journey (9.95): all they wish is to stay forever on this serene island and "to forget their homecoming" (νόστου τε λαθέσθαι 9.97). What the Lotophagi are actually offering to their visitors is more than just tasty food; it is no less than a constant present of oblivion marred neither by harrowing memories of the past nor by anxious anticipation of dangerous adventure in the future. Their island is therefore a haven totally devoid of the framing effects of time, no doubt an irresistible temptation to the already weary crew. Odysseus, however, immediately recognizes the pernicious nature of the forbidden fruit, and he forces the three crying men back to the ship where he binds them (9.98–99). He also accelerates the departure lest anyone again eat from the lotus and forget the homecoming (9.101–2).[20] And what is merely hinted at in the short scene of the Lotophagi is expanded in the episode of the Sirens.[21]

It is worth noting here that the meeting with the Sirens is Odysseus' first adventure after leaving the island of Circe for good (as the visit to Hades was a separate episode at the end of which the hero and his men returned to Circe). That departure, however, takes place after an entire year during which Odysseus himself has been oblivious of both past and future. Moreover, when Odysseus finally decides to terminate his stay on this blissful island it is not an outcome of his own will but rather in response to an initiative of his people (10.472–74).[22] It is in this seductive light of oblivion that one should examine the Sirens' episode and its significations.

During a relatively short span of text the Sirens are referred to three times, first by Circe to Odysseus in a prolepsis prophesying the dangerous potential of their encounter (12.39–54), then by Odysseus who partially recounts the words of Circe (12.158–64) to his comrades, and then once more as an analepsis by Odysseus who fully narrates the episode (12.181–200). When Circe describes the Sirens she emphasizes their ability to "exercise their enchantments" (*thelgousin* 12.40, 44) and she describes their power as based on a mixture of ignorance of their potential danger in approaching them (12.41) and the act of listening to their voices (12.41). The Sirens use their enchanting powers to deprive the listener of homecoming and consequently meeting his wife and children (12.42–43). And, although they do have "a sweet voice" (12.44), their abode is disgusting: They sit on a meadow surrounded by a great heap of bones of rotting men whose skin shrivels up. They therefore elicit contrasting reactions through different senses: appealing to the ear, they are revolting both to eye and nose. This is important, for it reflects—and this in a recited poem meant mainly for the ear—the supremacy of the auditory over the visual and the olfactory taken together.[23] What Circe does not tell Odysseus is how exactly the Sirens achieve their destructive end, the nature of their song that makes it so powerful that even the ghastly sight and smell cannot deter the sailor from approaching their deadly island. She does tell him, however, how he can know this for himself: the ears of all the rest of the crew being stopped with wax, he himself, with his ears open, will be firmly tied to the mast. Thus, he can both hear their song and be immune to its dangerous powers (12.47–52). When Odysseus prepares his people for the meeting with the Sirens, he omits most of the information regarding the exact nature of their danger, referring only to their voices and expanding on the way they should confront them (12.158–64).

They approach the island soon after, and Odysseus can hear their voices clearly for the wind has stopped blowing (12.168–69). Their first words indicate their knowledge of both the identity of the hero and of momentous events in his past. The words "come here quickly, much praised Odysseus, great fame of the Achaeans" (12.185) are a direct allusion to *Iliad* 9.673 in which Agamemnon accosts Odysseus after the failed embassy to Achilles.[24] It is now clear why Circe did not tell Odysseus more about the Sirens' song: they compose a new and personal song for every new arrival. Using a voice that has a tone as sweet as honey (12.187), they sing to Odysseus about his past or, to be more precise, about that moment in the Trojan War when Achilles' refusal to rejoin the battle cost the Greeks much misery. Yet, like so many dirgeful songs in the *Odyssey*, it is a pleasure to listen, and "no doubt, after enjoying it one returns with even more knowledge than he had before" (12.188). The Sirens therefore seem to embody the promise that Odysseus can acquire the two things he most desires: knowledge and homecoming. For the Sirens know not only all the suffering that took place earlier in Troy (12.189–90) but actually everything that happens all over the all-nourishing earth (12.191). The song is therefore carefully adapted to the listener, who is invited to join the Sirens only for a short while, to enjoy their song and knowledge, and then to return home much wiser than before.[25]

As predicted by Circe, Odysseus finds the temptation irresistible, and he wishes to disembark on the island and continue to listen to the Sirens. His wish is understandable, and I shall therefore not ponder it, but what still demands clarification is the way the song succeeds in subduing the revolting aspects of the Sirens' island. The text does not refer to this issue explicitly, but the emphasis on memory does invite consideration of the stark contrast between the seductive aural beauty and the disgusting visual and olfactory ugliness. On one level one might claim that the song is so beautiful and its content so tempting to Odysseus that he simply ignores the dead and their abhorrent smell. But this would be both too simple and too obtuse to the acuity of the text, for Odysseus is not like the other sailors in their ignorance of the danger of the place and the promises of its inhabitants. He knows all too well that the island is deadly and the Sirens' promise of return is a blunt lie. Consequently, if Odysseus still finds the island so alluring, this is not because he believes he would leave it but rather the opposite, because he is attracted by the death it portends.[26] The Sirens promise Odysseus such an intense experience of memory, offering such an overwhelming version of his suffering in the past that he would forget any wish to have a future. Immersed in bygone happenings, he will become oblivious of any notion of things to come, thus embracing the death that awaits him on the island. If the Lotophagi proposed forgetfulness of both past and future in exchange for a permanent heavenly present, then the Sirens suggest an extreme memory of the past that makes any future dispensable. Consequently even the present is annihilated in a realization of the death wish of the suffering hero.

To conclude the two parallel episodes, in order to return home Odysseus must relinquish both his paradisiacal aspirations and his suicidal wishes, continue remembering his past without succumbing to the daunting effects of memory, and finally adhere to the notion of a future, however difficult and full of woe. This is, no doubt, a task that is as heroic as it is deeply tragic, and I shall say more about it later. Now, however, I wish to resume my discussion of the *Odyssey*'s treatment of the past or, more precisely, of its emphasis on the importance of remembering as a constructive element of one's identity. All the cases I discuss in the following are hermeneutically opened by means of the same fissure, which is also an essential component of the tragic: the poem's various instances of recognition and their close link with the very distant past.

The first physical recognition of Odysseus after his return to Ithaca takes place in his home. Notably, the recognizing agent is not a human being but an animal, the dog Argus.[27] In order to fully perceive the signification of this animal in the recognition scenes, as well as its contribution to the tragic in the epic, I interrupt my discussion of this scene for an excursus regarding dogs. To begin with, this is not the first encounter of Odysseus with the dogs of the house. When the hero arrives home disguised as a beggar the dogs of the swineherd almost tear him to pieces, perceiving him as a stranger and therefore a potential enemy to the house (14.29–38).[28] Of course, he is a genuine stranger to them, since they were born long after he left home, but their reaction is emblematic, reflecting how deeply alienated from his home the master of the house has become. Argus, in contrast, remembers the master who reared him before leaving for Troy (17.292–94). The passage describing the meeting of the hero and his dog is rather long (17.291–327), and the poet has woven within it some of the central motifs of the epic. The first motif, physical recognition, appears already at the beginning of the passage when Argus lifts his head and perks his ears the moment he hears the conversation between Odysseus and Eumaeus (17.291). Later the poet states explicitly that the dog recognizes Odysseus when he is near (17.301) and wags his tail and drops his ears (17.301–2). For a dog, a life span of more than twenty years is almost, if not literally, mythical, and there is therefore little doubt that when Odysseus arrives Argus is on the threshold of death. Thus, the poet uses the very old dog as a symbol of the damage of passing time, on the one hand, and of the deterioration of a stale household, so impaired by the long absence of its master, on the other.

Between the phrase in which the dog notices his master and the phrase in which he recognizes him there is a passage depicting the abyss between past and present in the dog's life. The narrator opens with a brief description of Argus' frequent participation in hunting in the past (17.294–95) and then the contrasting present (*dê tote* 17.296), characterized by passive stability (17.296, 300), disability and disinclination to move (17.303–4), and humiliation: Argus is lying in a big dunghill (17.297), his body full of ticks (17.300). Odysseus weeps at this doleful sight (17.304) and accosts Eumaeus, comparing the marvelous dog to his squatting in the dung (17.306). In his answer Eumaeus emphasizes the contrast between past and present by associating the dog's former exceptional hunting capabilities (17.316–17) with the time of Odysseus' departure for Troy (17.313–14). The dog was then known for his speed and strength (17.315). Next Eumaeus links the ineluctable decline caused by time to the agonizing implications of Odysseus' absence, already apparent in the earlier description of Argus when the narrator uses the genitive absolute to associate the absence of Odysseus with Argus' pitiful condition both temporally and causally (ἀποιχομένοιο ἄνακτος 17.296). Now Eumaeus says the same thing, a concatenation of the dog's poor state (17.318) and his master's death far from home (17.318–19). He then goes on to describe the deterioration of the household in the absence of its ruler (17.319–23). These two aspects, the effects of passing time and the consequences of Odysseus' long absence, are not limited to the dog. They are also evident in the lives of the hero's parents, one of whom died of grief and longing for her son (11.202–3) and the other, though alive, is living like a dog (11.187–96); and when his son sees him in this condition for the first time (24.226–31), he reacts in the same way he reacted earlier to the sight of Argus: he weeps (24.232–34).

The dog is a recurrent motif in both epics, and its association with humiliation is not limited to the pitiful condition of the faithful old dog at the house of Odysseus. In the *Iliad* dogs regularly connote denigrating characteristics such as shamelessness and cruelty and sometimes unfaithfulness and even betrayal (22.74–76). Since this aspect of the dog motif is more pertinent to my discussion of the god Hephaestus, I refer the reader to its analysis in chapter 6. Despite the consistently negative depiction of dogs in the *Iliad,* there is also an extremely and no less pervasive positive portrayal of this animal that is relevant here, especially regarding its relationship with man. And in fact it is the positive perspective of the dog that is reflected in the archaeological evidence.[29]

In two important contexts in the *Iliad,* hunting and herding, dogs are constantly mentioned as cooperative and helpful. Skilled hunters themselves (10.360–64, 15.271–72, 579–80, 22.189–91), dogs accompany human hunters and assist them (11.292–93, 12.41, 147, 13.471–75, 17.725–29, 21.573–78) in pursuit of wild animals such as lions (3.21–26, 8.338–42) or boars (9.544, 11.414–18), which sometimes attack them (11.324–25). In like manner, dogs are extremely helpful in their function as guardians of herds. They are vigilant custodians (10.183–87), helping the peasants in general (12.302–3) and chasing away wild animals in particular (11.548–54, 17.108–11, 17.657–62). The task is difficult and occasionally ends in failure (13.198–200, 17.61–67, 18.577–86). It is also very risky since a dog can be devoured by the wild animal (15.586–87). This is a puzzlingly contradictory portrait, for the same animal is depicted as extremely good and extremely bad, the emblem of fidelity and the incarnation of treachery, man's best friend, willing to die protecting his interests, or his worst enemy, eating the corpse of its benefactor.[30] How, if at all, can one reconcile these two contrasting aspects of this motif?

The answer lies in the differentiation the poet makes between the contexts in which he uses this motif. The poet of the *Iliad* did not invent this dual potential of the dog motif, but he utilizes it for his own ends, not to create an uncanny effect based on equivocality but to clearly demarcate the distorting and distorted nature of war.[31] The *Iliad* consistently emphasizes the horrors of war and its terrible effects on all participants, regardless of their positions as winners or losers. Achilles' deterioration to bestiality when he turns into a slaughtering animal after the death of Patroclus is not the exception but rather the rule here, exemplifying the inevitable erosion of the humane in any human being participating in a long war. In this light it is easy to see the symbolic function of dogs in this epic: man's devoted friends and helpers in peacetime, they turn into his fiercest enemies during a time of war. This symbolic usage becomes even more salient when one takes into consideration the equivocality of the dog's status as a domesticated animal. In James Redfield's pithy formulation, "[T]he dog is the emblem of the imperfectly socialized. The dog is the most completely domesticated animal; he is capable even of such human feelings as love and shame. But he is only imperfectly capable; he remains an animal. The dog thus represents man's resistance to acculturation."[32] The majority of the derogatory references to the dog in the *Iliad* reflect the reality of the exposition, while positive mention is mainly in similes. Unlike metaphor, which tends to blur the boundary between tenor and vehicle, the simile preserves the marker separating the two, thereby reminding the audience of the gap between actual and imaginary presence. And since in the grim world of the *Iliad* the reality is that of atrocious war, actions associated with peace can be evoked as a potential reflected in figurative language, never to be realized in the actual events in the tale.

Given the inconclusiveness of the representation of the dog in the *Iliad,* one might wonder whether the *Odyssey* treats this animal in an essentially different way, despite its very different thematic and plot structure. In fact, the *Odyssey* is similar to the *Iliad* in the duality of its perception of the dog. True, its paramount emphasis on the animal's fidelity and devotion is positive, but this is because the *Odyssey,* despite occasional strife, is a postwar epic. In this context, as in the *Iliad,* the dog is man's best friend. Thus, in the midst of the treachery of the suitors, who will soon conspire to kill Odysseus' son, the dogs symbolize fidelity to both master and house. Note the recurrent image of Telemachus accompanied by his dogs in the epic (2.11, 16.4–5, 17.62, 20.145), an aspect that is strengthened by a simile that depicts the dogs' anticipation of their master in a more general context (10.214–19).

In another simile the bitch serves as a symbol for motherly affection and devotion to her puppies (20.13–16). In the same vein, the magic dogs created by Hephaestus for Alcinous' palace are a part of the doors, protecting and watching over the house (7.90–94), their immortality ensuring that they will adhere to their mission forever. In hunting, as well as in guarding the hearth, dogs are portrayed as actively assisting their masters. In the long scene recounting the pursuit of the boar that caused Odysseus' scar, dogs are frequently mentioned as giving aid to the hunters (19.429, 435, 438, 445). It is also worth mentioning that the fidelity of the dogs is expressed both directly in their function as guardians of the herd (14.21–22, 17.200–201) and ironically, when they almost tear Odysseus to pieces upon his first arrival home disguised as a beggar (14.29–38).[33]

From time to time, however, and in the appropriate circumstances, the negative aspects of this motif are also evoked. As in the *Iliad,* curses are prominent. Melanthius, the treacherous goatherd, calls the disguised Odysseus "dog versed in the pernicious arts" (17.248); Odysseus calls Melantho "bitch" (18.338), as does Penelope (19.91, using the Iliadic expression *kuon adees*). This abusive name recurs with reference to the women slaves who have shifted their fidelity from the house of Odysseus to the suitors, and it is uttered both by Penelope (19.91) and by Eurycleia (19.372). Odysseus also curses the suitors, calling them "dogs" (22.35).

However, it is interesting to note that, in contrast to the *Iliad,* where the horrifying aspects of the dog underline brutality and inhumanity, in the *Odyssey* even the negative characteristics of dogs are qualified by the general moral frame in which their behavior is perceived as punitive rather than merely aggressive.[34] Thus, Nestor tells Telemachus that if Menelaus had come on time he would have killed his brother's murderer, Aegisthus, and given his corpse as prey to dogs and birds (3.259). This would be a just punishment for a man who betrayed his king and seduced the latter's wife while her husband and his men were suffering in the grip of war (3.262–64). On a different occasion, the suitor Antinous threatens to send the beggar Irus to Epeirus, where the king, Echetus, will cut off his ears and nose and throw his testicles to the dogs (18.84–87). True, Antinous himself is basically no different from Aegisthus in his efforts to seduce the wife of a living though absent ruler, and his threat is incorporated in the order to Irus to fight with Odysseus, the disguised king of Ithaca. But in the context of Irus' haughty behavior toward Odysseus, this seems a just retaliation for his sins against the house he has betrayed. Moreover, it harbingers the punishment of another traitor to the house, Melanthius, who is about to suffer exactly this humiliation and torture after the suitors—and the conniving female slaves—are all killed (22.474–77).[35]

The dog, as indicated earlier, plays an important role in Odysseus' first physical recognition, and it will play that role once more in the unfolding of the hero's recognition by his wife. But before turning to that scene I wish first to discuss another physical recognition, that in which the hero is recognized by the governess Eurycleia.[36] This recognition is achieved through the memory of the old woman of an event that took place in Odysseus' youth, when he was severely wounded by a boar in a hunt during a visit to the house of his maternal grandfather (19.393–96). Since the visit is closely associated with Odysseus' birth (19.399–412), the story of the scar is, in a nutshell, the story of Odysseus' life from birth to maturity. Two aspects of this notable event should be emphasized. First, the past is physically inscribed on Odysseus' body; moreover, it is inscribed bodily in the shape of a healed wound that symbolizes the hero's primal experience. The scar is a sign of a literally painful past that both accompanies and characterizes the human agent as long as he lives. Odysseus is not merely recognized as Odysseus due to the traces of an old wound; he is also able to become Odysseus once again due to the inscription of this painful event both on his body and in the memory of his nearest and dearest. To put it differently, in order to successfully regain his former status in his household, Odysseus must be recognized as the same man who left it twenty years earlier, and this task is achieved by means of a representation of the past, first passively and against the hero's will when the scar is detected by Eurycleia and then actively and with full intent when he represents it to Eumaeus and the cowherd (21.207).[37]

By means of this representation Odysseus literally re-presents the past. It is therefore not, as claimed by Auerbach, due to a technique that conceals nothing, where there is "never a form left fragmentary or half-illuminated, never a lacuna, never a gap, never a glimpse of unplumbed depths,"[38] that the narrator gives the whole story of the scar in this episode. Rather, it is the bursting of the past into the present at such a crucial moment of reintegration that demands, both aesthetically and narratologically, to be presented in such length. The return of the past is not merely associated with Odysseus' homecoming. The theme of return is represented here, and it cannot but appear in a cicatrized form that makes one cry the moment it is recognized (19.471–72, 21.222–23).

The second aspect of the boar narrative that I wish to emphasize here is the close link between memory and the transformation of the past into a story.[39] Eurycleia was not in the house of Autolycus when the boar wounded

Odysseus; neither were his parents or the two herdsmen. They are told of this event by Odysseus, who presents the scar to his parents and, in a well-wrought story (*eu katelexen* [εὖ κατέλεξεν] 19.464), tells them all that happened. It is this act of encapsulating the past within a story that enables Odysseus not only to transfer past content to present time (when he tells his parents about the boar hunt, it is already an event of the past) but also to preserve it for the future, for a time when he will be able to retrieve it merely by presenting its physical inscription. The transparent resemblance of this aspect of the tale to the epic as a whole, the revivification of the past through its re-creation in verbal form, and the association between Odysseus and his poet creator, are discussed in depth in chapter 5.[40] For now, let us return to the text and the most complex of all the recognition scenes, the one between Odysseus and his wife.[41]

As noted previously, a crucial phase in this process utilizes the dog motif. It takes place when Odysseus, disguised as a beggar, recounts to his wife a meeting he supposedly had with Odysseus twenty years earlier. In order for Penelope to recognize the man he is portraying as Odysseus, he describes this man's clothing, which included a cloak woven entirely of purple wool (19.225). It had a brooch made of gold with double sheaths richly decorated (19.225–27).[42] On the face of it there was a dog gripping a dappled fawn with its front paws (19.228–29). The ornament was so lifelike that it used to arouse wonder in all who saw it (19.229–31). In this one small *ekphrasis* the poet has deftly intertwined two significations of the dog motif, one associated with hunting and one linked to fidelity. The hunting aspect of this motif functions on the level of the story, for the picture depicts a dog at the end of a successful chase. It can, however, function also on a symbolic level with Odysseus and the dog, on the one hand, and the suitors and the fawn on the other.[43] The association with fidelity is somewhat more abstruse, and it functions on the level of narration. When Odysseus narrates the story of the cloak, the latter no longer exists as a palpable object; it has been destroyed during its owner's lengthy absence. Yet in this case the erosive power of time is applicable only to the object itself, not to its power of signification. As the act of narration proves, Odysseus still remembers his wife's gift of twenty years earlier, thus indicating his loyalty to her despite their long separation. It is therefore pertinent here that Penelope says, in her response to her disguised husband, that the brooch was not a part of the cloak from the outset. It was she, Penelope, who had added it (19.256). In light of the discussion it is clear that what she pinned onto the cloak is not a mere brooch but an emblem of fidelity in the guise of a marvelous dog. It is, of course, a crucial aspect of this fidelity that it can outlive the object that bears its symbol, but even more important is the fact that its vitality is so essentially dependent on both memory and narration. And it is these features that are so striking in the final phase of the recognition scene between the spouses.

After the killing of the suitors, Eurycleia rushes upstairs to bring the good tidings to Penelope, revealing to her that the beggar was her husband in disguise (23.5–9). Going downstairs to meet him, Penelope is still hesitant (23.85–90), unsure whether the man in front of her is a beggar or her husband (23.93–95). She therefore sits in silence, a reaction that prompts her son to inveigh against her obtuseness (23.96–103). But Penelope knows better, and when she says that she still has to test the stranger with signs (*sêmath'* 23.110) that are known only to them both and are hidden from others (23.110), she gets Odysseus' approval (23.113–16).[44] Odysseus therefore goes to take a bath in order to look like his former self and then comes back and sits in front of his wife, who is, however, still silent (23.153–65).[45] This is Odysseus' breaking point, as he then rails against his wife's adamantine heart and asks Eurycleia to offer him a bed so he can sleep, even if alone (23.166–72),[46] a request to which the demure Penelope adds a small detail: that the bed should be the one that is currently inside their room (23.174–80).[47]

This, as soon becomes clear, is not an insignificant addition but rather Penelope's last test of Odysseus (23.181) before she finally recognizes him as her husband. For this bed, whose fixity is mentioned twice by the wife (23.177, 179), cannot be removed from its place in the couple's chamber. Moreover, it is literally rooted in the room since, as Odysseus says in response, one of the bedposts is the trunk of an olive tree that grew there before being cut by him for its present function (23.195–98). This story, like that of Odysseus' scar so closely linked to the beginning of the hero's history, is a piece of the couple's history that goes back to the beginning of their relationship.[48] Odysseus constructed the couple's bedroom around the tree, which was as thick as a pillar (23.191), and when he finished building the room he made a bedpost out of the tree. Nothing could be more symbolic of the solidity and rootedness of this couple's relationship: a secret known only to themselves and a single female slave (23.226–28), this bed is the sign (*sêma* 23.202) of the firmness of a bond that cannot be broken unless someone cuts it at the base (23.204). This bed, which has never been moved, is as steady as Penelope's bond with Odysseus and is therefore a representation of the wife's devotion to her husband. But it is much more than that. It is also a sign of the vividness of the past in the couple's shared memory. Twenty years after their separation, both husband and wife still remember this formative stage of their relationship. What Penelope tests here is Odysseus' memory, and his answer, which gives the story of this history in full detail, is the sign she is looking for in order to recognize her long-lost husband (23.206). As befits a tragic epic, the recognition, though joyous, is resonant with tragic echoes. The couple's embrace is full of tears (*dakrusasa* 23.207) and groans (23.231), and Penelope imagines her husband to be among those few who, having recently survived a shipwreck (23.236), happily reach shore after fleeing the evils (23.238) brought on them by Poseidon. This is an especially apt simile for the wife of a hero whose ship was wrecked by the hatred of this same god. In addition, there is still immense labor ahead (23.249), a task great and hard (23.250) that Odysseus must fully accomplish (23.250). In like manner, as fitting in a tragic epic, this event does not seal the narrative by means of a happy end. It is neither happy nor the end, merely a short respite in a long saga of suffering.

The last physical recognition in the epic is the one between father and son, and here again remembrance of things past is crucial to recognition of the son. At the beginning it is Odysseus who decides to test his father, Laertes, and see whether he recognizes his son after his long absence from home (24.217–18).[49] He goes to meet his father in the orchard, and seeing him from afar he starts crying at the sight of the old man's wretchedness and misery (24.233–34). Hesitating between instantly revealing himself to his father and first testing him verbally (24.235–38), Odysseus finally decides on a test (24.239–40). He therefore approaches the old man working in the orchard and starts talking to him. After complimenting him on his diligence (24.244–47), Odysseus asks the identity of the owner of the garden (24.256–57) and inquires about Odysseus, who is, he claims, an old acquaintance to whom he is strongly bound through links both personal and political (24.262–79). The father, ignorant of the true identity of the man querying him, begins weeping at the mention of his son (24.280) and refers to Odysseus as dead (24.289–96). He then asks the stranger's identity (24.297–301), a question his son answers with a fictive story of his fatherland and his relationship with Odysseus (24.304–14). Laertes, clouded with sorrow (24.315), pours dust upon himself and groans loudly (24.316–17), an act that prompts his son to disclose his true identity (24.318–26).[50] But the suspicious father does not immediately believe him and asks for a "manifest sign" (*sêma* [. . .] *ariphrades*) in order to be persuaded of this truth (24.328–29). Once again Odysseus uses shared memories of intimate moments in the distant past to regain his former position, this time as son and heir. He begins with the scar and a short version of the family tale that accompanies it (24.331–35) and then goes on to a more private story in their mutual history, identifying the different trees in the orchard that were first named to the son by the father and later given to him as a present (24.336–44). Odysseus remembers not only the names but also the exact number of the trees of each species that were given to him by his loving father. These are signs that cannot be refuted, and the persuaded father finally recognizes his son, embraces him, and faints (24.345–48), an act that attests not only to the father's emotional turmoil at this unexpected meeting with the son he has believed to be dead, but also to the great pain triggered by surfacing memories of lost time that cannot be retrieved.

To summarize: In this chapter I have focused on two main fissures, suffering and recognition, as a means of charting the tragic nature of the *Odyssey.* I have traced the motif of crying in the epic and demonstrated its close association with agonizing memories of characters who find themselves, once and again, in the midst of terrible events over which they have no control. This passive aspect of suffering is central to the general character of the *Odyssey,* an epic that accentuates the repeated victimization of its eponymous hero and where serene oblivion is frequently suggested as a seductive solution for the worn-out protagonist. And it is within this context of strong yearning to forget that one should locate the motif of recognition and its contribution to the tragic. Recognition, as a re-presentation of the past within the present, entails the return of painful memories of extreme suffering which, in their turn, severely afflict both the hero and his nearest and dearest. In order to discuss more thoroughly the nature of this suffering and its tragic implications, we shall now move to the seminal scene that sets the course of the hero's dismal postwar lot, the meeting with the Cyclops.

3

The Pivotal Scene and the Tragic

Heteroglossia, Focalization, and Colonialism in Odyssey 9

*I*n chapter 1, on a tragic pattern in the *Iliad,* I outlined the way human suffering is linked to divine intervention along the axis of time. The pattern also emphasizes the importance of the cognitive and the emotional by accentuating the role of psychological and metaphysical recognition in my model of the tragic. In this chapter, whose focus is the Cyclops scene in book nine of the *Odyssey,* the tragic will again be seen to consist of the emotional and the cognitive in addition to suffering due to the effects of time. It will also consider the component of recognition discussed in the previous chapters as well as an inherently related characteristic of the tragic: the complex notion of the heroic. Since the heroic is not a self-explanatory concept, and since it plays a significant role both in this chapter and the next, an exegetical excursus necessarily precedes my discussion of the Cyclops scene.

The tragic pattern in the *Iliad* granted the best of the Achaeans, Achilles, metaphysical recognition, which cast an extremely sad shadow over his achievements as a supreme warrior. In like manner, my discussion of the *Odyssey* mapping the ubiquity of crying in relation to the eponymous hero—as well as many minor characters—revealed the lugubrious undertone at the base of glorious heroic adventure. It therefore seems justified to regard the *Iliad*, and even more so the *Odyssey*, as epics that do not advocate a simple (let alone simplistic) ideology of force but rather as two sophisticated texts in which the poet undermines any heedless endorsement of power, suggesting instead a different set of values.[1] And it is in this context that one is invited to reflect on the refined concept of heroism as well as on its various manifestations in the epics. Note that my formulation does not deny either the existence of a heroic code of behavior or its importance; it rather aspires to accentuate its complexity, its dependence on changing and changeable contexts, and its subordination to a higher value system. Accordingly, my explication of heroism commences with what I term the crude-heroic code and then proceeds with some reservations and modifications to encompass the heroic in all its ramifications.

The main context in which the crude-heroic code of behavior is prevalent is, of course, war, and here the *Iliad* serves as my textbook of heroic characteristics, which include martial prowess and the appropriation by force of human beings, property, or both. In its rudimentary manifestation, the heroic man aspires to glory in battle, sometimes even at the price of self-sacrifice, and therefore shuns any sign of disgrace that might stain his name. This is why the εὖχος (*euchos*), the boasting of the Iliadic warrior in the face of his defeated enemy, is such an important component of the heroic. It is here that the hero asserts his appropriation, or reappropriation, of his superior martial status. This is also why the *euchos* frequently consists of the revelation of one's identity in general, and one's name in particular, for the boaster's greater public glorification.

Yet already in the *Iliad* the attitude toward the crude-heroic code is quite complex, and this exquisitely subtle text repeatedly articulates reservations about and criticism of such conduct. Thus, as I demonstrate in chapter 4, while the crude-heroic code demands heedless confrontation with the enemy and shames the warrior who flees from danger, the *Iliad* is rife with instances of heroic characters that either retreat or, worse still within the crude formulation, run for their lives. In like manner, chapter 4's discussion will pinpoint cases of the opposite of heroic self-sacrifice, namely, of survival ineluctably associated with disgrace. Moreover, the crude code of heroic behavior is inescapably violent, cruel, and bloody, aspects that are frequently criticized in this humane epic. No less important than these specific instances of critique is the more generally pervasive observation that, whatever values one ascribes to heroism, it is constantly conceived as a track that easily leads to that which is most abhorred in the *Iliad*, brutal massacre. This complex attitude toward heroism takes a further developmental step in the *Odyssey,* a postwar epic whose main theme is survival and whose main axis leads to domestic peace rather than foreign war. While the *Iliad* calls for a drastic modification of the crude-heroic code of behavior during wartime, the *Odyssey,* which takes place after war's end, conceives of this code as no longer applicable, something to be superseded by the values of its critique in the *Iliad.*

A pertinent example of the way the *Odyssey* complements the *Iliad* in critiquing crudely heroic conduct is its attitude toward flight. I have already mentioned the inherent equivocality in the treatment of this motif in the *Iliad* and the fact that, even within the frame of this war epic, flight is not necessarily negatively perceived. In the *Odyssey,* the postwar epic, flight is not merely not negative; it is even represented as a positive response that characterizes the conduct of almost all its heroes. This attitude is formulated by one of the oldest veterans of the Trojan War, Nestor, at a very early stage of the *Odyssey.* In book three, describing his own *nostos* to his guest Telemachus (3.153–85), Nestor repeatedly refers to his homecoming as flight. In Tenedos, after the army is split in two and part of it returns to Agamemnon (who is still in Troy), Nestor takes his ships and flees (*pheugon*) in anticipation of evil generated by some divine power (3.166). The same verb is used to describe Diomedes' departure with his men (*pheuge* 3.167), and it recurs in Nestor's story regarding the decision about which route to choose after arriving at Lesbos (*phugoimen* 3.175). This last case is especially revealing since it is Zeus himself who, in Nestor's words, counsels the army to choose a certain route "so that we flee (*phugoimen*) impending evil as quickly as possible" (3.175), as if divine protection is now extended through fleeing obstacles rather than in confronting them. This notion is reinforced in Nestor's depiction of Idomeneus and his comrades as "those who succeeded in fleeing (*hoi phugon*) from war" (3.190).

And what is true for Nestor is even more forcefully applicable to the epic's hero, whose lot (*aisa*) is defined by his archenemy Poseidon as "to flee (*ekphugeein*) from the great bond of misery" (5.289). Thus, the formula voiced by Nestor to describe Zeus' benevolent attitude toward flight, "so that we flee (*phogoimen*) impending evil" (3.175), recurs in Odysseus' description of his escape from the Cyclops' island (9.489) and once more, in reference to the Laestrygonians, when Odysseus flees with the crew of his ship (10.129).

Obviously, in a an epic that endorses survival, the worst possible evil is death (*thanatos* or *olethron*), which therefore keeps recurring in formulas associated with flight. It is in these terms that Odysseus describes those who escaped death on the island of the Cicones (φύγομεν θάνατόν [*phugomen thanaton*] τε μόρον τε 9.61) and in the Cyclops' cave (οἳ φύγομεν θάνατόν [*phugomen thanaton*] 9.467); a similar formula also occurs in the words of Eurylochus, who contradicts Odysseus' exhortation not to land on Thrinacia and urges the crew to stay there for the night (ὑπεκφύγοι αἰπὺν ὄλεθρον [*hupekphugoi* (. . .) *olethron*] 12.287). It resurfaces in Telemachus' description to his mother of his escape from the suitors (φυγόντι περ αἰπὺν ὄλεθρον [*phugonti* (. . .) *olethron*]17.47), and is also the expression the narrator utilizes in the opening of the epic to describe the warriors who succeeded in returning home from Troy (ὅσοι φύγον αἰπὺν ὄλεθρον [(. . .) *phugon* (. . .) *olethron*] 1.11). In addition, formulaic expressions regarding escape from death can be detected in admonitions such as the one before the Sirens' island, when Odysseus presents his crew with two options: either to die or "to escape doom by avoiding death" (ἀλευάμενοι θάνατον καὶ κῆρα φύγοιμεν [*thanaton* (. . .) *phugoimen*] 12.157). Another example occurs upon arrival at the rock of Scylla when Odysseus encourages his frightened crew by saying that Zeus might grant them escape and flight from death (τόνδε γ' ὄλεθρον ὑπεκφυγέειν [*olethron hupekphugeein*] καὶ ἀλύξαι 12.216). In the same vein, reference to extreme danger is expressed by means of negative formulations denoting the impossibility of flight or escape. Thus, the place of the wandering rocks is described as a locus "from which no man ever escaped (*phugen*) with a ship" (12.66) while Scylla is a monster from whom no sailor can boast of escaping (*parphugeein*) by ship (12.99).

This might lead one to conclude that the *Odyssey* is an epic epitomizing cowardice. And, indeed, with its constant affirmation of survival and its insistence on the value of life, how, one might wonder, can it be otherwise interpreted? Yet the *Odyssey*, despite its deferral of warlike heroism almost to its very end, is far from being the harbinger of a new age of cowardice. True, it sets "life" as one of its highest values, and consequently survival is a frequent phenomenon in the epic, but "life," as it is perceived and presented in the *Odyssey*, is a choice that cannot be regarded as the favored option of a coward.[2] In this tragic epic, "life" is first and foremost an almost impossibly long saga of arid suffering, the extreme cases of which make even death look appealing.[3] Take, for example, the waking Odysseus, who discovers that during his sleep his ship has been returned to the island of Aeolus due to his men's negligence and then weighs suicide against living in suffering (10.49–52).[4] In like manner Penelope, waking from a deep sleep, prays that Artemis give her immediate death so she would not have to waste her life in grief (18.202–5), a prayer she repeats with even greater intensity on a later occasion (20.60–82).⁵ I shall say more of this soon. For the time being, I will resume my discussion of the ninth book of the epic and expand on the methodology of my analysis.

My aim in this chapter is to present the Cyclops scene as a seminal episode in the *Odyssey*, the fulcrum for the most important process described in the epic, the arduous transition from one era (the Trojan War) to another (the postwar epoch). The passage from an antebellum to a postwar culture entails a lacerating move from one value system to another. The two poles of this extremely complex evolution are represented in the *Odyssey* by means of Odysseus' adherence to the crude-heroic code of behavior concomitant with and undermined by the text's construction of the need to renounce this selfsame code. To demonstrate the tension between two competing value systems, I have chosen heteroglossia as my hermeneutic fissure in this analysis. Heteroglossia is a neologism coined by Mikhail Bakhtin to describe

> a special type of *double-voiced discourse* [that] serves two speakers at the same time and expresses simultaneously two different intentions: the direct intention of the character who is speaking, and the refracted intention of the author. In such discourse there are two voices, two meanings and two expressions.⁶

Heteroglossia is perceived by Schechet as a primary fissure, marking "a narrative strategy that signals its reader to attend to the multivoiced potential of the text and to interpret it," whose usage is especially fertile in citations or first-person narratives where such multivocality is traced within a dominant-voiced narrative.⁷ The Cyclops scene invites heteroglossic interpretation in its first-person narration within a general context of third-person narration. It is here, more than anywhere else in the *Odyssey*, that one can detect the superb way in which the author forges a text that expresses simultaneously not merely "two different intentions" but rather two different worldviews based on two distinct value systems. In fact, as the following will demonstrate, the tragic is the offspring of these two contrasting worldviews, for it is their inevitable clash that fuses horrifically into a plangent poem about a tragic hero. In eliciting this realization of the tragic through the heteroglossic fissure of the Cyclops scene, I now wend my exegetical way to book nine of the *Odyssey*.⁸

Odysseus' return to Ithaca consists of a series of adventures in a new and wondrous world where he constantly confronts different values and different perceptions of order. Consequently, the hero's wanderings are a broadening of his epistemological, as well as his geographical, horizons, a process consisting of ineluctable crises. The Cyclops scene is consistent with this pattern, and Odysseus' visit to the ogre's cave elicits a variety of disturbing conflicts. Arrival in new territory raises the problem of colonization in general and intrusion in paradise in particular; contact with the monstrous Cyclops calls into question the validity of heroic codes of behavior while confrontation with cannibalism challenges concepts of civilization. The intensity of the experience and its ability to strike at the core of the identity of both the hero and his men account for the way this encounter is marked in the memory of Odysseus and his crew.

The originary event in a chain leading toward value change is the end of the Trojan War. As was claimed earlier, the transition from one era to another, or more precisely the transition from a code of behavior and set of values applicable to a time of war to a very different code of behavior and set of values applicable to a postwar period, instigates a profound transformation with far-reaching consequences. However, change is not immediate, for, although the end of the Trojan War marks the end of a historical era, it is not until Odysseus actually encounters the inhabitants of places reached on his journey that he can experience the change and its implications. It is therefore possible to regard the *Odyssey* as an epic describing its eponymous hero's travels on two different levels, temporal and spatial. Historically, Odysseus leaves wartime behind as he confronts the difficulties of a voyage home. Geographically, he sails away from a world famous and highly civilized city toward hitherto unknown territories whose native codes of behavior are sometimes very different from his own. Given the complexity of Odysseus' movement in both time and space, crisis is almost inevitable during his laborious adjustment to a changed reality.

The Cyclops scene is not the first realization of the problematic associated with this postwar transition, as analysis of the Cicones episode that precedes it will demonstrate. Yet it is in the Cyclops scene that Odysseus' attempts to behave and act according to codes that have suddenly become invalid bring such catastrophic outcomes that the hero is forced to start rethinking and revaluing his position in the world. The Cyclops scene, which represents repeated endeavors to act in the world and understand it according to a long-held and newly irrelevant code, is a transitional point triggering a process of profound change. It is apparent that Odysseus' suffering and loss are not outcomes of his negligence or imprudence. Rather, they are ineluctable and inherent aspects of his condition as a conscious human being who tries to live his life in the best possible way. What Odysseus must renounce in the Cyclops scene is a code of behavior that had until recently been a standard of excellence. Relinquishing this code is therefore giving up a measure of excellence, and such an act, though essential, cannot be realized without catastrophic effect.

My discussion of the Cyclops episode extends beyond the poet's deft treatment of characterization to reflect on the narratological ingenuity of the text in relation to this primary theme. I use two key narratological concepts in my discussion, focalization and narration. In *Narrative Discourse,* his highly influential book on narratology, Gérard Genette distinguishes between two questions that tend to be conflated, *"who is the character whose point of view orients the narrative perspective?* and the very different question *who is the narrator?—*or, more simply, the question *who sees?* and the question *who speaks?"*[9] Avoiding the restrictive visual connotations of terms such as *vision* or *point of view,* Genette coins the neologism *focalization.*[10] The term was further developed by Shlomith Rimmon-Kenan in her book *Narrative Fiction: Contemporary Poetics,* where she maps different facets of focalization: the sensory range of perception such as seeing or hearing; the psychological aspect, which includes cognitive and emotive components; and the ideological facet, which reflects values and norms.[11] It is in this comprehensive sense that focalization is used as the "prism" of presentation in this chapter.

Since any postwar era endures profound change, Odysseus' focalization both as an actor in his own story and as the narrator of events in his past reflects a process of reformation in which the hero's perception of the new world in general, and of himself in this new world in particular, is constantly changing. The new world is newly perceived, and actions are consequently given new interpretations and values. One of the most complex manifestations of focalization in this context reflects the attitude of both Odysseus and his crew toward the new world as a potential colony. This "colonial focalization," the perception of a recently discovered place as an optional settlement, is the primary vehicle for this book's representation of the highly problematic transition from war to a postwar reality. Carol Dougherty, whose accomplished treatment of the theme of colonialism in book nine of the *Odyssey* serves as the basis of my discussion of the topic, points out the deep affiliation between heroes and their code of behavior and *nostoi* legends that "have always provided a fertile ground for mythic traditions encompassing exploration, migration, and colonial settlement."[12] She notes that "Greek heroes returning home from Troy are easily recast as colonial founders: they are already on the road, and their success at Troy links the origins of these new Greek cities with the great heroes of the past.

The return of Odysseus is also a story well suited to this colonial tradition even though the *Odyssey* is not itself a settlement tale in the literal sense."[13]

While colonialism might have served Odysseus successfully in his postwar voyage, the *Odyssey* actually tells the opposite story of various failures in many attempts to establish dominance. There are two main reasons for these failures. First, the indigenous residents encountered along the way are not necessarily enthusiastic about their visitors; more often than not they treat their guests with blatant hostility that readily becomes deadly violence. Second, and even more important, the notion of a successful homecoming, which is the aspired aim of this specific *nostos,* as well as its highest virtue (to which the hero adheres assiduously), undermines from the outset any attempt to settle elsewhere. In this context, colonial focalization is double-edged: on the one hand it represents the attraction of the potential benefits of successful relocation, and on the other hand it reflects a grave danger to the hero's constant efforts to reach his fatherland. The colonial option offers a somewhat easier short-term transition from past to present, and its repeated thwarting (whether by voluntary renunciation initiated by leader and crew or involuntary yielding to external forces) worsens the already exacerbated crisis of adaptation to a new reality. The fact that even the astute Odysseus falls prey, more than once, to the enticements of colonialism is merely another indication of the power of this fantasy of a comfortable ensconcing in a new settlement away from the harrowing memories of the past and the anticipated labors of the future.

Narration is the second narratological aspect central to my interpretation of this pivotal moment in the protagonist's transition from one set of values to another. The meeting with the Cyclops, like most of Odysseus' adventures prior to his arrival in Phaeacia, is narrated by Odysseus. This feature, which differs from the rest of the *Odyssey,* where the narrative voice does not belong to any of the characters, raises two problems: the limits of the narrator's knowledge and the degree of the narrator's reliability. In a certain sense it is possible to regard Odysseus as an omniscient narrator, for the knowledge of the narrator Odysseus at the time of narration is much greater than that of the character Odysseus at the time of the events. Unlike the character, his younger self, the narrator knows both of future events (such as the outcome of the adventure in the Cyclops' cave) and of occurrences that take place in his absence (such as the first confrontation with Circe [10.208–43]).[14] But the narrator's omniscience cannot transcend human limitations, merely the limits of his own knowledge at a specific time. Thus, when Odysseus tells his audience about the habits of the Cyclopes and their general organization, he tells of things he does not know; how could he be informed of the fact that *all* the Cyclopes do not plant and do not plow but rather have everything from Zeus (9.108–11)? Moreover, how does Odysseus know, on the basis of a very short visit to the cave of a lone and lonely Cyclops, that the Cyclopes do not have councils (9.112) and that each Cyclops has autarkic rule over his own family (9.114–15)? In fact, Odysseus' final remark on the Cyclopes, his observation that they do not care for each other (9.115), is contradicted by his own narration; the Cyclopes do come to the aid of their neighbor Polyphemus when he cries in anguish (9.401–2).[15] To this one should add that, unlike the traditional epic narrator, Odysseus has no direct access to other people's thoughts or feelings and of course no direct knowledge of occurrences on Mount Olympus. He cannot know how a god reacts to an offering or a plea, and he cannot depict a divine conference or dispute. The fact that he gives his audience such information does not necessarily mean that he lies,[16] but it does raise the question of the reliability of his narrative.

Contemporary criticism has paid much attention to the similarity between poet and hero as a consequence of the decision to turn Odysseus into a narrator. Odysseus has become a kind of a surrogate for the poet, while his narration has turned into poetry. Moreover, since Jörgensen's law (which explains references to the gods by characters that have no access to the divine as nothing more than general remarks) and Suerbaum's article ("Die Ich-Erzählungen des Odysseus: Überlegungen zur epischen Technik der *Odyssee*"), many scholars have tended to assume that Odysseus' narrative is basically as reliable as that of the epic narrator.[17] This assumption, however, calls for modification, for one of the most conspicuous aspects of any narrative in the first person is the limited degree of reliability in comparison with a third-person narrative. This limitation is also true for Odysseus' narrative, and especially for a protagonist who boasts of his wiliness and expertise in lying.[18] In addition, Odysseus narrates his story to an audience that holds the key to his homecoming; similar to Scheherazade, his entire future depends on the effects of his storytelling. In other words, Odysseus' narration is highly motivated by his investment in a self-presentation that would bring about a specific and much desired consequence: his return home.

The reason for my emphasis on the protagonist's qualified reliability is not merely the close association between narration and focalization and the need to distinguish between them. The use of both an imperfectly reliable narrator and multiple focalization is the primary textual means of representation of the conflict between two competing value systems during a time of transition. Thus, while Odysseus aspires to relate his adventures in the most coherent way in order to facilitate his homecoming, the poet of the *Odyssey* sets his character's words in an extremely sophisticated heteroglossic text replete with contrasting attitudes and equivocal formulations that reflect the hero's confusion in this pivotal period of change.

The meeting with the Cyclops is the focal episode analyzed in this chapter, as noted earlier. However, I have decided to begin my reading of the text with a much shorter scene from the same book in order to give a succinct demonstration of the way narrative polyphony functions. Heteroglossia is already present in the tale of Odysseus' first postwar encounter, his arrival in the land of the Cicones. The narrative of this event, which precedes the encounter with the ogre, presents some aspects of the much more complex heteroglossia of the Cyclops scene.

When the crew reaches the Ciconian city of Ismaros, they destroy it, killing its men and taking a great amount of booty (9.39–42). Odysseus exhorts his people to leave the place, but they prefer to stay (9.43–46) and consequently have to face an attack by an army consisting of the neighbors of the Cicones, who were summoned by the survivors of the previous battle (9.47–59). Odysseus and his people lose the battle, and six people from each ship die while all the rest flee (9.60–61). Although told years after its occurrence, and therefore presumably consistent due to the benefit of hindsight, it is possible to locate traces of incoherence in Odysseus' narration of the episode. In other words, despite having a full temporal perspective of the entire sequence of this adventure, Odysseus as narrator is still somewhat hesitant in his description of the events that took place in his first encounter with the new world. These traces do not reflect an inadequate power of articulation; rather, they demonstrate a difficulty in defining a frame of reference within which the events just described take place.[19] The core of his wavering lies within the domain of Odysseus' own self-perception, where contrasting definitions compete in this transitional postwar phase. More precisely, the meeting with the Cicones generates a questioning of Odysseus' identity: Is he still a warrior whose main aim is glory in battle or has he already become a war veteran whose chief desire is to return safely home? Odysseus' uncertainty, implicit at this stage of the narrative, foreshadows the events of the Cyclops scene, where the protagonist will act out the clash between competing value systems.

As an immediate sequence to the Trojan War, the confrontation with the Cicones is described as no different from other battles of the Greeks either with the Trojans or with peoples in the vicinity. Such a battle is almost expected in this case, for in the *Iliad*, as one may recall, the Cicones were allies of the Trojans (2.846, 17.73). Both the beginning (9.40–42) and the major part of the end of the narration (9.54–59) are imbued with words taken from the Iliadic arsenal of military expeditions. The vast number of the enemies who come early in the morning and are likened to leaves ("they came later as many as leaves and flowers in springtime" [ἦλθον ἔπειθ' ὅσα φύλλα καὶ ἄνθεα γίγνεται ὥρῃ 9.51]) recalls the congregation of the Greek armies in the *Iliad*, which were "as many as leaves and flowers in springtime" (ὅσσα τε φύλλα καὶ ἄνθεα γίνεται ὥρῃ 2.468); the battle by the ships (9.54–55) resembles the battle scene inscribed on the shield of Achilles (18.533–34); and the reference to fighting over an entire day (9.56) echoes one in the *Iliad* (11.84), as does the association between the setting of the sun and defeat (9.58–59 and 16.779–80).[20] Yet into this discourse, replete with bellicose vocabulary and resonating with the crudely heroic code of behavior, Odysseus inserts its opposite, and he does this by means of a narrative in which words and expressions denoting shame and dishonor are prominent. Thus, soon after the victory Odysseus bids his people to leave the place as quickly as possible, using the expression "to flee with a nimble foot" (διερῷ ποδὶ φευγέμεν 9.43), while at the end of the story he says that the Cicones killed six people of each ship, "and the rest escaped the deadly doom" (οἱ δ' ἄλλοι φύγομεν θάνατόν [*phugomen thanaton*] τε μόρον τε 9.61). In the same vein, the expression "saved from death" (9.63), which recurs in 9.566 and 10.134, recalls the contemptuous reflection of Achilles on Aeneas' flight from him (*Il.* 20.344–50, with the above expression in line 350). Moreover, unlike the heroic discourse of the *Iliad*, in which soldiers dying in battle are mentioned by name,[21] here we have solely the number of the deceased. They have already sunk into anonymity and will soon be relegated to total oblivion.[22] Note also that the decision of the crew to remain and not flee the place after their victory leads Odysseus to call them *nêpioi* (9.44), namely, "with the flawed reasoning of a child," and that the sumptuous feast that soon follows this decision is, to say the least, dubious in its heroic implications under these circumstances.[23]

Confusion stemming from competing values will soon become even more acute when leader and men enter the Cyclops' cave. But before discussing the happenings in the ogre's abode I wish to consider the preceding events in order to demonstrate how the text utilizes focalization in order to frame this pivotal confrontation within a context of colonization. This context is not fortuitous; rather, it serves the poet in unraveling the complexity of the encounter between the homeward-bound Odysseus and the indigenous inhabitants met on the way. As the following analysis will demonstrate, the equivocality of colonial focalization reflects both the parochial interests of a homesick wanderer and the much grander potentiality of this crucial transitional phase. Above all, colonial focalization here reflects the general problematic inherent in the inescapably violent, cruel, and bloody crude-heroic code.

Odysseus' colonizing desires are aroused after reaching a no-man's-land located just opposite the territory of the Cyclopes. Both places are described as paradise, and both bear a strong resemblance to the state of the universe during the Golden Age depicted by Hesiod (*Erga* 109–26).²⁴ Thus, in the land of the Cyclopes "everything grows without sowing or plowing" (ἄσπ-αρτα καὶ ἀνήροτα πάντα φύονται 9.109); similarly, the island flourishes "without sowing or plowing" (ἄσπαρτος καὶ ἀνήροτος 9.123).²⁵ One of the most manifest features of this paradise is the absence of men (9.124).²⁶ In addition, the potential presence of man is perceived as limiting and curbing, for what grows and lives freely might be forced to submit to constraints: the island that is free of the plow and has countless goats (9.118) would become part of a place "dominated by herdsmen and plowmen" (9.122). In short, any intrusion by a human agent in this place precipitates its violation and the loss of its paradisiacal nature.

Odysseus' positive attitude toward the violation of the place, albeit uninhabited, is undoubtedly based on the crude-heroic code in which appropriation by force of inhabited places frequently implies some kind of violation. During the Trojan War, this valued violation was by no means limited to the beleaguered city; rather, it was constantly practiced on many nearby smaller cities in the long period of siege. Nothing demonstrates this more clearly than the opening of the *Iliad* itself, where the quarrel that breaks out between Achilles and Agamemnon is over a war prize that was recently gained in a victorious battle over the city of Chryse. No doubt, Odysseus' adherence to such a pale version of this code of behavior after the end of the war and under the very different circumstances of a voyage home is predictable. What is interesting here, in this initial postwar period, is the way Odysseus applies this rule of conduct to a reality that is so manifestly alien to the application of this code. With the great war over and its many heroes dispersed throughout the Greek world, Odysseus, a lone leader with a limited number of ships, contemplates possession of an uninhabited island in heroic terms. Through the focalization of martial glory that remains Odysseus' perspective at this point, the island is viewed as a potential colony within the wartime code of appropriation. The island's absent civilization is seen as an actual presence, allowing Odysseus to perceive himself as the heroic harbinger of civilization.

For, indeed, in this new place what is totally absent in reality has a very strong imaginary presence as Odysseus visualizes how it would look after being settled. In fact, as the narration evolves, more accentuation is placed on what the island is not and could be than on what is extant.[27] This emphatically subjective accent to imaginary amelioration culminates in focalization representing the island as a potential harbor for would-be settlers. This subjectivity, characteristic of all focalization by definition and heightened here, is especially evident in a colonizing context in which verbal appropriation reflects a fantasized subjugation. Similarly reflecting a narrow perspective and its consequent blindness, the narrator concludes his report (after describing in vivid detail the beauty and potential wealth of the island) by telling his audience that when he and his men actually reached the island they saw simply nothing: A god led them through the dark night when "it was impossible to perceive anything" (9.143). Even the moon was invisible, for it was hidden by a cloud (9.144–45). Nothing of the earlier account could therefore be seen at the time of arrival, as the anaphoric "not" (ou) that keeps recurring throughout the story continues to remind its audience (oude 9.143, 144; ou 9.146; oud' 9.147). The beauty of the would-be colony is literally in the focalization of the beholder, where perception has nothing to do with seeing. And this is not all, for the colonial focalization used here is closely linked with the notion of civilization and the legitimacy of violent heroic appropriation.

Odysseus claims that the Cyclopes did not settle the nearby island "for the Cyclopes did not have red-bowed ships" (9.125), a remark that allows him to expound on the merits of shipping. This is followed by an elaborate sentence full of subordinate clauses describing both the beauty and the utility of navigation, a phenomenon that enhances Odysseus' formulation of the highly civilized society.[28] Civilization is characterized by the presence of artisans, in this case carpenters, who can create the "red-bowed" (9.125) and "well-decked" (9.127) ships that contribute to communication between distant civilized peoples (9.128–29). The sentence abounds with verbs in the optative mood, thus denoting the options opened and opted for by maritime communication.[29] Moreover, even after Odysseus goes on to tell of the merits of the land and its potentially abundant crops (9.131–35), he concludes his narrative by describing not the fruits of the earth but rather the potential harbor of the island, imagining the impatient hearts of the sailors who eagerly anticipate their next navigation (9.136–39).

Since they land on the island at night, Odysseus and his comrades go to sleep until dawn (9.151). When they wake, they saunter around the island, marveling (*thaumazontes* 9.153).[30] Not for long, however, for the crew detects some mountain goats, which they hasten to hunt and eat, as the narrator proudly states (9.154–60). Thus, one of the first acts of the new visitors to paradise is killing accompanied by a feast. At this stage of the story this detail seems quite innocent and the victims are, after all, merely goats. Yet it will not be long before Odysseus and his men will again kill some animals in the Cyclops' cave; the act will then have sinister implications and catastrophic consequences. Before discussing that gruesome scene, I wish to again stress the active function of focalization in justifying the violent act of appropriation. Odysseus' focalization emphasizes divine protection of his deeds. In his narrative, the leader and his men did not simply encounter the goats and hunt them. It was the Nymphs, the daughters of Zeus who bears the Aegis, who provided the goats for the men "so that they would have something to eat" (9.155). Note that Odysseus says nothing about meeting the Nymphs. He only claims that it was they who were responsible for the meal, a fact that makes it plausible that it is his own focalization that adds divine providence to the episode.[31] There is also a subtle irony in the resonance of the sound "aig" in the story: "the daughters of Zeus who bears the Aegis, who provided the goats [. . .]" (κοῦραι Διὸς αἰγιόχοιο [*aigiochoio*] / αἶγας [*aigas*] [. . .] αἰρανέας [*aiganeas*] 9.154–56), as if, in Odysseus' eyes, the Aegis of Zeus protected the javelins that struck the goats.[32] Divine intervention is claimed again later when Odysseus says a god provided them with the hunt (9.158).

The next morning Odysseus divides his men, leaving most of them on the shore of the island and taking only the crew of his ship with him (9.170–80). They sail to the adjacent land and upon arrival Odysseus divides them once more, taking the twelve best with him and leaving the rest onshore (9.193–96). The small team reaches a cave that serves as a dwelling place, and, since its master is absent, they take the liberty of entering.[33] They see lambs and kids, as well as dairy products, separated from one another and ordered according to species (9.220–23). The greedy crew exhorts Odysseus to plunder the cave and flee as quickly as possible (9.224–27), but their leader has a better idea. Imagining himself contracting a *xenia* with the owner of the cave, he anticipates the gifts that are his due as a guest-friend, a *xenos* (9.229), deeming them more profitable than robbery (9.228).[34] They therefore stay, and while they wait inside the cave they offer a sacrifice and eat some of the cheese (9.231–32), an act resonant of the earlier appropriation of the goats.

The scene reflects deep confusion. To begin with, the cave triggers contrasting focalizations leading to contrasting possible actions. The twelve best men look at the wealth in the cave and react like robbers while their leader looks at the same place and reacts like a statesman. The crew observes the place and judges it beneath civilized society while Odysseus observes the area and thinks it is civilized enough for *xenia*. No doubt it is Odysseus who is wrong this time, for the knowledge of producing cheese and arranging things in order is hardly enough of a basis for presuming the presence of someone living according to the rules of civilized *xenia*.[35] The dweller's abode is not very promising either: it is neither a palace nor even a well-wrought building, merely a natural space turned, *tout court,* into a shelter. But surely the shrewd Odysseus could have easily perceived the true nature of the place and deduced the poor prospects for future *xenia*; if he did not do so, deeper reasons than folly must have played a part in his misjudgments.[36]

The same can be said about the far from prudent decision to wait for a total stranger inside a cave that could easily turn into a prison. It is highly unlikely that Odysseus, who had sufficient foresight to divide his people not once but twice before starting the journey into the cave, was suddenly a victim of carelessness. Odysseus' behavior undermines his own interpretation of the place and its owner: He waits for his host inside rather than outside the dwelling place, and, most outrageous of all, his sacrifice and meal are based on products belonging to his future *xenos*.[37] In this context, it is revealing that the hero's bewilderment is increased rather than diminished when he actually meets the Cyclops. One might have expected that direct confrontation with the monstrous dweller would immediately bring the resourceful Odysseus to his senses and make him acknowledge his mistake and respond suitably. What actually happens, however, is very different.

When the Cyclops arrives, the first reaction of Odysseus and his men is fright; they run away to hide in the inner part of the cave (9.236). At the beginning, the Cyclops does not see them and prepares his dinner, but after kindling a fire he perceives them and asks their identity. The Cyclops does not live in a very refined place, but his first words to the strangers attest to his refined awareness of their potential danger to him. He asks them where they sail from and the nature of their praxis and whether they are wandering pirates endangering their souls and bringing evil to strangers (9.252–55). The explicit reference to sailing (9.252), and the question, somewhat later, regarding Odysseus' ship (9.279–80) indicate a familiarity with shipping. Consequently, there is another plausible explanation for the absence of ships from the Cyclopes' life. Unlike Odysseus' focalization, which perceives the absence of ships as an index of a primitive society, the text offers another explanation according to which it is possible to regard the Cyclopes as people who have deliberately chosen not to introduce ships into their lives. In this case absence might reflect a choice based on knowledge instead of a lack of alternatives stemming from ignorance.[38] Living in their own paradise, they feel no need to launch colonial expeditions, not even to the nearby island, which they have no doubt detected from their own habitat (6.2–6). Through the Cyclopes' focalization, as reflected in the Cyclops' words, shipping is for merchandise or robbery, and they will have none of either.[39] This is the first direct reference to piracy in the story, and it is crucial to the reading of the episode as emblematic of the hero's identity crisis. For, although Odysseus never presents himself as a pirate, both his behavior in the land of the Cicones and his reaction to the products in the Cyclops' cave attest to this unflattering characterization.

Contemporary criticism tends to contradict a negative view of piracy in archaic society, claiming it as an occupation that brings honor rather than disgrace and is therefore compatible with the heroic code of behavior. This view has led readers of the Cicones episode to conclude that Odysseus' conduct in this case is laudable. Rainer Friedrich, for one, cautions, "If this adventure [the attack on the Cicones] strikes the reader as no better than a pirates' raid, he would do well to remember what Thucydides (1.5.2f) has written about piracy in an archaic warrior society: far from causing disgrace, it imparted reputation (*doxa*) and honor (*kosmos*) to its participants."[40] In like manner, W. B. Stanford, in his commentary on lines 39–40, states bluntly that Odysseus' behavior in this episode is nothing but piracy, but in his commentary on line 73 refers to the passage from Thucydides as evidence for a positive attitude toward piracy.[41] However, Thucydides' thoughts about archaic society and its relation to piracy must be weighed against the text of the *Odyssey*, where piracy is condemned both implicitly and explicitly. Thus, in 17.424–34, in a fictive tale told to Antinous, Odysseus describes pirates as "yielding to their hybristic impulses" (ὕβϱει εἴξαντες 17.431) and "giving rein to their passion" (17.431), hardly words of praise. The passage quoted earlier (17.427–41) is a repetition of 14.258–72, and since both have a striking correspondence to the episode of the Cicones,[42] a rereading of the Cicones passage cannot avoid the pejorative extension of Odysseus' own depiction of pirates, which appears much later. In 3.71–74, during his interrogation of Telemachus, the civilized Nestor uses exactly the same phrases as the Cyclops, a fact that makes the Cyclops' question look less uncivilized than it might at first seem. Note also that the Cyclops' interrogation links pirates with merchants; since there is little doubt that the latter's occupation is hardly a suitable one for the heroic man,[43] it sheds its negative light on piracy as well. In this context, let us reformulate the Cyclops' perspective: no longer a warrior participating in a glorious expedition, Odysseus is still wandering as a sea captain, endangering his own soul and bringing evil to others; what is he, then, if not a despicable pirate or a contemptible merchant?

Odysseus immediately refutes the allegation, claiming that he and his men are neither merchants nor pirates. They are ex-warriors, coming from Troy and heading home (9.259–62). But the status of an ex-warrior is not clearly defined, not even for Odysseus himself, as indicated by his own narrative. On the one hand, Odysseus presents himself as a war hero, taking pride in his association with the army of Agamemnon; he evokes the discourse of glory in his reference to the "greatest glory under heaven" (9.264) and recounts Agamemnon's successes as sacker of Troy and destroyer of peoples (9.265–66). Yet, on the other hand, Odysseus does not present himself and his crew as warriors; he stresses their humble state at present (9.266–67) and asks in a very cautious and modest way for some kind of gift (9.268). He then evokes the notion of *themis*, the established custom or law (9.268), and concludes with an implied threat referring to Zeus Xenios, protector of suppliants (*hiketai*) and *xeinoi* (9.269–71).

This is a very strange mélange. Until this point in the *Odyssey,* the narratees of the epic have encountered a meeting based on either *xenia* (Telemachus' meeting with Menelaus, 4.587–619) or supplication, *hiketeia* (Odysseus' supplication to the Phaeacian queen, 7.142–56), but never such a hybrid appeal conflating (in this order) pride, meekness, and threat. True, a *hiketes* (suppliant) can turn into a *xenos,* but only after total self-abasement; one cannot be a *hiketes* and a *xenos* at the same time: The former must precede the latter. Moreover, it is never the *hiketes* but only the other party that can initiate the change of status to a *xenos.*[44] In addition, one cannot proclaim oneself a *xenos* and demand gifts. The entire ritual of *xenia* is based on a seemingly mutual and voluntary donation, however rigid the rules of giving in this context.[45] There is no doubting Odysseus' acquaintance with all these facts, and his behavior in the Phaeacian court not long before attests to that. His speech is therefore not a testimony of ignorance but of confusion. What Odysseus does not know is whether he is a warrior who might claim equality, a humble *hiketes* who can be regarded as an inferior, or someone protected by Zeus who should therefore be revered.[46] The Cyclops, however, knows perfectly well how to treat both him and his crew, clarifying it immediately first in word and then in deed.

To begin with, he ignores Odysseus' claims of glory and responds with scorn to his threats. He tells him that the Cyclopes do not fear either Zeus or the other gods, for they deem themselves far mightier (9.275–76). Consequently, any plea for mercy depends solely on the Cyclops' will and has nothing to do with the future wrath of Zeus (9.277–78). This stated, the Cyclops queries the location of Odysseus' ship (9.279–80). Sensing the malevolent agenda hidden behind the inquiry, Odysseus replies "with crafty words" (*doliois epessi* 9.282), saying that Poseidon broke his ship into pieces and hurled it to the end of the earth; he and his men are refugees of this disaster (9.283–86). A wily present lie, yet a bitter and ironic future truth.[47]

This is actually the end of the conversation, for now the Cyclops takes two of Odysseus' men, throws them to the ground, and eats them. The description is both detailed and vivid (9.288–98), and much has been said about the Cyclops' cannibalism and uncivilized behavior toward his guests.[48] Two points, however, are worth mentioning here. First, Polyphemus' cannibalistic meal weaves the theme of colonization into the textual fabric of the episode. Dougherty's comments on the topic are cogent:

> Although the word "cannibalism" has obvious roots in a more recent historical encounter between European slave traders and indigenous Carib people, the term has come to represent a discursive practice that transcends the historical origins of the word. [. . .] Typically, tales of cannibalism operate as an index of savagery within an imperial or a colonial context to represent those capable of resisting conquest as themselves violent and voracious. The savagery of conquest is thus displaced onto those who are able to fight back. They are the ones who are truly transgressive since they eat human flesh and are therefore in need of being conquered. [. . .] Odysseus' encounter with the Cyclops conjures up the nightmare scenario of overseas settlement— the dangers and difficulties of subduing hostile native populations. In this way, Polyphemus' act of cannibalism and Odysseus' triumph over him belong to the larger framework of colonial discourse that first demonizes native populations and then celebrates their conquest as the victory of civilization over the forces of nature.[49]

In other words, the act of eating human flesh serves Odysseus as a means of focalizing himself as "hero" and Polyphemus as "cannibal," that is to say, to perceive himself in the flattering light of a civilized man who duly defeats a ferocious monster with terrible violence.

The second point of substance in the context of the Cyclops' cannibalism is the stark contrast between his eating of human flesh and what seem to be his routinely vegetarian meals. Note that in the rather detailed description of the Cyclops' preparations for his dinner before detecting his guests (9.244–49), there is no indication that he usually feeds on any kind of meat.[50] This is even more striking in light of his possession of many sheep and goats and the fact of his single-person household. There is little wonder in Odysseus' presentation of the Cyclops as uncivilized, the incarnation of despicable barbarity, a creature feeding on his guests instead of feeding them according to the rules of *xenia*. But Odysseus is far from a disinterested narrator, and the civilized nature of his motive for staying in the cave instead of looting it is at least questionable.[51]

It is thus that this heteroglossic text constructs an implied reader that is termed by Schechet a "resisting reader," namely, "one who is cued by a text to resist the text's narrator."[52] This "double-voiced discourse" consists of Odysseus' first-person narration, on the one hand, and the subtle net of muted voices and focalizations created by the poet on the other.[53] It is this constant construction of the other's voice and focalization that elicits the reader's resistance to the narrator, for the dialogical relationship between the two instructs the reader to keep interrogating Odysseus' reliability and motives rather than unquestioningly following him. This is, of course, not to deny the abhorrent aspects of the Cyclops' behavior but to emphasize the complex portrayal of the encounter limned by such an exquisite poet.[54]

After dinner, the Cyclops goes to sleep (9.298), and Odysseus intends to kill him on the spot but refrains from doing so, perceiving that the Cyclops' body would block the cave's exit and trap the men (9.299–305). Morning comes and with it another meal of human flesh (9.307–11); soon after, the Cyclops leaves the cave with his herds (9.312–16). Now it is time for Odysseus to devise his plan of both revenge and escape. He and his men take a big club left by the Cyclops to dry and turn it into a spike that will be heated in order to blind the Cyclops (9.316–35). The narrative is illuminating regarding both narration and focalization, and once more heroic values converge with colonial ideals. The narrator resumes the discourse of glory in his usage of the notion of *euchos* (εὖχος 9.317), boasting as if he is in the middle of a military expedition, and he adopts colonial focalization: what he and his men actually see is "a big club" (9.319), but seeing (εἰσορόωντες 9.321) is merely the starting point for imagining (ἐΐσκομεν 9.321) something else, "the mast of the ship" (9.322), the colonial object par excellence. This is an explicit and self-conscious focalization, as Odysseus acknowledges both the Cyclops' perception and his own; what was originally an olive tree (as the adjective "of olive wood" [ἐλαΐνεον 9.320] indicates) is deemed a potential club by the Cyclops and a potential mast and then spear by Odysseus. This association between colonialism and violence serves Odysseus as a means of presenting himself as a civilized hero who battles a primitive enemy that deserves brutal punishment.[55] The text, however, is more equivocal regarding Odysseus' civilized behavior, and the next episode enhances this equivocality.[56]

It is now evening, and the Cyclops is back for another cannibalistic dinner (9.336–44), after which Odysseus hands him the liquid that triggers his doom: the undiluted wine (9.345–46). Odysseus inebriates the Cyclops by filling his cup three more times (9.361–62), and soon afterward the Cyclops falls asleep (9.371). The narrator does not spare his audience the ghastly description of the drunkard's sleep, during which he vomits a mixture of wine and human flesh (9.373–74). Both the Cyclops' enthusiastic reaction to the wine and his subsequent repulsive drunkenness have served many critics as an indication of his primitive lack of sophistication.[57] No doubt there is more than a grain of truth here, but once more this heteroglossic text has other things to say.

To begin with, the Cyclops is not so primitive as to have no familiarity with wine; in his eager request for a refill, he states that the Cyclopes' land produces "wine that is made of fine grapes" (οἶνον ἐριστάφυλον 9.358). In contrast, what is given to him by Odysseus is something divine, "a distillation of nectar and ambrosia" (ἀλλὰ τόδ᾽ ἀμβροσίης καὶ νέκταρός ἐστιν ἀπορρώξ 9.359). This means that the essence of the Cyclops' current experience lies not in its novelty but in its intensity, for the Cyclops knows perfectly well that what he is given is a kind of wine.[58] Moreover, the wine itself has a sinister background; not merely a product of a civilized society, it is reminiscent of the bloody battle with the Cicones (9.197–200), a battle that led to the destruction of their city, the murder of their men, and the enslavement of their women.[59] Furthermore, there is nothing distinctly primitive about yielding to the power of this wine, for Odysseus himself describes it as irresistible (9.211). And this is not all, for the dialogue preceding the Cyclops' sleep has its own equivocality.

After his first cup, the Cyclops, craving more wine, suddenly adopts the discourse of *xenia:* he asks for more and wishes to know the stranger's name in order to give him the pleasing gifts a *xenos* receives (9.355–56). Odysseus inebriates the Cyclops, asks for the promised gift he deserves as a *xenos* (9.365), and then gives the ingenious false name Outis (nobody).[60] In response, the Cyclops promises to eat him last, thus keeping his promise of the guest's gift (9.370). This is a strange dialogue not only due to the fact that being eaten last is hardly a gift appropriate to *xenia* (the presentation of the Cyclops to this point prepares Odysseus' narratees for such a ghastly offer) but because of the Cyclops' resort to the discourse of *xenia*. He could easily have threatened Odysseus' life with immediate consequences if not given the rest of the wine. The sudden appearance of the codes of civility and courtesy is not expected from a creature that ended his earlier conversation with Odysseus by eating his comrades. Here, too, as in his knowledge of ships, merchants, and pirates, and his acquaintance with wine, the Cyclops reveals his familiarity with aspects of civilized society. Of course, this cognizance does not endow Polyphemus with civility, nor does it make him a civil character,[61] but it does imbue the ogre with complexity, which, in its turn, enriches the polyphony of the text.

It should also be noted that, like most colonial focalizations, Odysseus' perception of civilization does not necessarily embrace benevolence toward the unknown other; rather, it is much more likely that the encounter will bring suffering, if not annihilation, to the other party, a process in which civilization functions to justify intrusion, violence, and even barbarism.[62] Thus, when Odysseus narrates the insertion of the burned spike into the Cyclops' eye, he utilizes two similes; the first refers to the act of blinding itself while the second vivifies the noise of the burning socket. Both similes are taken from the field of civilized artistry, here subservient to violence.[63]

From this point on, the story moves quickly to its end. The neighbors arrive at the call of the wounded Cyclops and, due to Odysseus' deceptive name, leave without giving any help (9.398–412), the Cyclops bars the cave's entrance (9.413–19) while Odysseus binds his people and himself to the lower part of the sheep (9.420–36), they wait for dawn, and when it finally comes they all succeed in sneaking out (9.437–63). The Cyclops' words to his beloved ram (9.447–60), though spoken by Odysseus, are very moving and endow the text with tragic qualities that reveal the horrifying implications of the stranger's victory.[64] I shall return to this issue later in my discussion; meanwhile I would like to attend to the reference to Odysseus' invented name, Outis. The Cyclops mentions the name twice (9.455, 460) and associates it with an adjective denoting value: the stranger is "worth nothing" (*outidanos*). And it is these words that hit their target much deeper than the Cyclops could have hoped.[65]

What's in a name, then? As far as the poet's craftsmanship is concerned, it is worth mentioning that the name trick is absent from the various folktale versions of the story of the blinding of an ogre.[66] The poet, therefore, amalgamated two different stories into one consistent whole. What is more, the name "Nobody" is probably an ad hoc invention, for the name that appears in other versions of the folktale is either "me" or "myself."[67] And, indeed, at first reading the choice of Outis seems ingenious. Even retrospectively it seems an extremely clever means of securing the safety of Odysseus and his men after the blinding of the Cyclops (9.398–412), an indication of the leader's profound foresight regarding possible obstacles. This interpretation is also enhanced by the narrative when Odysseus relates to his audience how he laughed in his heart when he succeeded in deceiving the Cyclops about and through his name (9.413–14). But the false name has other implications, less benign and far from predictable, and it is they that loom large over the episode and its catastrophic consequences.[68]

To begin with, Outis substitutes not merely for the name Odysseus but also an entire range of significations. Outis is a lie, and its adoption implies an endorsement of lies and deceit in direct contrast to the absolute value of truth formulated by Achilles in his answer to Odysseus in the episode of the embassy in the *Iliad* (9.312–33).[69] But Outis is more than a substitution; it is an annulment of Odysseus. Signifying literally nothing, it is a total erasure of the hero's former self. What should be emphasized here is that this self-negation is as horrifying as it is indispensable. As claimed earlier, in the *Iliad* public self-identification is a necessary condition for sustaining one's glory, which, in itself, is an essential component of the heroic in its crudest form. But in the *Odyssey* such boasting can be obsolete if not pure folly. It is meaningless death rather than glory that awaits Odysseus if he fights the Cyclops in his cave, and he therefore must escape this lethal trap by all means. In this new postwar world, where survival frequently has greater merit than glory, Odysseus' self-annihilation is not just understandable, it is laudable, though not an easy or wished-for state of being.[70] On the contrary, as the conclusion of the episode reveals, Odysseus longs for his former self and former being. What is more, it is his strong desire to recuperate his lost status as Odysseus the warrior that will be the direct cause of his future prolonged suffering.

After releasing himself and his comrades from the sheep, Odysseus embarks with his men and starts rowing back to the island where the rest of the group awaits them (9.464–73). Still on the ship, Odysseus accosts the Cyclops "with mocking words" (9.474) referring both to his own prowess (9.475) and to the Cyclops' breaching of the rules of *xenia* (9.478–79). He concludes with a statement: it was Zeus and the rest of the gods who made the Cyclops pay for his ungodly behavior (9.479). The Cyclops is enraged and throws a big rock that almost crushes the ship and brings it back to shore

(9.480–86); Odysseus and his men recover and row back to sea, when again the leader is determined to speak. Ignoring the beseeching of his men, Odysseus opens his mouth once more, revealing his identity to his enemy (9.502–55). This essential component of the heroic code is an inalienable part of heroic revenge, and it is congruent with Odysseus' attempts throughout the narrative to regain his former status. Similar to Achilles, his great heart is not willing to be persuaded (9.500), and like Achilles he responds to the Cyclops with an angry heart (9.501). Both the angry outbursts and the revelation of his name recall the *euchos,* mentioned earlier, the boasting of the Iliadic warrior in the face of his defeated enemy,[71] and Odysseus, in a moment of self-assertion, describes himself by means of a heroic epithet, "city-destroyer" (9.504).[72]

This is a revelation to the Cyclops, who acknowledges the realization of a prophecy told him many years earlier, foretelling the arrival of an Odysseus who would blind him (9.507–12). The Cyclops' words are expository in two additional aspects. First, they undermine Odysseus' claim that the blinding is a consequence of the breach of *xenia*: the Cyclops' agonizing lot was determined much earlier, and Odysseus is therefore merely an agent of a divine scheme. The second important aspect is the Cyclops' refusal to treat Odysseus as a hero. Time and again he articulates the contrast between his former expectations regarding his would-be blinder and his present knowledge of the true identity of his tormentor. The prophecy accomplished, he still cannot see how someone so "small," so "frail," so "null" (*outidanos* 9.515) could do this to him.[73] Evidently, it was not Odysseus' prowess but the power of the wine that ultimately vanquished the Cyclops (9.516). In other words, far from being blinded by a hero, the Cyclops has lost the battle to a trickster.

In the vain hope of catching Odysseus, the Cyclops now offers him treatment "appropriate for a *xenia*" (9.517), promising to pray to his father, Poseidon, to escort Odysseus home (9.518–21). This comes too late, and Odysseus scornfully rejects the pathetic proposal (9.523–55). The prayer for Poseidon's escort, however, does take place (9.528–35), and it is this prayer that is responsible not only for Odysseus' very late and tortuous homecoming but also for a continuation of his wanderings even after he reaches his home.[74] The end of the *Odyssey* is not the end of Odysseus' odyssey: The hero will have wandered much more by the time he reaches a place where he can consecrate a temple to Poseidon (11.121–31). Only then will the god's wrath be appeased.

Characteristically, Odysseus' name is crucial to the Cyclops' curse; if Odysseus had not given the Cyclops his name and address, the Cyclops would not have been able to curse him.[75] But Odysseus' words, despite being his biggest error in the epic and the main cause of the dismal course of his postwar life, are not a consequence of negligence or ignorance. His relentlessness despite his comrades' exhortations before and, even more telling, after the Cyclops' first throwing of a rock attests to his need to adhere to the heroic code of his past.[76] At this early stage of his adventures, Odysseus simply cannot give up his former identity; he cannot be Nobody.[77] It is now that the Cyclops, who has denied Odysseus heroic honor to this point, restores it to him with a curse, calling him "city-destroyer" (9.530), thus associating Odysseus' consequent travail with the heroic code.[78]

As the unfolding of the narrative reveals, the renunciation of former heroic identity is a necessary condition for successful homecoming, and the hero will have to humiliate himself many times, both before and after coming to Ithaca, in order to regain his former position in his household.[79] No doubt, Odysseus is an exemplum of successful adaptation to new situations, but his transition from the Trojan War period to the postwar era could not have avoided a tortuous clash of values. Consequently, it could not have been realized without a painful process of learning through erroneous conduct and miscalculated action. The ten long years of his homecoming are bound with this kind of learning, as if Odysseus needs this period to leave behind a crucial portion of his past identity in order to acquire a new one. Like the biblical People of Israel who, after leaving Egypt, had to wander in the desert for forty years until the expiration of the generation born into slavery and the maturity of the generation born in liberty, Odysseus has to go through many adventures over a long span of time in order to become the very different man of the postwar era.[80] Odysseus, a skillful interpreter of fluctuating reality, eventually learns from this episode but not without paying the full price for his error.

Unsurprisingly, this learning curve is often deflected; value change provokes strong emotional and cognitive resistance. In fact, following the curse of the Cyclops, Odysseus shows no signs of regret for having revealed the crucial details of his identity. While Odysseus the narrator is quite aware of the dismal future that awaits him provoked by the Cyclops' words (9.536), Odysseus the character ignores them completely. Later both he and his men regale themselves with meat and sumptuous wine all day long as if they have completely mastered a difficult situation (9.556–57).[81] In like manner, Odysseus does not renounce his inquisitiveness when he reaches the land of the Laestrygonians (10.100–102, a repetition of the lines preceding the encounter with the Lotus-Eaters [9.88–90]). Despite Circe's admonitions not to arm himself against Scylla (12.116–22), he does so (12.226–30). And yet Odysseus does learn throughout, and the change he is undergoing can be traced in his focalization as narrator.[82] For, while Odysseus the character pays no heed to the Cyclops' words and deems the entire episode no more than an adventurous trial, Odysseus the narrator perceives it quite differently. From the vantage point of the storytelling present, he remarks grimly on the encounter with the Cyclops. He ends the narrative of the episode with a report of the return to the island opposite the Cyclopes' land, where he and his crew sacrifice to Zeus. But the narrating Odysseus notes that the god refuses to accept their offering (9.553), contriving instead a total loss of ships and comrades (9.554–55). Although the actual cause of the loss instigated by Zeus was the eating of Helios' cattle, which occurred later (12.374–88), the narrator recognizes the present scene as the turning point in the destruction of men and fleet alike.[83]

While the Cyclops scene is characterized by Odysseus' adherence to heroic self-identification and by his fascination with the marvelous options of colonization, the final scene of his overseas adventures, his landing in Phaeacia and his visit to the rulers' court, exemplifies a very different attitude regarding the hero's psychological recognition of his state in the world. Note that in the sequence of the narrative, this final scene precedes the narration of Odysseus' adventures. In other words, the poet has chosen to frame the depiction of the hero's development and change narratively by an event that takes place chronologically after that development and the change have already been achieved. Since we can fully appreciate Odysseus' words and behavior in this final stage of his wanderings only after being informed of the long mental process through which he has gone during his adventures, the narrative activates us to reread and reinterpret this episode in light of the information acquired in the process of listening to Odysseus' story. This is the reason I have postponed my discussion of this early episode to such a late stage of my analysis.

As implied by a statement of the poet at the beginning of the narration of Odysseus' arrival in Scheria (6.2–6), there might be a close colonial link between the land of the Cyclopes, the adjacent island where the hero's meditations regarding fitness for settlement were initially aroused, and Phaeacia. It is quite probable that Odysseus' first paradise, the island facing the land of the Cyclopes, was once the home of the Phaeacians. The latter were forced by the Cyclopes to leave their native land and wander the seas in order to found a new settlement in Scheria.[84] Odysseus' last station before he reaches his fatherland is therefore literally colonial, and, if we accept the assumption regarding the Phaeacians' former country, then it is also closely associated with the hero's first colonial thoughts and experiences.[85] The historical implications of these links, that is to say, their potential to reflect the time of the text's composition, are beyond the scope of this analysis.[86] What is relevant here, however, is Odysseus' focalization of this potential second paradise and the way it reflects the profound change the hero has gone through regarding crude heroic values and colonialism.

When Odysseus finally reaches the land of Scheria, bereft of all and half dead after his long battle with the sea, Athena pours sleep on his eyes (5.491–93). Awakened by the voices of Nausicaa and her girls, his first reaction is a rueful cry, "Oh woe is me" (Ὢ μοι ἐγώ), followed by a question, "to the country of which mortals have I come this time?" (τέων αὖτε βροτῶν ἐς γαῖαν ἱκάνω 6.119). He then goes on to ask himself whether the inhabitants of this new land are "insolent" (ὑβρισταί), "savage" (ἄγριοι), and "unjust" (οὐδὲ δίκαιοι) or rather "hospitable to strangers" (φιλόξεινοι) and "with a god-fearing disposition" (νόος [. . .] θεουδής [6.120–21]). The last two lines are the same formula used by Odysseus to describe his expectations before embarking on the Cyclops adventure (9.175–76), an adventure to which he was prompted by the mixture of curiosity and boldness that characterizes the conduct of the hero, pirate, and colonizer. The addition of the emphatic first line indicates the deep change in focalization. In contrast with the enthusiasm of the earlier episode, Odysseus is no longer anticipating a future encounter with strangers but rather dreading it. Unlike the voyage to the land of the Cyclopes, where Odysseus initiated a voluntary expedition to satisfy acquisitive needs that were far from essential, here his decision to approach the ruler's daughter is based on pure necessity, on his total dependence on her for saving his life and salvaging the possibility of his homecoming. We can see here how Odysseus, whose epithet was once "the city-destroyer," has relinquished his former colonial and heroic focalization, substituting the anxious focalization of the Odysseus whose other epithet, "the one who has suffered so much" (*polutlas*), reflects his new psychological recognition. Not even the experience with the Phaeacians, albeit encouraging and beneficial, has changed this basic attitude, as Odysseus' reaction to his arrival at Ithaca can attest. Waking in a new place that he does not recognize as his fatherland, Odysseus cries in anguish, reiterating the anxious formula he utters in Scheria and not the rather neutral one he uses before going to meet the Cyclops (13.200–202).

The intense memory of the experience with the Cyclops and the consequent profound psychological recognition in Odysseus can also be detected on the level of narration. Odysseus' newly cautious self-representation is most evident regarding his name. After entering the rulers' palace the hero is interrogated by Queen Arete, who asks his identity (7.237–39). The phrase that opens her question, "who are you and who was your father?" (τίς πόθεν εἰς ἀνδρῶν 7.238) is formulaic, but the second phrase, "who gave you these garments?" (τίς τοι τάδε εἵματ᾽ ἔδωκεν) is not. The formulaic inquiry is "which is your *polis* and who are your ancestors?" (πόθι τοι πόλις ἠδὲ τοκῆες).[87] Arete's second phrase therefore leaves Odysseus enough room to be evasive about his identity and especially about his name. Odysseus, however, is more than evasive. In his very long answer (7.241–97) he completely ignores Arete's first question referring to his identity, depicting nothing more than the events leading to his arrival in Scheria and his acquisition of the garments. As many critics have observed, this lack of reference is extremely intriguing and important.[88] Not unexpectedly, at least one of these significations has a direct association with the Cyclops scene. Odysseus finally reveals his name to his generous hosts only after a direct question from the king insisting on the disclosure of the name (8.548–51). Neither the form nor the content of the question is formulaic, and their shockingly uncouth character can be detected only in one more instance in the *Odyssey*, the Cyclops' brutish question regarding the identity of the intruder in his cave (9.355–56).[89] The analogy between the two occasions is telling: Odysseus' present reluctance to reveal his name reflects what he has learned from the catastrophic revelation of his name in the past. The swaggering Odysseus who insisted on reasserting his heroic identity by means of the utterance of his name has turned into a diffident person, one who prefers to be as abstruse as possible.[90]

I would like to return briefly to the notions of change and constant readaptation that this transitional scene represents. Although there is little doubt that the end of the war marked the end of an era, the nature of the new age is still obfuscated when Odysseus starts his wandering. Moreover, the brisk movement from war to a postwar world necessitates a comparable move away from martial heroic values.[91] To restate, one of the main tasks of Odysseus, and, in fact, of the *Odyssey* as a whole, is to move, over time, from one code of behavior to another, abandoning old notions that are already invalid in favor of new values yet to be formulated. Once more, the two focal domains where this reformulation is realized are colonization and military valor; both occur after the return of Odysseus to Ithaca, and both manifest the extent of the transformation Odysseus has undergone.

Obviously, Ithaca is not a colony founded by Odysseus. It is his former home, to which he returns at the end of a long and arduous journey. But, as demonstrated by Carol Dougherty, the return of Odysseus after such a long interval can be regarded as a refounding of Ithaca. His landing there is like a landing on unfamiliar and unknown shores (13.187–96), and the descriptions of Ithaca, both by the narrator and by Athena, who meets Odysseus in disguise (13.242–49), echo the description of the island opposite the land of the Cyclopes.[92] Like the monstrous Cyclops, the suitors, the current inhabitants of Ithaca, are described by Telemachus (1.250–51) and Penelope (21.332–33) as greedy and monstrous, while their eating of raw flesh, an act with cannibalistic resonance, symbolizes their degradation and loss of humanity (20.347–49).[93] In this interpretative vein, claims Dougherty, "There is a certain logic [. . .] to the fact that the colonist's (here Odysseus') tools of revenge against the indigenous cannibal are the very nautical skills and tools that enabled him to cross the sea to settle new lands in the first place."[94] To reiterate, this does not mean that Odysseus literally refounds Ithaca:

[R]ather, the themes and issues of colonial discourse articulate the terms of his return to represent it as a kind of re-foundation. [. . .] In other words, Odysseus metaphorically re-founds Ithaca, and the fertile connections between this re-foundation and scenes from his encounters at Phaeacia and in the land of the Cyclopes imbue this new foundation with some of the productive qualities of the New World and the Golden Age.[95]

The seeming recuperation of Odysseus' heroic self in book twenty-two of the epic during his fight with the suitors (22.1–389) should be similarly interpreted. The narrative of this battle, which echoes so many passages of the *Iliad*, is not a harbinger of the return of the crude-heroic code.[96] On the contrary, it is merely its final appearance in a very different version and a very different context. The battle with the suitors, however valorous and dangerous, is not held within the context of a glorious expedition like that of the Trojan War; it is a battle literally confined to the limits of a house, a domestic aspect salient in its description. In addition, the veteran and his son, accompanied by two herdsmen, are as remote from Achilles and Patroclus, with their Myrmidons, as Antinous and the suitors are from Hector and the Trojans. If, as some critics contend, the last book of the *Odyssey* may be regarded as a part of the whole epic (and not a dissociated late interpolation),[97] then Odysseus' rejoicing at Athena's proposal for peace in 24.545 is revealing; unlike the typical Iliadic hero, who aspires to battle, Odysseus welcomes peace as soon as it is offered him.[98]

However, the battle with the suitors is not merely a courageous act of Odysseus and his helpers. It is also an act of revenge and carnage that costs the lives of many, a fact that again problematizes the question of the poem's attitude toward the heroic value of martial prowess. Divine intervention is once more a key to interpretation. Athena, who to this point has constantly supported Odysseus both in practical preparation for battle and by emotionally encouraging him when he showed signs of despondence, is now both chastising his seeming indecisiveness and exhorting him to kill the suitors (22.225–35). This imperative does not leave the master of the house much choice, and he therefore plunges into this final mortal combat (22.265–329).[99] One should also recall that the killing of the suitors is almost his prerogative due to the latter's persistently insolent behavior toward his property (24.451–60), to say nothing of their attempt to murder both Odysseus and his son. The killing of the suitors, however, might have been the inchoate stage of a tragic cycle of bloodshed and feuding. Although this is not the road taken by the poet of the *Odyssey*, it is explicitly apparent as an option in the last book of the text as we have it (24.413–37, 463–71). Thus, this battle, and with it the notion of martial heroic valor, is represented as a necessary and just evil that terminates rather than commences a long period of suffering.[100] It is in this light that one should interpret Odysseus' reaction to the joy of Eurycleia after the death of the suitors: In contrast to the traditional heroic *euchos,* Odysseus does not boast in his victory but, on the contrary, mutes the old woman, forbidding her to rejoice while emphasizing the death of the suitors as a manifestation of divine justice (22.408–16).[101]

Such an Odysseus cannot be regarded as the same character who tried so hard to adhere to the heroic code after leaving the Cyclops' cave. This is, as deftly described by Richard B. Rutherford, a deeply changed Odysseus:

In the course of the poem [. . .] Odysseus acquires greater severity and self-control, and wins a deeper understanding of human feelings and motives, perhaps even of the wider condition of man. In this sense, and in his role as avenger and instrument of divine justice, he is a hero with special moral authority. This is not the whole story, however. The "philosophic" Odysseus never totally displaces the older, wilier Odysseus; rather, the moral side coincides with and controls his instinctive sense of curiosity [. . .], his greed [. . .], and his vanity [. . .]. The moral task of testing and dealing out justice offer a suitable channel for Odysseus' native character and talents [. . .]. The older, craftier side of his personality is not dead [. . .], but it is *controlled* in a way that it was not always before (most conspicuously not in the Cyclops episode).[102]

And it is with this change, culminating in a new kind of "hero with special moral authority," that I conclude my discussion of this pivotal episode. The process undergone by Odysseus, the process that has enabled him to acquire "a deeper understanding of human feelings and motives, perhaps even of the wider condition of man," is an inherent element of the tragic.

To begin, it is worth postulating once more that while suffering is an inalienable element of the tragic it is not, in itself, tragic. The sufferings of Odysseus, like those of Achilles, acquire their tragic dimension due to their specific relation with time or, more precisely, because they are anchored in unavoidably ill synchronization or a missed opportunity of *kairos* as the right time to do a thing. As demonstrated earlier, Odysseus' behavior in the Cyclops scene exemplifies this principle. Two of his acts, the catastrophic decision to stay in the cave of the ogre and the even more disastrous revelation of his name to Polyphemus, are inevitable tragic errors since Odysseus could not have avoided these decisions at the time they were made. The errors were unavoidable not because of the protagonist's idiosyncratic personality but due to the values of an entire era that were deeply rooted in him. To elucidate the tragic in this context more succinctly, this unsuccessful adherence to the crude-heroic code of behavior—like the failed attempts to focalize experience through heroic or colonizing lenses—does not reflect a recalcitrant character foolishly clinging to the past. Rather, it symbolizes the extreme difficulty of individual movement both in and with time, a movement that necessarily entails an irretrievable loss that must be recognized and acknowledged. It is here that one perceives quite clearly how the tragic associates time, suffering, and recognition, for the tragic recognition is a perception of the human condition according to which great suffering and terrible loss are an ineluctable component of human life. Yet this suffering and loss are not merely the outcome of a miscalculation of an individual within a specific context but rather a result of the ineludible contusive effects of time. To summarize this point: tragic time can be either closely linked with malevolent divine intervention, as is the case with Achilles, or independent of any concrete powers, as happens with Odysseus. In both cases, however, what contributes to time's tragic nature is its emblematic quality, an aspect that sheds light on painful and unavoidable characteristics of life in general formulated in what I have termed metaphysical recognition.

Here, again, the two epics exhibit a marked similarity regarding their heroes, for both Achilles and Odysseus have to go through a long and painful process, which finally leads to a psychological and metaphysical recognition that is both cognitive and emotional. In both cases this process necessitates relinquishing an essential aspect of the heroic personality, for it is only on the basis of such renunciation that a new perspective can be built. This metaphysical recognition is tragic, for it implies the understanding that one has to live and act in a world dictated by powers that are essentially hostile to one's aims and similarly obstructive to one's happiness. This comprehension is reflected in Achilles' ability to formulate the tale of the two jars, and it is similarly expressed in Odysseus' tortuous apprehension of his behavior toward the Cyclops many years after the event. Such recognition does not facilitate crude heroism, where the ego and its blind belief in its superiority stand at the center. On the contrary, it leads to an opposite understanding of the importance of humility and meekness, as well as of an acceptance of one's unavoidable tragic lot. Such recognition, however, is not solely positive. Although it can, as is the case with Odysseus and Achilles, generate a new value scale for human life, its harrowing aspects can also undermine any value system as such by exposing the inherent futility of human endeavor. This aspect of the tragic is the focus of the next chapter on the association between the tragic and the absurd.

4

Hector in Flight

The Absurd and the Tragic
in the Iliad

*T*he discussion of the Cyclops scene has indicated the tragic problematic entailed in the notion of heroism for a hero in a transitional phase. The problematic, however, is rooted in a context of the end of the Trojan War and the beginning of a postwar era, that is to say, in a context in which war has only recently ceased to be an essential component. My aim in this chapter is to broaden the textual and epistemological horizons of this problematic presence not only in an epic of the postwar period but also in the epic set in the age of its antecedent "classical" heroism, the *Iliad*. I pointed out the complexity of the notion of heroism in the *Iliad* in the previous chapter, and what was merely outlined there will be fully elaborated in the following discussion. I therefore return here to the *Iliad* in order to track the same path I analyzed earlier in the *Odyssey*, attending to the same involution of the notion of heroism that was mapped there. I intend to present a chasm at the core of the notion of heroism in the epic where it is most heavily value charged, where excellence and prestige are almost totally dependent on crude heroic notions such as valor and prowess in war. My three central fissures—the textual entries through which I intend to delve into the representation of heroism in the *Iliad*—are the motif of flight, characterization, and permanent textual gaps.[1] I open my discussion with a survey of the motif of flight in the *Iliad,* noting its various appearances in the epic while underlining the essential difference between flight and retreat. I then investigate the characterization of Hector in this respect, focusing on his behavior in several exemplary events to reveal his repeated flights as a quintessential aspect of his portrayal. The final fissure through which I enter this text is the narratological technique of "permanent gaps," which are gaps in the story created by the narrative that remain unresolved at the text's conclusion. I examine this technique in the context of Hector's last flight in the epic, when he runs from Achilles in book twenty-two. All three fissures illuminate the intricate representation of heroism in the *Iliad* and shed a disturbing light on Troy's most prominent hero. Moreover, these fissures expose the insoluble tensions that lead me to incorporate a new notion into the model of the tragic developed in this book, namely, the absurd as it is formulated by Albert Camus in his book *The Myth of Sisyphus.*

I commence with the motif of flight. In the *Odyssey,* as shown in chapter 3, flight is represented positively as a preferred option for the returning heroes in the face of the constant threats and dangerous obstacles confronting them on their way home. In the *Iliad,* in contrast, flight is basically an index of cowardice and shame. This maxim is formulated by various characters on different occasions and is already implied at the beginning of the epic when the angry Agamemnon answers Achilles' threat to return home (1.169–70) by calling it a flight ("flee then" [*pheuge mal'*] 1.173). True, somewhat later he does refer to Achilles' possible act as a homecoming ("go home, then" 1.179), yet the derogatory tone of his initial reaction should not be ignored. The shameful aspect of flight from war is explicitly articulated by Agamemnon himself in the second book of the epic. After Zeus sends Agamemnon a false dream with the promise that he will capture Troy, Agamemnon recounts it to the assembly of the elders, adding that first he wants to test the people in words because this is the custom (2.73). The trial will be his order "to flee (*pheugein*) with the ships" (2.74). His suggestion accepted, Agamemnon later exhorts the people in the general assembly "to flee (*pheugômen*) home with their ships" (2.140), hoping to attain the opposite result by his explicit references both to the personal and private shame inherent in such an act (2.115) and to the collective future shame of all the Greeks (2.119). His plan backfires, and the army, exhausted after a long and fruitless war, rushes toward the ships. The possibility of such an end to the war horrifies Hera who, in her speech to Athena, refers to this act as flight ("they will flee" [*pheuxontai*]

2.159) and to the Greeks as those who might leave Priam and the Trojans a glory to boast of (2.160). These aspersive expressions are reiterated in Athena's words to Odysseus asking him to intervene and prevent this shameful act (2.173–78). Odysseus himself, who immediately afterward stops the army from going to the ships, accosts each leader with the reproach that it is not seemly to be afraid like "a coward" (*kakon* 2.190).

Repeatedly the epic presents exhortations against flight that are strongly associated with the discourse of honor and shame. So Agamemnon, in words that are later used by Ajax (15.561–64) and reverberate in Nestor's speech (15.661–66), exhorts his people "to be men" (5.529) and remember "their pride and sense of shame" (5.530), "for there is neither glory nor prowess for those who flee" (*pheugontôn* 5.532).[2] In like manner, in a dialogue regarding virtue (13.274–91), Idomeneus tells Meriones that his, Meriones', virtue is impeccable, for if he were wounded in battle it would always be somewhere in the front of his body and never in his back, implying that Meriones never turned his back to his enemies in flight. These concepts are not restricted to the Greek army. When Paris, defeated in a duel, flees from Menelaus he is reproached by Hector as "a source of shame to himself" (3.51) as well as "a source of malignant joy to the Achaeans" (8.43, *charma* 3.51). The same expression of "becoming a malignant joy (*charma*) to the enemies" (6.82) reappears in Helenus' words to Hector regarding the possible flight of the Trojans.[3]

One should, however, carefully demarcate the line separating fleeing from retreat. On several occasions combatants encourage their fellow warriors to retreat from fighting because the odds seem so greatly against them. In those cases it would be mere folly to stay and fight a battle leading to an unpreventable loss. Thus, Diomedes, seeing Hector accompanied by Ares (5.592), confronts his people with the following words.

> Friends, how we used to marvel at godly Hector
> for being a warlike and audacious warrior.
> Indeed there is always one of the gods at his side to keep him from
>   destruction,
> as Ares there is just now, in the likeness of a mortal.
> So, turning constantly toward the Trojans, retreat,
> and do not desire eagerly to battle in full force with the gods.
>
> (5.601–6)

Since it is Ares that helps Hector in his war, any direct fight with the Trojan hero means a fight with a god, which is why the Greeks must retreat. But retreat is not flight, and Diomedes insists on the prolongation of the battle during the act of retreat.[4] The emphasis on retreat as an action taken while facing the enemy and continuing to fight is essential to his discourse, for it proves the Greeks reasonable without being sullied by cowardice.[5]

Retreat, however, is justified not only when a god stands by the enemy. When Ajax kills Amphius (5.611–17) he rushes to strip off his armor, yet soon after he refrains from doing so for "he was afraid" (5.623) of the strong Trojans that surround him. He is therefore "driven from his post and retreats" (5.626).[6] Note that, although Ajax is afraid, he is not reproached here by the narrator, and, as indicated by the use of the passive voice, the narrator perceives Ajax' retreat as something forced upon him and therefore inevitable.[7] In the same vein the Trojans did not "flee (*phobeonto*) with headlong speed" (16.303–4) from the Greek ships but rather "retreated from them due to necessity" (16.305). So Menelaus, who leaves behind Patroclus' corpse in order to seek a messenger to bring the bad tidings to Achilles, is likened to a lion, the emblem of force and courage, forced to give up his prey (17.657–65).[8]

This is not to say that a retreat, even a justified and temporary one, is devoid of conflict. When Hector, spurned by Apollo, rushes to take the armor of the recently dead Patroclus, Menelaus, who stands beside the body, hesitates between leaving the body and defending it (17.91–105). On the one hand, he states that if he deserts Patroclus he will deserve the shameful blame by any of the Danaoi who might see him (17.93), for, after all, Patroclus lies here dead because of his, Menelaus', "prestige" (*timês* 17.92). And yet, if he yields to "his sense of shame" and goes alone to fight Hector and his men, he will surely die. A second thought then follows, in which Menelaus conceives himself beyond reproach by any of the Danaoi who might see him (17.100) if he withdraws from Hector (17.101), for Hector fights with the help of a god (17.101). Here, again, the retreating Menelaus is described by means of the flattering simile of a lion (17.108–13).

Of course, whether an act should be regarded as retreat or flight is open to interpretation as, for example, in the dialogue between Sthenelus and Diomedes. When the former, seeing Pandarus and Aeneas approaching, advises Diomedes to "withdraw together in chariots" (5.249) for otherwise they will surely die, the angry Diomedes "looks superciliously at him" (5.251) and tells him that he, Diomedes, is not a coward and therefore will go on fighting (5.252–58). Unlike Sthenelus, Diomedes regards such an act as mere flight and not retreat, and he therefore orders Sthenelus "not to mention anything associated with flight" (*phobond'* 5.252). Moreover, even in cases in which retreat from battle does seem reasonable, a hero might decide to regard it as flight and therefore stay for reasons of prestige. Thus, Odysseus is left alone to confront the throng of Trojans after the rest of the Greeks leave the scene in fear (11.401–2). His decision is an outcome of internal debate: on the one hand it would be "a terrible evil" (*mega kakon* 11.404) "if he flees in terror due to fear of the throng" (11.404–5), and on the other hand, it would be "even more horrible" (11.405) to be captured alone (11.405–6). Although the comparative "more horrible" indicates that the second option is the less desirable one in this quagmire, Odysseus chooses it nevertheless, for he knows that only cowards (*kakoi* 11.408) avoid fighting, while one who is noble and brave stays in his place, heedless of consequences (11.409–10). The naming of the act as "fleeing in terror" is, of course, telling, revealing Odysseus' preconception of it.[9]

As noted by Stephen Scully, Odysseus' soliloquy is representative of what I have termed the crude-heroic code of the *Iliad:*

The private thoughts of a hero question the values of heroic activity as he could never do publicly. Thus, it is the privileged domain of the soliloquy to convey the anxiety of the hero as he moves from indecision to resolution, from fear to courage, from thought to reaffirmation of heroic action. Although the soliloquy calls into question the values of society, it also serves to highlight the particular nature of heroism as conceived in the *Iliad.* Iliadic heroism is not only action, but action born from consciousness of death and recognition of the limits of human existence.[10]

This soliloquy, however, is by no means a portrayal of the only possible avenue for a hero in the *Iliad.* In two important passages that, like Odysseus' deliberation, take place within a context of general fleeing of the army, shameful flight is seriously considered by a hero as an option. In the first case Zeus intervenes on behalf of the Trojans and throws his lightning at the feet of the horses that carry Diomedes' chariot (8.132–36). Nestor, who sees it and recognizes in the lightning the hand of Zeus, who has already decreed glory for Hector (8.140–44), quails (8.138) and calls out to Diomedes to "turn his horses and flee" (*phobond'* 8.139). Diomedes agrees with this assessment (8.146) but dreads the enemy's interpretation of such an act as flight: if he did retreat, Hector would boast that he, frightened (*phobeomenos*), went to the ships (8.147–50). This is an important passage for it proves that the same act can be represented both as a justified decision of calculated retreat

and as a manifestation of cowardice.[11] Note that there is actually no difference between the retreats mentioned earlier and the present occasion: Hector, who is challenging the Greek army, is aided by Zeus and is consequently
unconquerable. It is futile to fight him, and if Diomedes decides to do so
nevertheless he will benefit neither himself nor his fellow warriors.

Nestor's answer to Diomedes' hesitation is instructive, for what he
chooses to stress is not the nature of the act itself (which is probably indisputable) but its interpretation: being the hero that he is, the slaughterer of
so many Trojans, Diomedes will never be deemed a coward by Hector's
people. In short, opines Nestor, nobody could possibly believe Hector's
bragging (8.152–56). Following these words, Nestor "turns his horses to flee"
([*phugad*] 8.157). The old man's claim for a universal and irrevocably heroic
view of Diomedes is, of course, impossibly unattainable and willfully oblivious to questions of point of view, for Diomedes' flight has so many eyewit-
nesses that it would be impossible to contradict interpretations of it as cowardice. And, indeed, the moment the two Greeks turn their backs to the
Trojans, Hector starts scoffing at Diomedes, telling him that he "always was
a woman at heart" (8.163),[12] and calling him "a disdained plaything" (8.164).
Three times the exasperated Diomedes ponders turning his face to his
enemy, and three times Zeus gives a sign that the day is Hector's (8.167–
71).[13] The narrator is reticent about Diomedes' final decision, but his obfus-
cating silence cannot conceal the fact that the Greek hero eventually did flee
the Trojan leader, thus yielding to the reasonable, though antiheroic and
shameful, argument in favor of running away from an unnecessary death.

The second example of serious consideration of shameful flight takes
place at a later stage of the story after Achilles resumes fighting in order to
avenge the death of his beloved friend Patroclus. While throngs of Trojans
are running for their lives from the wrathful Achilles (21.527–29), Priam orders the gates of the city opened and admits the refugees (21.531–33). This
would have been the end of Troy if Apollo had not inserted courage into the
heart of Agenor so that he would confront Achilles (21.543–47). The narrator tells his audience not only that Agenor's decision to face Achilles was an
outcome of Apollo's intervention but also that the god would save the hero
from certain death (21.547–48). Agenor, however, is ignorant of all this, and
both his cogitations and his decision are uninformed by, and hence independent of, his future guaranteed salvation. Like Odysseus and Diomedes,
Agenor wavers between two options, yet, unlike them, he thinks solely of
flight. What troubles Agenor is not the shameful aspect of flight but rather
its prospects for success: in the first case he considers fleeing in the same way

that all the others have chosen, yet then, he thinks, he will surely be caught and killed by Achilles (21.553–55); next he considers running in a different direction and hiding in order to come later, in stealth, to Troy (21.556–61). However, since the prospects for this second plan seem no brighter than those of the first (21.562–66), he decides to face Achilles and fight him (21.567–70). In other words, Agenor's decision is pragmatic and has nothing to do with the crude-heroic code, which bids fighting the enemy for the sake of one's prestige: if he could have chosen a shameful yet successful flight, he would have surely done so. Only after acknowledging that fleeing would lead to inevitable death whatever route he chose, does he decide in favor of an honorable fight with Achilles.[14] And it is this tendency to embrace flight that leads us straight toward the most complex of all the flights in the epic, that of Hector from Achilles.

I shall consider this astonishing act before long, but first I wish to locate it within the broader context of Hector's behavior in warfare in general. For, although Hector is no doubt the most distinguished hero among the Trojans and the one whose death symbolizes more than anything else Troy's approaching doom, his association with retreat and flight from the enemy is a recurring motif in the *Iliad*.[15] To begin with, a day after the failed embassy to Achilles, when the Greeks resume fighting, Zeus orders Iris to tell Hector "to withdraw" (11.189) as long as Agamemnon participates in the battle. He also adds that the moment the latter is forced to retire by a wound, Hector may regain his former position as the leader of the fighting Trojans (11.191–93). What is interesting in this episode is not so much Hector's withdrawal during Agamemnon's *aristeia* as his flight from Diomedes after he reemerges as the unconquerable hero. According to Zeus' promise, Hector has the upper hand in battle, and he bursts into the Greek army like a storm wind, bringing death to anyone in his way (11.297–309). But then Diomedes hurls his spear and hits him in the helmet, and Hector runs back and mixes in the throng (11.354) before falling into a swoon (11.355–56). Diomedes runs after him, but Hector recuperates and mingles with the crowd, thus shunning the black lot of death (11.360). The narrator eschews the incriminating vocabulary of flight in describing this scene, but Diomedes uses it fastidiously, telling Hector that he has "again succeeded in escaping death" (*ephuges thanaton*) and addressing him as the emblem of shamelessness, a "dog" (11.362). In like manner, after unsuccessfully casting his spear at Ajax (14.402–6), Hector "shrank back" (14.408) before falling to the ground unconscious, hit by a stone hurled at him by Ajax (14.409–20). He is then led away by his people, rallies for a while, and faints again (14.427–39).

On a different occasion, soon after the death of Sarpedon, Zeus implants "a feeble heart" (16.656) in Hector. Consequently, Hector "took a flight" ([*phugad'*] 16.657) and "called on the rest of the Trojans to flee as well" (*pheugemenai* 16.657–58). Again, the narrator does not inveigh against Hector for this act, especially since it is a direct outcome of a decision by Zeus, yet Glaucus, Sarpedon's comrade in arms, blemishes him later for exactly this reason. He says that Hector is "good-looking but falls short as a warrior" (17.142),[16] contemptuously calling into question the glory of a coward (17.143). He reminds the Trojan leader of Sarpedon's contributions to Troy and spurns Hector's desertion of such a hero (17.150–53).

No doubt each of these examples can be justified, and Hector cannot be characterized solely on their basis. Yet, in combination with the flight before his last duel with Achilles, the motif of flight does contribute to a puzzling and extremely complex aspect of the characterization of the Trojan hero. It is also notable that Hector's flight from Achilles toward the end of the epic is not the first one. In book nine Achilles mentions another occasion on which they met outside the gates of Troy (9.352–55) and Hector "barely succeeded in fleeing (*ekphugen*)" from Achilles' assault (9.355). It is in light of this episode that one should read both Hector's declaration that he would engage Achilles if he met him near the ships (18.305–9) and the long scene in book twenty-two where he deliberates whether to flee Achilles or face him.[17] And it is to this internal monologue and the pivotal flight scene that follows it immediately that I shall now turn.

While the frightened Trojans run to their city (21.606–7) and dare not stay outside its walls (21.607–11), deadly doom (*oloiê moir'*) binds Hector outside the city walls (22.5–6). Both his father (22.38–76) and mother (22.82–89) plead with him to enter but to no avail; Hector resists their pleas and refuses to yield (22.91–96). He does, however, recognize his inauspicious situation, as indicated by the opening words of his internal debate: "Oh woe is me" (*oi moi egôn* 22.99). He considers entering the city (22.99) but drops this idea as soon as it is raised both because Polydamas, whose good council he had rejected the previous day, might repudiate him (22.100) and because he is ashamed that an inferior Trojan might chastise him for causing terrible loss (22.105–7).[18] From this perspective, he thinks it better to fight Achilles in a glorious battle whatever the consequences (22.108–10). But then he becomes frightened and therefore ponders another option: offering Achilles the return of Helen to the Greeks and the compensation of half the treasures of Troy for the insult of her kidnapping (22.111–20). This is illusory, as Hector himself acknowledges (22.122), for Achilles will undoubtedly not listen and kill him on the spot (22.123–25). In any case, this is not time for a chat, as if they were a boy and a girl standing by a rock or a tree (22.126–28); better to engage in fighting as soon as possible and see to whom Zeus will grant victory (22.129–30). The notion of shame pervades the discourse in its entirety. Polydamas might "lay disgrace" (22.100) upon Hector, Hector himself is "ashamed" of what a Trojan might say (22.105), and Achilles will not honor Hector if he offers him Helen (22.124) but rather will kill him like a woman (22.125). There is also something despicable in the simile of a flirting chat between a boy and a girl within a warlike context, an aspect emphasized in Hector's account (22.127, 128).[19]

But then, after a long cogitation, Hector sees Achilles and runs away.

And trembling caught Hector when he saw him, and indeed he did
    not dare anymore
to stay there, so he left the gates behind and ran, terrified (*phobêtheis*
    22.136–37).

This is extraordinary. Two lines and nothing more? The main hero of the Trojan army runs for his life, a coward in his own terms who, worst of all, is being watched by both armies during this shameful act, and the narrator is silent regarding the implications of such a deed?

No less surprising is the reticence of many critics, ancient and modern alike, on the subject. The Scholia prefer to concentrate on philological questions about the order of the words (bT on line 136); on logical issues such as the causal connection between fear, running, and flight (TA on line 137); or on geographical aspects signaled by the word *behind* (bT on line 137). Among modern critics Nicholas Richardson notes the aesthetic merit of these lines,[20] and Von der Mühll expands on the possible archaeological implications of the description as well as on the poet's extensive topographical knowledge.[21] Fenik's attitude is representative in this context, for his subtle reading of the episode ends with an unexplained absolution of Hector. Fenik opens his discussion with a comparison between Hector and Agenor: "Sheer terror of the enemy consumes Hector's attention. In this he is like Agenor, and we realize with a start: Hector is not deciding whether to resist or flee. Like Agenor, he is casting for a way out."[22] Fenik justly pinpoints the exceptional nature of the simile that likens Hector to a serpent and contrasts it with the other three examples that belong to the same group of warriors' speeches.[23]

Odysseus, Agenor and Menelaus are likened to noble beasts of prey, all holding their ground against attack or in grudging retreat. The serpent representing Hector coils itself around its whole, but no fight occurs and none is described. The placement of the comparison tells even more. For the other men it comes right after the monologue, illustrating the resolution just made. Hector's comes *before* he addresses himself. As usual, the poet's hand is sure. The simile would be badly inappropriate at the end of his deliberation since the decision to fight will be abandoned. He is not, in fact, like the others, an intrepid beast, hard to dislodge.[24]

Yet, after adducing the unheroic aspects of Hector's decision and, which is even more compelling, attending to the fact that Hector's decision to fight lacks "genuine resolve" and consequently "there is no surprise when he turns and runs,"[25] Fenik concludes his discussion with the following benign words:

In short, the whole episode dramatically expounds the meaning of Hector's death—for his city and as a personal fate. The monologue is part of this, and is thereby weightier and more revealing than the others. The decision it records, falteringly made and immediately abandoned, is only a piece of something larger, the wonderfully probing and moving depiction of Hector in his last moments, of his character and fate in their setting.[26]

Fenik's efforts to underplay the significance of Hector's flight by viewing it as a "piece of something larger" are far from convincing. And, while this suits his romantic portrayal of this magnificent hero ("the man driven by vain dreams and generous enthusiasms"),[27] it cannot dispel the implications of such a disturbing aspect of Hector's characterization for his heroic stature.[28]

But let us go back to the narrator who leisurely particularizes the route of the two warriors. Once more a disturbing question surfaces: are we really to believe that a watchtower and a wild fig tree (22.145) or two springs and their adjacent washing troughs (22.147–56) are the most important things for a narrator to report in this context? In order to clarify this seemly incomprehensible narratological decision, let us deviate for a moment to one of the most famous analyses of the narrative of a Greek epic, Erich Auerbach's *Mimesis*. In the opening chapter of his masterpiece, Auerbach claims that the narrator of the *Iliad* and the *Odyssey* makes no distinction between foreground and background, and in fact "[his] style knows only a foreground, only a uniformly illuminated, uniformly objective present."[29] Consequently, "a continuous rhythmic procession of phenomena passes by, and never is there a form left fragmentary or half illuminated, never a lacuna, never a gap, never a glimpse of unplumbed depths."³⁰ According to Auerbach, the antipode of this narrative technique is that of the Bible, where the narrator eliminates many important details of the story. Thus, for example, in his description of the sacrifice of Isaac, the narrator does not provide his narratees with even an inkling regarding the thoughts and feelings of father and son during the three days preceding the sacrifice.³¹ This is how Auerbach summarizes the biblical style:

[T]he externalization of only so much of the phenomena as is necessary for the purpose of the narrative, all else left in obscurity; the decisive points of the narrative alone are emphasized, what lies between is non-existent [. . .] the whole permeated with the most unrelieved suspense and directed toward a single goal (and to that extent far more a unity), remains mysterious and "fraught with background."³²

Although Auerbach's somewhat derisory assessment of the narrative technique of the Greek epics has been much criticized since the publication of his book, one must concede that his observation is, at least partially, correct. Often the narrator expounds on a detail of his narrative and deviates in order to shed light on a topic that is loosely associated with the main narrative. The description of the objects and places passed by Achilles and Hector in the passage quoted earlier is not exceptional, although their relation to the main topics of the epic in general and to this specific flight in particular can be presented as less artificial than they might seem at first sight. Yet what is so exceptional in this passage is the unusual combination of the "Greek" narrative style, characterized by Auerbach as fully detailed and rich with information, and what he terms the biblical narrative style, replete with elisions and absent crucial information. Hector's reflections and those of Abraham and Isaac are similarly presented. In both cases the narrator withholds crucial details, leaving permanent textual gaps. Hector's flight is therefore both excessively detailed and extremely scant, self-reflexively delineating a void at the center of the field of information in order to fill it with data that cannot but give an impression of redundancy. The similes in this narrative reinforce the reflexivity of this gap, for they do not add to the information the narratee already has. Whether the runners are likened to a hawk and a dove (22.139–40) or a dog and a fawn (22.189), whether the situation is likened to a horse race (22.162) or a dream (22.199), the effect is the same: the similes merely vivify the act of flight and pursuit.³³ The text remains silent about its central characters at this crucial moment and even highlights that silence. Entering the narrative through the fissure of this permanent gap, we can reconsider the motif of flight.[34]

The centrality of the flight motif to the epic in general and its place within the pivotal scene of Hector's death in particular lead to the conclusion that the narrative of this episode is tendentious. And even if, according to Horace's dictum (*Ars Poetica,* verse 359), one can detect some passages tainted with negligence in the *Iliad* and the *Odyssey,* Hector's flight is surely not one of them. The hermeneutically inviting fissure of a permanent gap furthers this reading of the motif of flight and the question of heroic characterization. Putting these elements together in reflecting on their tragic signification now brings us to consider the notion of the absurd.

In his highly influential treatise, first published in 1942 and entitled *Le Mythe de Sisyphe,* Albert Camus discusses various aspects of what he terms "an absurd reasoning" ("un raisonnement absurde," the title of the first section of his book).[35] The absurd, as the following will demonstrate, is a perception of reality that is closely associated with my notion of the tragic. Like the tragic, Camus' absurd comprises both suffering and psychological recognition while at its highest degree it also includes a certain kind of recognition that cannot be termed metaphysical—Camus' world is alien to entities such as gods and fate—but is akin to it. In fact, it is Camus himself who defines this moment of highest recognition as tragic, when one is able to acquire tragic depth through direct confrontation with and unmitigated acknowledgment of the horrifying aspects of the human condition.

Although at first sight Camus' book seems remote from the culture that generated the focal texts of my investigation,[36] it is interesting to note that the book is almost literally coated in ancient Greek thought: its motto is taken from Pindar's third Pythian ode, and its final essay gives the book its title. The French translation used by Camus for the excerpt from the ode reads:

Ô mon âme, n'aspire pas à la vie immortelle,
mais épuise le champ du possible.

*[O my soul, do not aspire to immortal life,
but exhaust the domain of the possible.]*

Thus, the book begins with a statement calling for renunciation (of immortal life located in the domain of the impossible), on the one hand, and adherence (to real, quotidian life located within the limits of the possible) on the other. Absurd reasoning is therefore conditioned by a certain abandonment of high aspirations and by concentration on a much more limited field of achievement.[37] The exact nature of both field and achievements is mapped throughout the book, and one of its most succinct formulations appears in the chapter on the myth of Sisyphus. Camus sees in Sisyphus, a mortal doomed forever to roll a rock up a hill from which it is destined to roll down, the absurd hero ("le héros absurde," 302). This eternal punishment is the price he has to pay for his adherence to life, for his cheating of Hades, to whose abode he refused to return despite his promise (301–2). The most horrible moment in this futile and repetitive action is undoubtedly when the rock rolls down:

> Tout au bout de ce long effort mesuré par l'espace sans ciel et le temps sans profondeur, le but est atteint. Sisyphe regarde alors la pierre dévaler en quelques instants vers ce monde inférieur d'où il faudra la remonter vers les sommets. (302)
>
> *[In the end of this long effort, which is measured through space without sky and time without depth, the goal is achieved. And so Sisyphus watches the rock hurtling down in a few minutes toward this lower world from which he will have to roll it up once more toward the summits.]*

And yet, for Camus, it is exactly this moment that enables his hero to make sense of his existence by achieving tragic depth.[38] For when Sisyphus slowly descends toward his endless torture ("vers le tourment dont il ne connaîtra la fin," 302), he is fully aware of his situation ("cette heure est celle de la conscience," 302), which is why he is superior to his destiny ("il est supérieur à son destin," 302). Camus associates Sisyphus' recognition of his situation with the tragic ("Si ce mythe est tragique, c'est que son héros est conscient," 302), and the existential value of his distress lies precisely in its being devoid of any hope for success ("Où serait en effet sa peine, si à chaque pas l'espoir de réussir le soutenait?" 302). In fact, concludes Camus, the clarity of Sisyphus' perception, his full awareness of his miserable condition ("Sisyphe [. . .] connaît toute l'étendue de sa misérable condition," 302–3), the components and the source of his torture, are concomitantly the realization of his victory ("La clairvoyance qui devait faire son tourment consomme du même coup sa victoire," 303).

Characteristically, Camus' notion of the absurd is basically secular. Not only does the absurd man silence all idols in contemplating his torture ("l'homme absurde, quand il contemple son tourment, fait taire toutes les idoles," 303), but Sisyphus, the emblem of absurd reasoning, teaches a superior fidelity that negates the gods and uplifts the rocks ("Sisyphe enseigne la fidélité supérieure qui nie les dieux et soulève les rochers,"304). Yet his perception does not necessarily exclude religious thinking from the absurd:[39] Thus, while Camus himself epitomizes the notion of contempt for gods and destiny,[40] he notes the absurd reasoning that takes place within a religious framework, where reverence toward the gods, however cruel and incomprehensible, is an inalienable part of beliefs and perceptions of the world. And it is this conception of the absurd that I would like to apply to Hector's flight.

Technically, the poet has succeeded in creating a text so suggestive of absurd reasoning by working simultaneously on two levels: that of the narrative and that of the actual events. On the level of narrative, the poet suddenly abandons the heroic discourse in order to substitute a detailed description of flight. Both aspects of the narrative, the disappearance of heroic discourse at this crucial point and the detailed description of flight, point toward an indelible crisis of values. Since the crude-heroic code of behavior is deeply rooted in a system that endorses excellence according to which a face-to-face battle is laudable while running for one's life is cowardly, Hector's deed cannot but be interpreted as a chasm at the foundation of heroic valuation. In fact, Hector's flight can be regarded not merely as a diminution of his own private status as a glorious hero but as something much graver, as an evisceration of heroic signification in general. For what this greatest of Trojan heroes does—and here it is of crucial importance that his act is not merely impudent but also in blunt contradiction of his own conclusion, achieved after a long cogitation—is so shocking and incomprehensible that the episode may be conceived as undermining heroic values and possibly subverting them altogether. And it is this strike at the core of signification itself that resonates so strongly with absurd reasoning.

The second level on which the poet works in order to create the absurd is that of the actual event, the flight itself. For unlike the flights discussed earlier, this specific run is futile from its outset. On the one hand, the gates of Troy are barred, so Hector cannot run inside; on the other hand, there is no refuge outside, so Hector cannot possibly escape Achilles. The simile of the dream concretizes the absurd aspects of the chase:[41]

just as in a dream it is impossible to chase someone who runs
away—
for indeed neither the one is able to withdraw in flight from the
other, nor the other to chase—
so was Achilles unable to catch the fugitive by means of his legs, nor
was Hector able to flee.   (22.199–201)

Both warriors are caught in a movement that is interminable and leads
nowhere, a dreamlike reality the absurd aspects of which are reemphasized by
means of repetitive circling.[42] The route of the race is adjacent to the walls of
Troy, so its end is its beginning both spatially and temporally: the runners
end where they literally began just to begin running again.[43] The parallel
with Sisyphus' route up and down the hill is evident.

Yet Hector's flight from Achilles is not the end of the episode, nor do the
human agents play the sole significant role in this scene. The human arena,
where the chase takes place, is but a stage watched by the gods.[44] It is they
who are the crucial actors in the execrable drama at Troy, and it is their mischievous intervention that gives the scene its tragic signification. This is val-
idated by the narrative, where a divine conversation between Zeus and
Athena is inserted into the description of the flight. In fact, the two sections
of the flight narrative (22.138–66, 188–207) serve as another manifestation of
the repetition motif—so fundamental in absurd thinking—since both describe the same event, the encircling of Troy, which is itself repeated three
times (22.165, 208). The short conversation is indicative of the nature of divine intervention. It begins with Zeus' seemingly genuine concern for Hector ("woe [. . .] my heart moans for the ills of Hector" 22.168–70), which
leads to his consultation with the rest of the gods over whether to save the
Trojan's life. Yet it takes only the grumpy response of Athena (who claims
that all the rest of the gods do not approve of such an act [22.181]) for Zeus
to say that his suggestion was not in earnest (22.183–84), a declaration followed not only by his permission to Athena, willingly given (22.184), to do
whatever she likes (22.185) but also by an exhortation not to linger any
longer (22.185). His answer, besides being another manifestation of the all
too divine characteristic of frivolity, is again a revelation of the cruelty of
divine intervention in human affairs.[45] The harshness of Hector's inevitable
death, so sadly realized in Zeus' golden scales, which decree his doom
(22.209–13), is compounded by Athena's misleading posturing in her disguise as Hector's helping brother Deiphobus (22.226–27).

The narrative is unreserved about the true nature of the goddess's

action.[46] Before offering Hector her precarious support, Athena surrepti-
tiously accosts Achilles in her real form, promising him glory through Hector's death (22.216–21). She also tells Achilles that she will personally go and
persuade Hector to fight against him (22.223–24); after Hector is easily persuaded, the narrator states that the goddess gained his assent "through
treacherous cunning" (22.247). She also intervenes in the battle, returning
Achilles' spear without the notice of Hector (22.276–77) while disappearing
from the scene when Hector is in need of one (22.294–95). It is the absence
of Deiphobus at this crucial moment that leads Hector to the metaphysical
recognition of the bitter truth at the core of the preceding events. He realizes that Deiphobus had been behind the walls of Troy when Athena took
his shape and "deceived him thoroughly" (*exapatêsen* 22.299). Here again,
the resemblance between Hector's recognition and Camus' formulation of
absurd feeling is striking:

[D]ans un univers soudain privé d'illusions et de lumières, l'homme
se sent un étranger. Cet exil est sans recours puisqu'il est privé des
souvenirs d'une patrie perdue ou de l'espoir d'une terre promise. Ce
divorce entre l'homme et sa vie, l'acteur et son décor, c'est propre-
ment le sentiment de l'absurdité. (223)

[*In a world suddenly deprived of illusions and lights, man feels himself a
stranger. This exile has no remedy, for he is deprived of the memories of
his lost fatherland or the hope of a promised land. This divorce between
the man and his life, the actor and his decoration, this is exactly the feeling of absurdity.*]

Acknowledging the treacherous interventions in the world by the hostile
gods and fully aware of his impending death (22.297, 300), Hector determines, nevertheless, not to die without struggle or glory (22.304) but rather
to do some great deed that will be recalled by future generations (22.305).
What is exceptional here is not so much the combination of a hero's apprehension of the daunting nature of human life under the reign of the gods,
on the one hand, and adherence to the heroic code on the other. Many
Iliadic heroes can be regarded as representatives of this combination. In fact,
Hector himself formulates it at a much earlier stage of the epic in his conversation with Andromache (6.440–55). What is exceptional here is the resumption of this code after its blunt transgression by means of a shameful
flight. Note that Hector's perception of flight as an antiheroic act appears

not only before but also after its occurrence: Hector's initial words to Achilles refer directly to his running away as a result of fear, as the verbs "I will not fear" (*ou phobêsomai* 22.250) and "I did not dare then" (22.251) attest. Moreover, in the middle of the duel, after Achilles hurls his spear and misses, Hector declares that he, Achilles, will not "hit him in the back while fleeing (*pheugonti*)" (22.283). Of course, one might claim that Hector's words are nothing more than an indication of his change of mind or, to be more precise, his return to his heroic senses, which finds its expression in a renewed validation of the so recently abandoned code. Yet this simplistic explanation, if not totally unconvincing, is surely too meager for such a refined text as that of the *Iliad*. As demonstrated earlier, Hector's complex status regarding flight is delineated by the poet long before book twenty-two, while running away from Achilles is, in itself, much more than a mere breach of the crude-heroic code. It is also worth recalling that even Achilles, the embodiment of the notion of the hero in the epic, is willing to relinquish the battle and turn his back on Troy in order to avenge his humiliation and that his return to the battle owes much more to his love for his deceased friend than to his commitment to heroic glory. To reformulate the analysis of the previous chapter, since the *Iliad* is a plangent dirge to the human condition as manifested in the atrocities of war rather than a hymn to the glories of battle, its attitude toward the heroic code is ambivalent from the outset. Note that even here Hector's main motivation in eliciting this code is pragmatic. His concern is not its inherent merit but its utility as a basis for negotiation regarding the dead body of the loser: heroic reciprocity would vouchsafe the burial of the deceased (22.254–59). It is in this light that one should view Hector's readoption of the heroic code on the verge of his end. Neither a blind adoration of glory nor a valorous embrace of death, the resurfacing of the heroic code in this context hints, once more, at tragic signification, which is based on absurd reasoning.

Hector's final adherence to the value of heroic prowess is essentially congruent with absurd thinking. Hector's first reaction to Achilles' imminent threat is to run for his life, a mission impossible as his lot had already been divinely decreed. The ineffectiveness of his efforts is symbolized by the useless circling of Troy, which leads from nowhere to nowhere. Moreover, the end of his running is not the outcome of a voluntary decision but the achievement of a sly divine trick that leaves Hector somewhat blind to his real situation. Yet, after Athena's disappearance, when on the threshold of death and recognizing the truth of his desperate situation, Hector's decision to face Achilles reflects a genuine choice. This choice, and his profound ab-

surd heroism, is not to face Achilles in a suicidal act but to face his lot as a
human being in courageous and absurd revolt. Camus defines the absurd revolt as "this constant presence of man to himself. It is not aspiration, it has
no hope. This revolt is nothing but the assurance of an overwhelming destiny, yet without the resignation that should have accompanied it" ("cette
présence constante de l'homme à lui-même. Elle [la révolte] n'est pas aspiration, elle est sans espoir. Cette révolte n'est que l'assurance d'un destin écras-
ant, moins la résignation qui devrait l'accompagner," 256). The act of revolt,
according to Camus, is one that gives value to life and restores its grandeur
("Cette révolte donne son prix à la vie. Étendue sur toute la longueur d'une
existence, elle lui restitue sa grandeur," 256). It is also heroic, and in a much
deeper sense than that of the crude-heroic code of behavior, for the spirit
that dictates this discipline to itself, this forged will and direct confrontation
with a disheartening reality, is as forceful as it is unique ("Cette discipline
que l'esprit se dicte à lui-même, cette volonté forgée de toutes pièces, ce
face-à-face, ont quelque chose de puissant et de singulier," 256–57).[47]

To conclude, the case of Hector is exemplary of the human condition,
which is unavoidably replete with suffering and inevitable loss while heavily
influenced by hostile divine powers. It is also paradigmatic of the fragility of
the value systems to which a human being tries to adhere in order to endow
life with meaning, which are, in light of the characteristics described earlier,
in constant danger of dissipation. In engaging with the enormity of the difficulty of his situation, Hector resists the temptation to despair and chooses instead to instill value in the very short span of life remaining to him. And it is
this valorous decision, this forceful embrace of the absurd and the tragic, that
illuminates his horrific human condition with its dazzling heroism.

5

Mise en abyme and the Tragic

Metaphysical Recognition in the
Three Songs of Demodocus

$\mathcal{T}$o this point in outlining my tragic model, I have traced central motifs in the *Iliad* and the *Odyssey* and their diverse functions. Thus, the motif of flight in its various appearances in both epics serves my construction of the complex notion of heroism, which, in its turn, contributes to the depiction of the precarious status of the human being in a world dominated by hostile powers. In like manner, the narratological device of heteroglossia, where contrasting voices are intertwined in a subtle textual fabric, enables me to shed light on the extreme difficulty of movement in time. The preceding chapters of this book offer various perspectives on the same model, where three main components (time, suffering, and recognition) mark the zone of tragic signification. *Kairos* (time in its association with action, especially missed action) is a recurrent phenomenon in both the *Iliad* and the *Odyssey*; the central role given to a deeply flawed—albeit inevitable—synchronization in the epics reflects their essential tragic nature. This missed or lost time is the source of much of the suffering that is the stuff of human lives. Time and suffering converge in the tragic by means of recognition when characters acknowledge that this indissoluble nexus can be an outcome of divine intervention, which is inexplicable and unyielding to human understanding.

Thus far I have concentrated on textual fissures such as framing, repetition, and heteroglossia in developing my tragic model. In this chapter and the next I deal with a different kind of fissure generated by reflexivity, evidenced in strategies established and displayed by the poem as keys to its own reading.[1] In other words, these chapters investigate ways suggested by the poem itself as a means of reflecting upon its own tragic nature, starting here with the narratological technique of *mise en abyme* in the three songs of Demodocus.

The concept of *mise en abyme,* first coined by André Gide in his *Journal,* was thoroughly mapped and developed by Lucien Dällenbach in his book *Le Récit spéculaire: Essai sur la mise en abyme.*[2] Originally, the word *abyme* signified the center of the shield and *en abyme* the figure depicted in its center. What Gide probably had in mind in adapting this concept was something more emblematic, namely, a miniature image of the whole shield that was replicated in its center.

Hence *mise en abyme* has become a narratological term denoting a certain part of a literary work of art that represents the work as a whole.[3] One of the best-known examples of *mise en abyme* is the one given by Gide himself in the passage from his *Journal* where he coined the notion. Gide cites *Hamlet,* where the play directed by the eponymous hero is a kind of miniature of the play as a whole. This "play within a play," the staging of the murder of the Duke of Gonzaga by his brother and that brother's subsequent marriage to the victim's wife, reflects and refracts both the murder of King Hamlet by his brother Claudius and Claudius' marriage to his newly widowed sister-in-law Gertrud. Thus, the short play presented to the Danish court by the traveling troupe of actors can be conceived as a concise representation of the play within which it is presented.

My focus here is on three aspects of *mise en abyme* in book eight of the *Odyssey* exemplified by means of Demodocus' three songs. I begin my presentation with the first song of Demodocus as a *mise en abyme* of the *Odyssey* as an epic in dialogue with the *Iliad.* I then move to the second song, treating it as a *mise en abyme* of the *Odyssey* at two points, the epic as a story and a poetic creation. In other words, the second song serves me as a *mise en abyme* of both the content of the *Odyssey* and its poetic form. The last of the bard's songs enhances the perception of *mise en abyme,* viewing the *Odyssey* as an act of communication between poet and audience where the song and its responding listeners suggest emotional and cognitive reactions to the narratees of the

Odyssey.[4] This third manifestation of *mise en abyme* is also relevant to the first two songs of the bard, where different responses of different narratees are recorded. It is the dialogic relationship between the reactions to the bard's three songs that contributes most to the construction of tragic signification.

Demodocus' first song is a *mise en abyme* of the interepic dialogue of the *Odyssey* with the *Iliad.*[5] The beginning of the song refers to the singing of the glories of men, (*klea andrôn* 8.73), and soon afterward the notion of glory, *kleos,* is mentioned again (8.74). The emphasis on *kleos* alludes directly to the *Iliad* both thematically (glory in battle) and lexically: The phrase *klea andrôn* is used by the poet of the *Iliad* in reference to the theme of Achilles' song in book nine (189).[6] In addition, the sportive games that follow the song constantly allude to the most famous artifact of the *Iliad,* the shield of Achilles created by Hephaestus, thus associating the fictive world within the *Iliad* with the real world within the *Odyssey.*[7] Note that the first song of Demodocus appears in very condensed form (8.75–82),[8] and there is therefore a crucial difference between the information conveyed to Demodocus' narratees and that acquired by the narratees of the poet of the *Odyssey:* The audience of the *Odyssey* is given a mere synopsis of the events while Demodocus' listeners hear a whole poem. The compression of the song, however, enables one to see its resemblance to the *Iliad* more clearly. The strife between Achilles and Odysseus recalls that between Achilles and Agamemnon: the verb δηρίσαντο (*dêrisanto* 8.76) recalls the verb ἐρίσαντε (*erisante Il.* 1.6), the phrase referring to the beginning of woes in 8.81 recalls the phrase in *Il.* 1.6, and the phrase denoting Zeus' council in 8.82 alludes to the one in *Il.* 1.5. To this one might add the mention of Apollo (8.79), which recalls his prominent role in the first book of the *Iliad,* and the mention of the gods' banquet in 8.76, which evokes their banquet at the end of the first book of the *Iliad.* The main difference between Demodocus' song and the *Iliad* is the prominent role of Odysseus in the latter, in contrast to his rather minor presence in the opening quarrel of the *Iliad.*[9] Yet even this contrast reflects the dialogue of the *Odyssey* with the *Iliad,* for one of the main characteristics of the former epic is the prominence it gives this somewhat minor figure in the latter.

The second song of the bard, which tells a tale of adultery, shame, anger, and cunning, serves as a sophisticated *mise en abyme* of the *Odyssey's* main themes and motifs;[10] although Odysseus himself does not have an adulterous wife, adultery is one of the main threats to his successful homecoming. Demodocus' poem recites a divine story of adultery where the goddess Aphrodite, Hephaestus' wife, betrays him with Ares, the god of war. Hephaestus discovers their secret and contrives invisible fetters that catch and chain them in the sexual act. He then invites the rest of the gods to see them in their shame and demands retribution. The motif of the treacherous wife looms large in the *Odyssey* from its start, for already in the beginning of the epic Zeus recounts the adulterous relationship of Aegisthus and Clytemnestra as an exemplum of his moral attitude (1.32–43). The same motif recurs in book eleven, when Odysseus visits the underworld and meets Agamemnon, who tells him how he died by the treacherous hand of his wife's lover (11.409–30). In response, Odysseus compares the behavior of Clytemnestra to that of Helen (11.436–39), thus strengthening the connection between the disastrous act that initiated the *Iliad* and one that might bring catastrophe to the hero of the *Odyssey.*

Adultery is also the cause of Hephaestus' anger and the instigator of his cunning. It was anger that prompted Hephaestus to devise the trick (*dolon*) of the invisible fetters (8.276), which is a recurring motif in the story (*doloenta* 8.281, *dolon* 8.282, and *dolos* 8.317). Cunning is, of course, one of the main characteristics of Odysseus in the epic, and by stressing its association with Hephaestus the poet of the *Odyssey* creates a strong bond between the hero of his poem and the protagonist of Demodocus' song.[11] In addition, the god's cunning in the creation of a special marriage bed that chains the adulterers so they cannot move associates him with Odysseus, who built a marriage bed that could not be removed from its place and is used by his cunning wife as a final identification test (23.177–204).[12] Hephaestus is therefore also analogous to Penelope, since both utilize their marriage beds as a way to test the fidelity of their spouses, an analogy that becomes even stronger when one notes the comparison of Hephaestus' invisible fetters to the weaving of a spider (8.280), another allusion to Penelope, master weaver of the shrouds that were cunningly unraveled away from the eyes of the suitors.[13]

In addition to the above manifestations of the *mise en abyme* in the bard's second song, there is another important level on which the song serves as a miniature reflection of the epic as a whole, and that is its representation of the nature of the poet and his poetry.[14] The first song of Demodocus, in which Odysseus functions as a prominent figure, mirrors the poet of the epic who sings the adventures of the same character; the bard's second song weaves a much more complex net of interconnections between its content and that of the epic as a whole, for here Hephaestus, the main protagonist of the poem, is closely associated with the bard who sings his tale. The first association is created through the epithets, since Demodocus is called *periklutos* ("highly renowned," 8.83), which is the epithet of Hephaestus at 8.287,

300, 349, and 357.[15] In addition, the two are artists, and both are connected with the divine: Hephaestus is a god, and Demodocus is "a godlike (*theion*) singer" (8.43), "for the god gave him song as a gift" (8.44). The second association is based on one of the most prominent features shared by the two: their disabilities. Demodocus is blind, and his blindness is noted soon after he is first mentioned (8.64) and subsequently hinted at in several places (8.105–7, 256–62, 482–83). Hephaestus is also extremely limited by one of his organs, his legs.[16] The motif of his lameness is central to Demodocus' second song, for the main contrast between Hephaestus and Ares is based on Ares' preeminence in the same limbs in which Hephaestus is deformed (8.310–11, 329–32).

To this point I have concentrated on the manifestations of *mise en abyme* in the content of the two poems. However, this narratological device can also be detected on another level, the responses elicited by the songs of the bard. As noted earlier, one of the prominent features of Demodocus' first song is its concision. The brevity of the song, however, contrasts strikingly with the lengthy description of Odysseus' response to it: eight lines are dedicated to the song (8.75–82) while the response of the protagonist occupies thirteen lines (8.83–95). The response to the song is therefore at least as important as its substance, and in this context the poet of the *Odyssey* lingers mainly on the emotional aspect of the response. The song is supposed to give its listeners pleasure, and as far as the Phaeacians are concerned it does so quite successfully; they enjoy (*terpont'*) the words and ask the bard to resume his singing (8.90–91). Odysseus' response, however, is quite the opposite: he groans deeply as he listens (8.95), time and again he wails (8.92), and he cries (8.86, 93). Crying in this context is a source of shame for Odysseus (8.86), which is why he hides his face (8.85, 92). The bard's song can therefore elicit different reactions from different listeners, and according to the principles of *mise en abyme* these divergent responses to the song of Demodocus formulate two possible attitudes to the epic poem in general.[17] Two questions must be addressed at this point. The first regards the reason for two contrasting reactions to one and the same song, and the second ponders the relation of each of the reactions to the audience of the *Odyssey*.

It is clear that the difference between the Phaeacians' and Odysseus' responses to the first song is a function of their different involvement in the narrated events. The Phaeacians listen to a work of art depicting the suffering of another and enjoy its beauty while Odysseus hears the tale of his own suffering, remembers his former agony, feels pain, and weeps. A certain distance from narrated events is therefore needed in order to enjoy their artistic formulation; affinity, like Odysseus' to Demodocus' first song, leads to a different response.[18] Yet if, as I claim, the response of the listeners to the bard's song is a *mise en abyme* of that of the *Odyssey*'s addressees, it should teach us something about our own responses to the epic. And since the narrated events are much farther from our world than from that of Odysseus' audience, we are probably meant to enjoy them just as the Phaeacians did. Probably but not surely, for the poet of the *Odyssey* will again turn his screw before the end of this episode.

Unlike Demodocus' first song, which bifurcated its listeners, the second song, about Ares and Aphrodite, elicits the same reaction from both Odysseus and the Phaeacians: they enjoy (*terpet'*) the song (8.367–69). This seems reasonable, for the song tells the tale of the afflictions of a god who is remote from both Odysseus and his hosts. Moreover, the song itself seems to call for such a response, for the audience within it reacts twice with laughter to two different speakers: the male gods exhibit "inextinguishable laughter" (*asbestos* [. . .] *gelôs* 8.326) after Hephaestus summons them and depicts the adultery, and they laugh again after hearing the conversation between Hermes and Apollo, when the former confesses his wish to lie beside Aphrodite even if the fetters were stronger and the humiliation much greater (8.339–43). The two occurrences of laughter among the gods stress their lightheartedness in a most inappropriate context, for they prefer to concentrate on the risible aspects of the entrapment of the adulterous couple rather than on the far-reaching implications of their deed.[19]

In the *Odyssey*, inappropriate laughter is not restricted to the divine domain. It also occurs in the human arena. In book eighteen there is an episode depicting the clash between Odysseus, who is disguised as a beggar, and Irus, a genuine beggar. The scene is accompanied by laughter from its inception, when Antinous laughs in his heart at seeing the two beggars exchanging invectives following his suggestion that the two fight (18.35), which arouses the laughter of the suitors (18.40), to the victory of Odysseus, which makes the suitors "die by laughter" (*gelôi ekthanon* 18.100).[20] Yet, unlike divine laughter, which reflects the gods' levity and carefree way of life, the suitors' laughter serves as an unconscious premonition of their dismal destiny.[21] This notion is given concrete expression in book twenty, where the narrator states explicitly that it was Athena who induced "inextinguishable laughter" (*asbeston gelô* 20.346) in the suitors and "drove them out of their wits" (20.346). Their laughter is, of course, inappropriate, for the suitors are actually crying and their hearts are full of grief (20.350); they cannot control their hysterical behavior, not even when they hear the prophecy of

Theoclymenus, who vividly foretells their approaching doom (20.351–57). Their continuous laughter (20.358), instigated by the goddess and in direct contrast to their own feelings, is another indication of their inability to resist the doom that awaits them. To reiterate, while adultery counts for nothing when a god sleeps with the golden goddess, in the human sphere such an act cannot be taken lightly. Consequently, it is the afflicted Hephaestus who should be regarded as an emblem of the human situation and not his wife, "the lover of smiles" (*philommeidês* 8.362), who easily washes away her adulterous past in all its shameful aspects.[22]

But if Hephaestus is the focal character of this song, if his affliction is meant to elicit empathy rather than scorn, and if his position is portentous for human conduct then the lighthearted reaction of Demodocus' audience is called into question. The strong analogy between Odysseus and Hephaestus, which is partly based on suffering, also hints at a certain problematic in the pleasure the former derives from the agony of the latter. Note also that the bard resumes his song not with the laughing gods but with Poseidon, who does not laugh (8.344) and treats the situation with grave seriousness. Of course, Odysseus is not aware of the analogy between himself and the god, and Hephaestus' story seems to have no direct connection with his own life story. But, as I will demonstrate, the epic calls for exactly this personal application of a story that initially seems distant. To put this in Horace's words:

quid rides? mutato nomine de te
fabula narratur

[what are you laughing at? If you change the name,
it is you the story is about.]   (S.I.1.69–70)[23]

To conclude this point, in Demodocus' first two songs the poet of the *Odyssey* constructs two possible reactions to a poem. The first is based on pleasure while the second is based on pain. I say possible and not contrasting because the two are not necessarily mutually exclusive.[24] But there is a difference in emphasis, and it is to this difference that I now turn in my discussion of the third and last of Demodocus' songs.

It is worth noting that, unlike the first two songs, which were sung at Alcinous' request and whose content was the bard's choice, here it is Odysseus who both asks the bard to sing and determines the subject of the song: the building of the wooden horse that led to the complete destruction of Troy (8.492–95). Odysseus' initiative functions to recall the connection between

Odysseus, Demodocus, Hephaestus, and the poet of the *Odyssey*. Odysseus, like a bard, decides on the topic of the song, and, like Hephaestus, he consciously associates himself with tricks. In like manner, *kosmos*, the word that indicates the narration of the fashioning of the horse by Odysseus (8.492), is also used to describe the excellence of the bard's fashioning of his song, "for he sings it in extremely good order (*liên gar kata kosmon*)" (8.489). This means that both are presented in extremely good order, as the equivalent expression, *kata moiran*, implies.[25] The story of the wooden horse is also a means of reestablishing the connection between Demodocus' song and the two epics in general, for it refers to the central topic of the *Iliad*—the war with Troy—and to a specific episode already encountered by the audience of the *Odyssey* (4.265–89).[26]

But the most important aspect of Odysseus' choice of both the timing and the substance of the song is the expected reaction. Obviously, Odysseus does not wish to reproduce the painful and shameful experience of his crying. His call for a new topic (8.492) seems, therefore, to reflect his desire to return to the subject of the first song, the Trojan War, but to derive from it the same pleasure he derived from the second song. This wish, however, is so strongly thwarted that Odysseus not only cries (as he did before) but is also forced to disclose his true identity to his hosts. This unexpected reaction is revealing regarding both the miscalculating protagonist (who is, one may recall, a master of disguise and an archcalculator) and the narratee of the *Odyssey*, who is earlier presented with two optional responses to the epic.[27] If, as claimed earlier, good order (*kata moiran*) is one of the greatest merits of a poem, then the decision to present the reactions to the poems in the sequence pain-pleasure-pain is significant. The nature of this significance will be revealed shortly, but first I wish to consider the sequence of events within Demodocus' third song.

The bard opens his song at the point where the wooden horse is already in the *agora* of Troy, indicating that it was the Trojans themselves who brought him there. He then goes on to depict the events preceding the opening stage of his tale and describes the Trojans' deliberations on the treatment of the horse. Of course, analepsis is a recurrent technique in the *Odyssey*, and its appearance within the epic context of the bard's poem is not unanticipated. And yet, if this song of the bard is supposed to be "very well ordered" (*liên gar kata kosmon* 8.489), then this analepsis does call for explanation, for such a reversal of chronological order is probably not without cause. And, indeed, the bard's song is actually about this reversed causality, for while the Trojans were debating about the future of the wooden horse their decision had long been preordained, "for it was Troy's *aisa* to be destroyed" (8.511).²⁸ In other words, it is not the present that breeds the future but rather the distant past; the Trojans, who believe they can affect the future by means of their decisions, are gravely mistaken. They cannot do this, and their entire deliberation is a sham, for the decision had been made for them many years before they started the present debate. Thus, the causal connection between present and future is broken, and in its stead a direct connection between past and future is established. This sequence reveals the illusory aspect of human beliefs as regards their power to influence the future. This is not to deny any causal connection between what one does and what happens, but the action that determines the future is not a result of human choice; it is rather an outcome of a much stronger agent whose past decisions cannot be changed by the present. What is interesting here is the fact that this tragic aspect does not seem to apply to either the Achaeans or Odysseus. On the contrary, it tells the story of the Greeks' victory over their foes in general and of Odysseus' *aristeia* in particular (8.519–20). Why, then, does Odysseus react as he does? The answer is connected, again, with the epic's tragic perception of the human lot.

When Odysseus asks the bard to sing the destiny of the Achaeans, he formulates his request in the words "the *oitos* of the Achaeans" (8.489). However, *oitos* usually indicates bad destiny,²⁹ and Odysseus' choice of word therefore has an unconscious ironic level; for, although the bard's song does not report the afflictions of the Achaeans, it does evoke in Odysseus the proper response to such afflictions. There is also an ironic level in another expression of the protagonist, namely, his reference to the bard's song as sung *kata moiran* (8.496). No doubt, in using this phrase Odysseus refers solely to the aesthetic aspect of the poem that has nothing to do with fate,³⁰ but in light of the role of *aisa* in the song, *kata moiran* can be retrospectively understood also as *kata Moiran*. In this usage, the phrase refers to the content of the song, where everything happens according to *Moira*. Demodocus' song is therefore a song subordinated to order both in its aesthetics and in its content. In this preordained world the human factor is no more than an unknowing agent and, what is worse, an agent that brings destruction on fellow human beings. It is to this horrifying aspect of *Moira* that Odysseus responds with tears, understanding that even his own *aristeia* is merely an illusion of victory in a world where every human being is essentially at the mercy of potent and cruel powers. This tragic notion is further substantiated by the simile used by the poet of the *Odyssey* to portray the protagonist's reaction.³¹

Demodocus describes in his song how the Greeks brought death to the Trojans and how they destroyed the city (8.513–14). The simile that depicts Odysseus' crying is, in some respects, the song's sequel, lingering on the terrible fate of a victim of a conquered city and the way she is treated by the victorious army. But the simile is incongruous with the song's content, for in the song Odysseus belongs to the victorious army while in the simile he is likened to a defeated citizen of the city. What is more, in the poem he arrives at the house of Deiphobus with Menelaus (8.517–18), there displaying his manly virtue by means of a fierce battle (8.519); in contrast, in the simile he is compared to a loyal wife who sees her husband dying and clings to him in vain (8.526–27).[32] In other words, while Demodocus' song describes Odysseus as a virile hero, the simile portrays him as a desperate feminine protagonist. What is more, Odysseus' arrival at the house of Deiphobus hints not at his faithful wife Penelope but rather at the adulterous Helen, who was Deiphobus' wife after the death of Paris; in the same vein, the woman who bewails her beloved husband, and to whom Odysseus is likened, is reminiscent of Andromache, the faithful wife of the Greeks' archenemy, Hector. We have already seen the centrality of adultery to Demodocus' second song and its implications for Odysseus' life; here the difference between the song and the simile underlines not only the chasm between Helen and Andromache but also the theme we have already encountered in chapter 3's discussion of the Cyclops scene, namely, the evolution of the conception of the hero during the transition from the world of the *Iliad* to that of the *Odyssey*. Let me explain.

If the *Iliad* is primarily the story of adultery and its grim consequences while the *Odyssey* concentrates on the story of faithful marriage, if the Odysseus of the *Iliad* stands by the betrayed husband Menelaus and the Odysseus of the *Odyssey* is, in principle, on the side of the loyal wife, then the Odyssean hero, whose identity is literally revealed through his expression of empathy, is quintessentially different from the Iliadic hero, whose virtue is based on prowess and valor.[33] This is consonant with Achilles' words to Odysseus in the eleventh book of the *Odyssey* where the two meet in Hades and Achilles says he would prefer being the lowest of the low among the living rather than the primary ruler of men in Hades (11.489–91).[34] In the *Odyssey*, an epic of survival, there is a strong link between survival and suffering, and in this simile it is the woman who represents this link: what awaits the woman now crying "in anguish" (*achei* 8.530) is a future of "labor and misery (*oïzun*)" (8.529), which is what actually awaited Odysseus after the sack of Troy and what still awaits him after leaving

Phaeacia. What is more, Alcinous, who is obviously unaware of the simile, perceives Odysseus in just the same way: he claims that from the moment the bard started singing his guest "never ceased his miserable (*o'izuroio*) wailing" (8.540) and that he was emotionally surrounded by "anguish" (*achos* 8.541). The woman elicits empathy because her anguish is "extremely pitiful" (*eleeinotatôi* 8.530), and Odysseus arouses Alcinous' response because his tears are "pitiful" (*eleeinon* 8.531). We are far from the beginning of the episode in the Phaeacian palace, where Odysseus' epithet was "sacker of cities" (8.3).[35]

It is now time to return to the question posed at the beginning of the discussion of Demodocus' third song, namely, how the *Odyssey* constructs the response of its narratees in light of the two possible reactions to the songs of the Phaeacian bard.[36] The first point to be considered in this context is the differentiation between the two internal narratees, Odysseus and the Phaeacians. The Phaeacians respond with identical pleasure to all of Demodocus' three songs while the reaction of Odysseus fluctuates from crying via pleasure to crying again. Now if, as I claim, not only the songs but also the reaction they elicit should be considered part of the *mise en abyme*, then both Odysseus and the Phaeacians represent a possible understanding of the relevance of the song for its audience; the Phaeacians regard the song as no more than a source of pleasure, while Odysseus' different reactions demonstrate his movement toward deeper comprehension of his human nature. In other words, for the Phaeacians the songs are mere entertainment; for Odysseus they also serve as a means of learning and growth.

Up to this point the two options seem no more than two variations on a single theme since, on hearing a song, one can choose to yield to pleasure or learning. But the poet of the *Odyssey* offers more than that, for the eighth book of the epic implies a hierarchical conception of the two options; that is to say, there is something wrong in regarding poetry as no more than entertainment, as can be deduced from the representation of the Phaeacians.[37] After he sees Odysseus crying a second time, Alcinous accosts him and asks him to reveal his identity. This is actually the condition for Odysseus' return to Ithaca with the Phaeacians' ships (8.555–56). Then comes a digression describing the magical nature of these ships (they have their own minds and sail without sailors [8.557–63]), followed quite abruptly by Alcinous telling a story he once heard from his father about the dismal lot of the Phaeacians, who would arouse the rage of Poseidon by taking someone home in their ships (8.564–70). This passage gives the impression of a *non sequitur,* and its recurrence with slight differences at 13.172–78 has caused editors from

Aristarchus onward to suspect its authenticity;[38] but a *non sequitur* in a poem that has recently stressed the importance and applauded the occurrence of *kata kosmon* and *kata moiran* is even more suspect. It is much more plausible to think that the poet of the *Odyssey* deliberately planted this passage in order to foreshadow the grim future of the Phaeacians,[39] a future that sheds new light on their two main characteristics: their connection with the divine and their frivolity. That the Phaeacians are both somewhat divine and somewhat frivolous has been noted by many critics,[40] and the pleasure they derive from the poems is congruous with both features. But Alcinous' sudden remembrance of his father's story points to the fact that the Phaeacians are closely connected with the human and that suffering and distress will also be part of their lives.

In light of this it would be plausible to claim that the *Odyssey* emphasizes the painful aspect of human life and that poetry, which is essentially a representation of this life, leads its audience to reflect on the connection between the fictive lives of the protagonists and their own lives.[41] This is not to diminish the importance of pleasure in the experience of poetry, but pleasure is either a component or a phase of a much more complex process toward painful learning that the audience should undergo. And this process is relevant not only to the internal narratee of the epic, whose tears attest to his deep understanding of the afflictions of the human lot, but also to the audience of the epic, both past and present. As can be deduced from the example of the Phaeacians, one should not be misled by one's distance from narrated events; in essence, human lives are all constructed by the same cruel and immortal forces that make mortals suffer in exchange for divine pleasure. In this light, poetry, as formulated succinctly by the Phaeacian king, is not merely nourished by human suffering; poetry is actually the aim of this suffering from the outset. The gods devise our ruin in order for it to be transformed into song:

> For indeed the gods devised this [fate], namely they assigned destruction
> to human beings, so that a song will be for future generations too.
>
> (8.579–80)

This metaphysical recognition of Alcinous, which echoes that of Helen in the *Iliad* (6.357–58), starkly illuminates all of the bard's songs. It is a recognition caustically formulated by the Sophoclean Odysseus in his rejection of Athena's exhortations to enjoy Ajax' fall:

> for now I see that we, living creatures, are nothing but
> phantoms or unsubstantial shadow.   (Sophocles, *Ajax* 125–26)[42]

Laughter at another's suffering is restricted to the gods while we mortals should not forget that it is our lives that are the stuff of their evil dreams.

In this chapter I have configured the use of *mise en abyme* in the three songs of Demodocus and explicated its different functions. I have also demonstrated how this narratological technique aids the poet in constructing two possible reactions of his narratees—pleasure, on the one hand, and painful self-recognition on the other—and how the poem leads its narratees toward a hierarchical ordering of these two options. According to this hierarchy, it is self-recognition, however painful, rather than mere pleasure that is the right response to the epic. The self-recognition attained by Odysseus through the cognitive and emotional processing of the three songs leads him to a higher level of understanding regarding his vulnerable existence in a woeful world. Moreover, Odysseus' deep apprehension of the basic similarity between his enemies and himself serves as a foundation for his metaphysical recognition, which is a profound discernment of the tragic essence of the human condition characterized by a shared lot of immense and ineluctable suffering.

6

Tragic Hephaestus

The Humanized God in the
Iliad *and the* Odyssey

*I*n the previous chapter I examined the role of the reflexive technique of *mise en abyme* in building tragic signification in the *Odyssey*. In this chapter I consider another aspect of reflexivity and the tragic through the fissure of characterization in the portrayal of Hephaestus in both the *Iliad* and the *Odyssey*. I have already analyzed Hephaestus' characterization as an object of derision in the second song of Demodocus, and this song will serve me once more in the following discussion. The emphasis, however, will be different, for I now intend to examine the contribution of Hephaestus' artistic creativity to the construction of tragic signification and to illuminate the association between art, especially poetry, and the humane from a new angle. The fact that among the gods who live on Mount Olympus Hephaestus is exceptional both in form and status is germane to my argument, for it is through these characteristics above all that the poet succeeds in presenting this god as a tragic figure. Note that Hephaestus' maimed body is the sole instance of crippling in this lofty kingdom, and as for status, his profession of divine artist, one generally occupied with hard physical labor, contrasts with the occupation of the rest of the gods, who usually devote themselves to pleasure. Hard work and bodily limitations are not merely inherently ungodly; they are also closely linked to the lives of human beings, whose odious lot is often delineated by these factors.

Endowing Hephaestus with human characteristics enables the poet to present him as a character who, despite his divinity, possesses emotional and cognitive capacities that make him especially sensitive to the human condition and its tragic aspects. He is also closely acquainted with pain and irretrievable loss, two tragic features discussed in previous chapters. As the following argument will demonstrate, Hephaestus' lameness is also strongly linked with his perception of time as consisting of an irrevocable past, a human and ungodly aspect that enriches this god's humanized characterization and, thereby, his tragic signification.

Hephaestus' first appearance in the *Iliad* is at the end of book one, where he speaks to his mother, Hera. His speech is prompted by a quarrel between Zeus and Hera over Zeus' conversation with Thetis, a conversation in which Zeus promised Thetis to aid the Trojans in retaliation for the profound insult to her son, Achilles. Hephaestus opens with a general remark concerning the impropriety of a divine quarrel over human affairs: such destructive things are not to be endured (1.573) since they would spoil the feast of the gods (1.575–76). He then goes on to more practical reasoning, claiming that Zeus is the mightiest of the gods and could rudely thrust the others from their seats (1.580–81). At this stage he pours wine into a chalice, hands it to his mother, and starts the second part of his speech, where he gives a concrete example of Zeus' power, manifested in similar circumstances. He opens with a general notion of the impossibility of aid to his stricken mother (1.587–89) and continues reasoning on the basis of a specific example. In an earlier quarrel between the divine couple he had been eager to protect his mother from Zeus, but the latter, seizing Hephaestus' leg, hurled him over the divine threshold (1.590–91). The fall took an entire day, and when it ended in Lemnos Hephaestus was left with very little life force (1.593).

The consequences of that earlier intervention were far from happy, and yet the transformation of that intervention into a story is the source of the happy outcome of Hephaestus' present mediation in the royal quarrel. For not only does Hera smile after this story,[1] but all Olympus reacts with "inextinguishable laughter" (*asbestos* [. . .] *gelôs* 1.599) when Hephaestus, limping, goes on to distribute wine to the other gods. Hephaestus is therefore quite consciously playing the role of the laughingstock of the laughing gods, and he does so both through his story and by means of his handicap.[2] Note that his decision to act as wine server, already an act of self-humiliation,[3] becomes even more derisory in the inevitable comparison between his ugly shape and that of the handsome Olympic wine server, Ganymede.[4] Story, history, and present action combine as Hephaestus easily dispels the Olympians' gloom, giving them the opportunity to go back to the pleasures of the feast, which continues until sunset (1.601–4).[5]

Much later (in book eighteen) Hephaestus describes his other fall.[6] That context, however, is very different. Mention of Thetis, who arrives at Hephaestus' home to ask him to prepare new weapons for her son, elicits the painful memory of Hephaestus' second plummet to earth. The addressee of this story is his wife, and under these intimate circumstances the storyteller prefers to concentrate on the agonizing aspects of the incident. Hephaestus describes Thetis as his savior after his very long fall, mentioning how painful the experience had been (18.395) and how much more painful it would have been without her and Eurynome's intervention (18.397–98).[7]

Presumably, the two falls reflect two variant, and to some extent contradictory, etiological tales of the origin of Hephaestus' lameness.[8] Yet the poet of the *Iliad* did not merely decide to represent both in his poem in order to motivate Hephaestus' words and behavior in different contexts; rather, he integrated them into a unified whole by inventing a causal association between the fall mentioned in book eighteen and the fall mentioned in book one. Since Hera could not bear the sight of her crippled son, she wanted him literally to disappear (18.396–97) and therefore threw him away once more. Note that the existence of not one but two etiological stories of the fall attests to the fact that tradition perceived Hephaestus as a god who, quite probably, was not born a cripple but became one at a later stage in his life. Therefore, if the fall in book eighteen happened because Hera wanted Hephaestus to disappear, "since he was lame (*chôlon eonta*)," the fall that maimed him in the first place must have occurred previously. Since Hephaestus fell only twice, it is the fall mentioned in book one that both preceded the fall mentioned in book eighteen and instigated it. The second hurling is hardly surprising in the Olympian context, where Hera's wish and action are eminently reasonable: the mere presence of Hephaestus is a disgusting reflection of the goddess's failure in the quarrel with her husband, for her defeat is eternally inscribed in her son's deformed legs. The fact that his maimed legs are a source of incessant agony for Hephaestus himself is irrelevant to Hera, inasmuch as the real cause of his deformity, his voluntary intervention against his father on her behalf, has been completely forgotten.[9] The sole things that matter are her feelings and memories: with syllogistic logic, Hephaestus is forever blamed for Hera's defeat in the quarrel with Zeus because Hephaestus did not succeed in helping her.

The poet of the *Iliad* does not give us any comments by Hephaestus' wife on his story; in like manner, Hephaestus does not give any details concerning the circumstances and the conversations he had with his two benefactresses, Thetis and Eurynome. He does, however, refer metaphorically to their connection with him. They "took him to their bosom," which hints at their maternal role in this stage of his life: for nine long years they functioned as his surrogate mothers. Such descriptions invite pity and compassion, not laughter, and the poet of the *Iliad* directs his audience to the appropriate reaction first by emphasizing the god's lameness when he continues his story (18.411) and then by describing Thetis as full of tears (18.428), weaving into her speech many words denoting agonizing suffering and mourning.[10]

The association between the two narratives of the two falls is not limited to story, where the same act happens twice. It can also be detected in the technique of the poet, where echoes of one of the most conventional features of oral craftsmanship in book one, the noun-adjective epithet, can be traced in book eighteen. Since Milman Parry's classic study on the traditional epithet in Homer,[11] research on the subject has hovered between two poles: one concentrates on the conventional aspect of the epithet in the *Iliad* and the *Odyssey* while the other focuses on the innovative features of the poet's craftsmanship.[12] These two aspects are not mutually exclusive, for it is clear that even in the work of that most innovative poet of the *Iliad* and the *Odyssey* there is a strong conventional component at the core of his technique. What should therefore be investigated is the poet's creative process in which he uses the conventional tool of the formula in order to transmit something new, a process especially noticeable in the stories of Hera and Hephaestus.[13] The most frequent epithets of Hera are "mistress Hera" (πότνια Ἥρη) and its variation the "ox-eyed mistress Hera" (βοῶπις πότνια Ἥρη),[14] both of Mycenaean origin, implying a strong conventional basis.[15] It is therefore not surprising to find the expression "ox-eyed mistress Hera" twice in the Hera-Hephaestus episode in book one (1.551, 568). What is surprising, however, is the adjective "dog-eyed" (or "dog-faced," *kunôpis*) attributed to Hera by Hephaestus in book eighteen (18.396).

Characteristically, the choice of the dog is far from contingent, and the poet, who employs this epithet in order to represent the focalization of the wounded son, has selected a blatantly abusive word for this purpose. Dogs and their revolting behavior are constantly mentioned in both epics, and it is not without cause that it is this animal, so closely associated with abhorrent action, that is repeatedly used by different speakers as especially effective disparagement.[16] Thus, the *Iliad*, an epic depicting the unfolding of a quarrel the inception of which was a verbal insult, is rife with curses, among which *dog* and its cognates are utilized regularly in order to reflect the speaker's turmoil and indignation.[17] Already in the opening book of the epic Achilles calls Agamemnon both "dog-eyed" (or "dog-faced," κμνῶπα 1.159) and "having the eyes of a dog" (1.225), an insult he repeats in book nine (9.373). Patroclus likens the Trojans to dogs (11.816–18), and Hector, who calls the Greeks "death (or plague) bearers' dogs" (κύνας κηρεσσιφορήτους 8.527), is himself called "dog" by Ajax (8.299), Diomedes, (11.362) and Achilles (20.449). The term is not limited to the human arena: Zeus tells Hera "nothing is more bitchlike than you" (8.483), and Hera calls Artemis "shameless (*adees*) bitch" (21.481). And there are other examples.[18] The adjective of the last phrase, "shameless" (*adees*), is revealing in hinting at the essence of the derogatory nature of this metaphor.[19] Dogs are shameless and therefore heedless of shameful acts, even the abysmal deed of mutilating corpses.[20] In the *Iliad,* the repeated mention of dogs, occasionally in tandem with birds of prey,[21] formulates either an eerie threat or a grim reality for the dead bodies of distinguished warriors. Indeed, the opening of the epic itself refers to this fact explicitly when the narrator recounts the outcome of the quarrel between Achilles and Agamemnon (1.4–5). Warriors, as an essential part of their victory, aspire to further disgrace their dead enemies by means of throwing the latters' cadavers to the dogs, as can be deduced from Hector's wish to donate the headless corpse of Patroclus to the dogs of Troy (17.126–27). The contagious nature of this shame is clearly perceived by Athena who, disguised as Phoenix, warns Menelaus that if Hector succeeds it will be a disgrace to Menelaus (17.556–57). Athena is not the only god who loathes such a destiny for this distinguished warrior. Zeus, who is usually on the side of the Trojans, hates the idea that the Greek Patroclus will become prey to the dogs of his enemies (17.272) and therefore encourages Patroclus' companions to shield his corpse (17.268–70).

Dogs are drawn to human corpses (17.153, 23.184–86); they drag them (15.351), treat them as playthings (18.178–80), and then eat them (13.831; 17.240–41 and 255; 18.271 and 283; 22.43, 88–89, 335–36, 347, 354, and 509–10; 23.21 and 183; 14.211; 408–9 and 411). It is this last characteristic, so bluntly emphasized by means of frequent repetition, that is perceived by Priam as the symbol of this animal's treacherous nature. In a doleful passage (22.60–76), the Trojan king pleads with Hector to enter the city walls instead of fighting Achilles. He tries to persuade him to do so by means of a description of his (Priam's) bleak future after the fall of Troy. A considerable part of this passage is dedicated to portraying the behavior of the palace dogs, which, Priam is sure, will inflict horrors on their own master. The description could not be more terse: the same dogs that were nourished by Priam as warders of the gates (22.69) will savagely drag his corpse to the portals (22.66–67) and then drink his blood (22.70).[22] Thus, those who were fed will feed on their feeder at the very site that symbolizes their former protective function. And, while the death of a young man in battle, Priam concludes, has at least a certain nobility (22.71–73), when dogs disfigure the gray hair and beard of an old man and, worst of all, maim his private parts, there is nothing more lamentable to wretched mortals (22.74–76).[23]

In light of this, the inclusion of the dog in the phrase used by Hephaestus to describe his mother (18.396) appears to be more than a mere outburst of anger. It denotes a wide range of execrable associations that reflect the despicable behavior of the unmaternal mother. The choice of word, of course, does not belong solely to the character. It is first and foremost the choice of the poet, whose art is conditioned by the conventions of his poetic heritage. True, the phrase is not a formula, but the novel adjective does shockingly echo the formulaic, as can be deduced from the conventional variant "ox-eyed" (βοώπιδος) attested by Scholium T. Consequently, what the poet does in this phrasing of Hephaestus is to take one of Hera's most conventional epithets and distort it completely in service of a new idea.[24] In other words, while breaking formulaic form and changing its content, the poet has retained the formula's background resonance so that it can continue functioning in its new context: the beautiful mistress, ox-eyed Hera, is a dog-eyed mother.

As noted earlier, Hephaestus' falls and his crippling, ugliness, and pain characterize his exceptional status among the Olympians, an exceptionality that becomes even more conspicuous in the context of his spatial and temporal characteristics. One of the main features of the Greek gods is their aloofness, and their dwelling place, Mount Olympus, is a symbol of both their high status and their remoteness from men.[25] Men, in contrast, live on earth, which is a reflection of their low rank and mortality: the dead are buried in it, and their souls dwell beneath it. Of course, the Olympians have the prerogative to visit men whenever they wish, but this is merely another demonstration of their power over humans, whose mobility is much more limited: not only is Mount Olympus barred to them, but their movement on earth is much slower than that of the gods. In addition, divine calls are usually very short; most often the gods tend to return home as soon as possible.

Hephaestus, as already noted, is an exception. To begin with, there is something bizarre in his first fall to earth. In the *Iliad* the divine status of the

Olympians is quite stable. Unlike the upheavals described in Hesiod's *Theogony*, the world of the *Iliad* gives a more constant impression; the gods who live on Mount Olympus are presumably there forever.[26] And yet Hephaestus is expelled from Olympus as if he did not really belong there. What is more, his fall is everything but godlike: it took him an entire day to come to earth, and when he finally hit Lemnos he needed to be healed by its human inhabitants, the Sintians (1.592–94).[27] This is very strange when one considers the normal speed of divine journeys to earth: Thetis jumps swiftly from Mount Olympus to the depths of the ocean (1.531–32), Athena sinks to earth like a bright star (4.73–79), and Apollo descends like a hawk to Troy (15.236–38) while Iris goes down quickly to Troy (15.168–72), jumps to the surface of the sea, and then plunges into it (24.77–82). Hephaestus, by contrast, took a whole day. Why did he need so much time to reach the earth and why could he not stop his fall? The poet of the *Iliad* does not provide answers to these troubling questions, and the shift to the comic that immediately follows this story tends somewhat to blur these intriguing aspects. And yet even in this comic atmosphere the text does emphasize the difference between Hephaestus' sad past and the other gods' happy present: while his fall took an entire day, lasting until sunset (1.592), their feast lasted until sunset (1.601–2); and, while he had very little spirit (*thumos*) left in him, their heart (*thumos*) did not lack anything in the feast (1.602). And it is this contrast that reemerges so powerfully in book eighteen, for here the second fall is embedded in Hephaestus' most ungodly aspect, the humiliating limitation of his lameness.

True, Hephaestus is already crippled in book one, but the frivolous atmosphere of the banquet offers only a light view of this fact, especially since Hephaestus himself initiates the laughter. The second fall endows the first one with gravity. On the level of the story, the second fall leads to Hephaestus' long disappearance from the divine scene; for nine years he stayed with Thetis and Eurynome (18.400), and neither gods nor men knew where he was (18.403–4). He then resumed his role among the Olympians, for we know he is now again on the gods' mountain; quite disturbingly left beyond the limits of our knowledge is the exact manner of his return. This is disturbing because one of the main myths connected with Hephaestus is precisely that of his return to Mount Olympus after his expulsion by Hera. According to this myth, Hephaestus stays with the Nereids after his fall from heaven. Many years afterward he sends Hera a beautiful throne in which he installs a secret mechanism so that when she sits on it she is trapped, unable to move.[28] None of the gods can release her or persuade Hephaestus to do so until Dionysus makes him drunk and leads him in a jolly procession to the mountain where he finally releases his mother. The myth was very popular from around 600 B.C. and much favored in Archaic and classical Greek art.[29] It was probably also a part of the *Homeric Hymn to Dionysus,* which is usually dated to the later seventh century B.C.[30] Whether the myth was known to the poet of the *Iliad* is a more complicated question, but there is no reason to assume that he was wholly ignorant of its existence.[31] If this version of the myth of Hephaestus were known to the composer of the *Iliad,* the decision to excise it would be even more telling regarding the special nature of the god in the epic; the poet has chosen deliberately to suppress not only the vengeful aspects of Hephaestus' character but also his triumphant return to Olympus after his victory over his mother. The *Iliad* would have none of that and not without cause. Its poet's interest is not the happy integration of Hephaestus within the divine community but rather the reverse, his fundamental differentiation from the other Olympians, a difference closely associated with the god's exceptional conception of time and pain.

The fact that Hera was so easily consoled by Hephaestus' words testifies, among other things, to her basically happy situation; like the rest of the gods she is forever happy, and nothing can essentially change this fact. Consequently, all her past sufferings, as well as her present quarrels with her husband, are reversible. This is not to deny that they are unpleasant but to assert that they are merely unpleasant and therefore easily forgotten. The same criterion can be applied to many other phenomena, to human beings, for example; they can be very annoying and incur terrible wrath, but from the point of view of eternity, which is literally the divine point of view, all such phenomena are no more than trifles.[32] Hera's relation to time, which is also that of her fellow gods, is therefore one of serene indifference.[33]

Hephaestus' situation, however, is quite the opposite. Those painful nine years with his surrogate mothers, so bitterly remembered and so easily revived by the mere appearance of Thetis, are a constant part of his present, and they will be so forever. Unlike his mother's past, his is irreversible: the first fall has left an eternal physical flaw in his body, and the second has scarred his soul, apparently forever. The irreversible is also unforgettable, and consequently Hephaestus' conception of time is based on an unforgettable past imbuing his present and future with pain. Temporal and spatial limitation, in addition to pain and irreversibility, are human and not divine, and it is these traits that reveal Hephaestus as a god hovering between the human and the divine.[34]

Pain and irreversibility, however, are also the traits of Thetis, who mourns the forthcoming death of her beloved only son, Achilles. No wonder, then, that the meeting between Hephaestus and Thetis is a meeting of fellow sufferers who share a strong bond based on a mutual understanding of pain. I have already mentioned the painful atmosphere of the meeting of the two, an atmosphere created by the dense verbal environment of words denoting various manifestations of suffering. Like Hephaestus, whose pain has a human aspect, Thetis' agony is closely connected with the human condition. In fact, her self-description in the meeting resembles a mortal's lot much more than a god's, and, although in the first book of the *Iliad* Thetis is depicted by Achilles as the benefactress of Zeus, the one who brought the giant Briareus to help him when the rest of the gods wanted to bind him (1.396–406), in her self-presentation in book eighteen she perceives herself a victim of Zeus. It is Zeus who apportioned her so many miseries (18.431); who forced her, a goddess, to be married to and ruled by a mortal (18.432–33); and who also provided her with a son to breed and nourish only to see him die young (18.436–41).[35] Marriage is not a common phenomenon among the gods, which is understandable in light of the selfish and self-centered character of the immortals. The *Iliad* is rife with quarrels between Zeus and Hera, and their dispute in the opening of the epic is emblematic not only of their life as a couple but also of the acute conflict between self and surroundings inherent in any divine personality. In her status as a married goddess Thetis, like Hephaestus, is therefore an exception among those who are forever happy, an exceptionality that becomes even more striking in light of her strong emotional bond with her son.

Thetis is not the only divine parent of a human being in the *Iliad,* and the poet does give other examples of gods' emotional attitudes toward their mortal children, especially after the children's deaths. Thus, Ares considers defying Zeus' command not to intervene in the battle after he hears of his son's death (15.115–20), and Zeus pours a rain of blood before the death of his son Sarpedon (16.459–61) and takes care of the special honors after his death (16.666–83).[36] But none of these reactions is comparable to the deep sorrow of Thetis over her son, a sorrow that is already referred to in her first meeting with Achilles (1.414–18) and persists until her meeting with Hephaestus (18.436–41),[37] continuing ceaselessly to the end of the epic when, in the midst of her grief, she is summoned from the depth of the ocean to Mount Olympus, where she is the only one grieving among the ever-merry immortals (24.83–91, 104–5).[38]

Note how the poet incorporates the epithets of the two in the narrative:

Thetis is described as "silver-footed" in the last word of 18.369 while He-phaestus is named "the clubfooted" in the last word of 18.371. In some of the manuscripts Thetis' epithet recurs at the end of line 18.381. Two lines later Hephaestus is named "the one with both feet crooked." The end of a line is at least partially a locus of emphasis, and the juxtaposition of the two epi-thets, the one signifying the foot's perfection and the other its deformity, cre-ates another association between the two gods, an association based on their former intimacy and powerful enough to transcend the risible aspect of the disfigured legs. Moreover, the silver of Thetis' foot is connected with the beautiful objects created by Hephaestus, which are also made of silver: first the throne, which is "silver-studded" (18.389); and then the shield (18.475, 480, 563, 588). These epithets, which hint at the possible transformation of pain into beauty, are associated with another aspect of Hephaestus' character-ization in the *Iliad,* the palliative nature of his art.

In his speech to his wife in book eighteen, Hephaestus summarizes his stay with Thetis and Eurynome. His account is very brief, but what he does say refers specifically to his artistic activity: he "used to forge many beautiful artistically wrought (*daidala*) objects" (18.400) for them. These objects were jewels, as can be seen from their enumeration in the next line, and they rep-resent the transformation of his pain into art. The epithet "artistically wrought" (*daidala*), however, alludes to other artifacts described at the begin-ning of this scene: the ears of his tripods are "artistically wrought" (*daidalea* 18.379) and Thetis is invited to sit on a throne that is "beautiful and artisti-cally wrought" (*kalou daidaleou* 18.390). Hephaestus' artistic activity is there-fore deeply connected to his fall, and it is in this light that one should read back to both the first epithet about Hephaestus in the *Iliad,* where he is re-ferred to as "Hephaestus who is renowned for his art" (1.571), and the other two characterizing adjectives that conclude the Olympian scene in book one, "the renowned one with both feet crooked" (1.607).[39] Hephaestus is both no-torious among the gods due to his maiming and famous among the gods because of his artistry.[40] This combination is evident in Hephaestus' most celebrated artifact, the shield of Achilles.

Much has already been written about the uniqueness of this object and its outstanding engravings.[41] What I would like to emphasize, however, is not so much the aesthetic qualities of the shield or its status as an object hovering between the real and the fantastic but rather its tragic signification, a signification that bears a special association with its creator, Hephaestus. In fact, the tragic is intertwined with the shield from the outset, for the fu-ture bearer of this protective object is destined to die soon. The shield is ordered with full knowledge of this limitation, and Thetis, who is aware of the association between her son's return to the battlefield and his inevitable death, tells this to Hephaestus when pleading with him to make new armor for Achilles (18.440–41). Of course, Achilles must have a shield in order to resume fighting, but his dubious prospects shed a tragic light on the whole scene. And it is here that Hephaestus, who acknowledges Thetis' agonizing situation by referring to the unavoidable death of her son, binds once again deep pain and helplessness with the palliative power of his art: he explicitly juxtaposes his inability to protect her son from woeful death and his ability to create beautiful armor:

> I wish I were capable of hiding him
> away from dismal death, when a dreadful lot approaches him,
> as I am capable of preparing him beautiful armor.   (18.464–66)

The armor might be limited in its power to protect its bearer, but it is powerful enough to strongly affect its beholder:[42] it will not be merely beautiful; it will be so beautiful that it will astonish everyone who sees it (18.466–67).[43]

However, the experience of beholding this beautiful artifact is not limited to the emotional sphere of wonder and astonishment; it is also aimed at the cognitive level where seeing leads to understanding.[44] Moreover, the mimetic qualities of the shield remind one of the close associations between the scenes depicted on this weapon of war and the world in which it is intended to function, a world in strife where war is part of a much larger sequence of events embedded in misery and suffering. The shield abounds with irresolvable tensions,[45] and even the peacetime scenes either lead to some kind of catastrophe or imply a lurking destructive potential waiting to be realized. Thus, the lawsuit over a murder is not resolved (18.497–500),[46] while the strife (*neikos* 18.497) it entails involves many other people in addition to the two litigants (18.503),[47] and an ambush awaits peaceful shepherds before they reach the river (18.520–22), attacking them, to their utmost surprise, while they are absorbed in the pleasures of music (18.526–27).[48] Even the last scene on the shield, the seemingly optimistic depiction of young dancers, the future brides and grooms (18.590–606), is inauspicious: the floor on which they dance is like the one that Daedalus built for the fair-haired Ariadne (18.591–92), the same Ariadne who, after saving her lover from the Minotaur, was abducted and deserted by him, dying soon after.[49] If this dance floor is associated with the one in Knossus, then those who dance on it are at least potentially vulnerable to the same dismal fate as that of their predecessors in Crete: brides can be abducted and then deserted by their abductors while couples can die a monstrous death by the Minotaur.[50]

Yet the tragic, as has been demonstrated more than once during this treatise, is not confined to catastrophic deaths and inevitable suffering. It also has metaphysical implications realized in the destructive and active role of the gods in the agonizing lot of mortals. This kind of evil intervention in human affairs finds salient artistic expression in the battle scene by the river, which is perpetrated under divine aegis: Ares and Athena are in charge of the attack (18.516). The choice of Athena seems self-evident due to her inclination toward the attacking side in the *Iliad,* but Ares' appearance as her companion is not, for he is identified with the besieged in the epic and usually sides against Athena.[51] The obvious explanation for his appearance is his role as the god of war, which means that any battle is within his domain. But there is another reason for his active part in this scene. Although motives for attacking the shepherds are not explicitly mentioned, the sequence of the assault and the appearance of the gods give the impression that there is a causal connection between the two: it is the gods who have pushed the mortals to this disastrous decision, and it is they who are personally involved in its realization.

By emphasizing the contrast between the greatness and splendor of the gods and the small proportions of the humans in this picture (18.517–19), Hephaestus reinforces the notion that the latter are but a tiny game for those who cruelly decree their lot. The inclusion of Ares therefore emphasizes the perception that human beings should not be misled by being temporarily preferred by one god or another.[52] This apprehension has tragic implications that are applicable to the *Iliad* as a whole, for, although Paris abducted Helen with Aphrodite's help and approval, his act doomed both him and his city, and what seemed to be tactics whose success was guaranteed by the gods turned out to be part of a much broader divine scheme, the outcome of which was the complete destruction of its human agents.[53] To conclude, the shield, like the poem in which it appears, is an artistic representation of the tragic. The main aim of the shield is therefore didactic, and its marvelous features are in the service of a tragic signification. In this context the human aspects of its creator are crucial, for Hephaestus' affinity with the tragic emphasizes the effect of his artifact: constructed by a divine yet humane artist who is well aware of pain and suffering, the shield leads its human beholders to a deeper understanding of their own tragic condition.

Hephaestus' unique status, so stressed in the *Iliad,* is echoed and developed in the *Odyssey.* Here, however, he appears not as a real character in the story of Odysseus' wanderings but as a fictive persona in a song that the protagonist hears at the court of the Phaeacian king. As noted in the previous chapter, the song concentrating on Hephaestus (8.266–366) is the second of three songs that are sung by the blind bard Demodocus during Odysseus' stay in Phaeacia. The song stresses two of Hephaestus' characteristics that appear in the *Iliad*: shame and anger. There is constant allusion to shame, either implicitly or explicitly. The adulterous act "is done secretly" (8.269), and the verb describing it, *êischune* (8.269), refers to the notion of shame; in like manner, the goddesses do not come to see the couple in fetters "because they are ashamed" (8.324). In addition, Hephaestus' punishment of the adulterers is mainly the infliction of visible shame on those who have tried hard to avoid the public eye, which explains why the story is replete with references to seeing: Helios "watched the adulterers" (8.302), the fetters contrived by Hephaestus "cannot be seen by anyone" (8.280), Ares sees Hephaestus leaving his home (8.286), and the gods are summoned to see Ares and Aphrodite (8.307,313). Hephaestus himself associates his pain with the act of seeing (8.314), and seeing is the explicit source of the initial laughter of the gods (8.327–28) and the implicit source of its second eruption (8.341).

In addition to shame and anger, Demodocus intertwines a third aspect, which is Odyssean in nature: cunning. Adultery is both the cause of Hephaestus' anger and the instigator of his cunning: it is anger that prompts Hephaestus to devise the trick, *dolon,* of the invisible fetters (8.276). As already mentioned, cunning is a recurring motif not only in the story of Hephaestus (*doloenta* 8.281, *dolon* 8.282, and *dolos* 8.317) but also in the *Odyssey* as a whole, a poem whose focal character is a master of treacherous tricks and wily programs. Cunning and invisible fetters are also an important part of the myth of Hephaestus' return to Mount Olympus in order to release Hera from the throne to which she is bound due to his machinations. Once more textual reticence is illuminating, for Ares has an eminent role in the myth: he is the first to try to fetch Hephaestus by force and is thwarted by means of the god's fire.[54] Thus, unlike the myth that represents Hephaestus as an equal match for Ares, a myth in which Hephaestus is an able god who succeeds in overpowering his strong opponent, the poet of the *Odyssey* stresses Hephaestus' inferiority and weakness, characteristics that caused him to resort to cunning and trickery in the first place. As in the *Iliad,* where Hephaestus' human traits served as the basis for his tragic characterization, so here inferiority, weakness, and trickery, the traits associating the god first with Odysseus and then with humanity in general, contribute to his presentation as a tragic figure. The emphasis on the human aspect of the

god becomes even more conspicuous when one traces the strong analogy between Hephaestus and the poet who sings his song.

Both artists are disabled; the god is maimed in his legs, and the singer is
blind. Demodocus' blindness is stressed no less than Hephaestus' crippling:
it is stated soon after he is first mentioned (8.64) and is hinted at several
more times. After he finishes his first song, he is led out by the herald
(8.105–7), who later brings him his instrument before the second song
(8.256–62) and hands him food at the banquet (8.482–83).[55] In like manner,
the motif of Hephaestus' lameness, which had so prominent a role in the
Iliad, is also central to Demodocus' second song, and the recurrent references to walking keep reminding the audience of Hephaestus' limited mobility.[56] In addition, the main contrast between Hephaestus and Ares is
based on Ares' preeminence in the same limbs in which Hephaestus is deformed. The comparison is explicitly made by Hephaestus himself, who
claims that Aphrodite despises him "because he is lame (*chôlos*)" (8.308), and
while Ares "is sound of limb" (8.310) he, "in contrast, is feeble" (8.310–11).
This notion is strengthened later in the remarks of the gods after the couple
is caught. The slow overtakes the quick: Hephaestus, "despite being slow,"
catches Ares, "although he is the quickest of the gods." In sum, the lame one
(*chôlos*) succeeds by means of his craft and cunning (*technêsi* 8.329–32).[57]
The connection between Hephaestus and Demodocus has another facet: for
both physically handicapped artists, art serves as compensation and consolation for limitation.[58] I have already demonstrated how art functions in this
way for Hephaestus in the *Iliad* during his long and painful stay with his
two surrogate mothers. The poet of the *Odyssey* hints at the same idea as regards Demodocus, whom the Muse loved so much and gave both good and
bad (8.63): she took his eyes but gave him sweet song (8.64).[59]

As claimed in the opening of this chapter, the overt associations between
Hephaestus and central human figures in the poem, such as Demodocus
and Odysseus, are essential to the poet's construction of Hephaestus as a
character full of empathy for the tragic human lot. There is, however, another aspect, somewhat more covert, of Hephaestus' tragic association with
the human. This aspect, which is based on the prominence of the notion of
charis in this context, is also a manifestation of the *Odyssey*'s dialogue with
the *Iliad.* Between the first and second songs of Demodocus, the *Odyssey* describes a verbal quarrel between Odysseus and one of the Phaeacian nobles,
Euryalus, who chides him for his refusal to participate in the Phaeacian
games (8.158–85). In his angry reply to Euryalus' chastisements, Odysseus
utilizes two opposing exempla, one of a man who has excellent speech and

another of a man who has physical perfection. These are presented as mutually exclusive: the one who has the former does not have the latter and vice versa (*allos men* [. . .] *alla* [. . .] *allos d' au* [. . .] *all'* 8.169–70, 174–75). Regarding Hephaestus, this is another echo of the recurring motif of limited blessing. However, it is also an allusion to the god's complex association with *charis*. Odysseus describes the speech of the handsome man as lacking *charis* (literally, "*charis* does not crown and garland his words," 8.175).[60] The notion of *charis* is first and foremost divine, as can be deduced from the fact that Athena pours "divine *charis*" (*thespesiên charin*) on Odysseus, her favorite (8.18–19). In both epics poets and poetry are also conceived as strongly associated with the divine, which is why the adjective describing divine *charis* in the above phrase—*thepesiê*—appears in the description of poets and poetry both in the *Iliad* (2.600) and the *Odyssey* (12.158, referring to the song of the Sirens). In like manner, *thespis* describes the poet (*Od.* 17.385) and his song (*Od.* 1.328, 8.498). The connection between poets and poetry, on the one hand, and Hephaestus and his craft, on the other, has already been stated. The notion of *charis*, however, adds another layer to this aspect, for the deification of the concept of *charis*, namely, Charis, is literally connected to the Iliadic Hephaestus: Charis is Hephaestus' wife in book eighteen of the *Iliad*.

The exceptional nature of Hephaestus' marriage was noted in my discussion of his role in the *Iliad*. The *Odyssey* highlights this irregularity even more by means of the song of the bard: the marriage of Hephaestus and Aphrodite is most likely the poet's innovation.[61] Now, if Hephaestus is married to both Charis and Aphrodite, his double marriage can have one of two explanations: he had two wives either simultaneously or serially. Presumed bigamy has no foundation in the text. Serial marriage, however, is hinted at in Demodocus' song by means of the discussion concerning the return of the *eedna*, the gifts Hephaestus gave Zeus as part of the marriage contract (8.318–19, 347, 355–56).[62] The *Odyssey*, therefore, makes Charis of the *Iliad* Hephaestus' second wife after he has divorced Aphrodite. The poet of the *Odyssey* alludes to the second marriage by ending the bard's song with mention of the bathing and clothing of Aphrodite by none other than the Charites (8.364–66). Thus, Hephaestus' second wife is directly connected with the beauty of the first and yet is essentially different from her; she serves as the responsive addressee of his complaints about a painful past and not as the source of present or future suffering.[63]

The innovative power of the poet in this case is not confined to his insertion of the probably new story of Ares and Aphrodite; nor is it restricted to the compelling dialogue between the two epics, where the *Odyssey* turns a god's marriage, already an exception among the immortals, into a second marriage, unprecedented on Mount Olympus. The poet's creativity is also manifest in his combination of divine and human aspects in order to emphasize the intermediary status of an exceptional god who hovers between the divine and human realms. Thus, by utilizing the notion of divine *charis,* the poet both alludes to Hephaestus' godly nature and associates him with human beings such as himself and Odysseus, while the implied reference to the goddess Charis both associates Hephaestus with human institutions such as marriage and divorce and establishes that these institutions are realized among gods. What is more, both *charis* and Charis reflect the tragic aspect of Hephaestus' life through their allusion to pain and suffering. They also hint at his exceptional ability to recover from great loss and affliction.

Already in the *Iliad,* Hephaestus' tragic character as an object of derision stands in complete contrast to the frivolous laughter that ends the Olympian quarrel. The poet of the *Odyssey,* well aware of the basic chasm between the lame god and the other immortals, reemphasizes this characteristic in order to restate the unbridgeable gap between Hephaestus and his fellow Olympians. The two incidents of laughter among the gods that reveal divine lightheartedness in a most inappropriate context contrast starkly with the reaction of the divine victim of adultery. Once again the poet, with his superb sensitivity to the power of words to reflect the complexity of reality, utilizes his language in a very effective way. In Greek, the word denoting lameness, χωλός (*chôlos* with a long *o*), is very similar to the word denoting anger, χόλος (*cholos* with a short *o*). Hephaestus, who is lame—*chôlos*—and consequently despised and betrayed by Aphrodite, is also full of anger—*cholos*—due to his wife's behavior. This connection between the physical and the emotional is stressed by the close proximity of the two words (8.304, 308), thus giving additional weight to Hephaestus' expectation of a serious response. But the gods' reaction is not the desired one, for they prefer to concentrate on the amusing aspects of the entrapment of the adulterous couple rather than on the far-reaching implications of their deed. Thus, the gods' initial laughter focuses on the contrast between the lame and the quick-footed instead of feeling empathy for a betrayed husband. The second laughter (like the second fall) is even worse, for here Hermes says to Apollo that he is ready to suffer an even greater humiliation than Ares if only he could sleep with Aphrodite (8.335–42). In other words, adultery counts for nothing when the golden goddess is at stake. This is a typical divine reaction that conforms with the gods' general behavior toward Hephaestus in the opening section of the *Iliad,* and in like manner the comic surface covers a much more disturbed and disturbing attitude.[64]

For what is typical for the gods is not applicable to mortals, as the epithet describing Aphrodite connotes: Hephaestus states that he gave Zeus many wedding gifts for his dog-eyed (or dog-faced) daughter (8.319). As noted in the previous chapter, in the *Iliad* Hephaestus deliberately tags Hera with the epithet "dog-eyed" (or "dog-faced") in order to emphasize her shameless and unseemly behavior. The *Odyssey* again employs the adjective when Hephaestus' describes his shameless and unseemly wife, thus associating her not only with the previous epic but also with the focal theme of the later text: this epithet is applied to Helen at 4.145 and to Clytemnestra at 11.424, the two sisters whose most notorious deed in the *Odyssey* is adultery.[65] In the human sphere, however, the consequences of such an act are far from risible, and the afflicted Hephaestus, the most humanlike of all the gods, serves here once again as an emblem of the human situation. Unlike his first wife, the "lover of smiles" (*philommeidês* 8.362),[66] who easily washes away her adulterous past, including all its shameful aspects, Hephaestus' insistence on retaliation remains a bitter reminder to his audience of the constant outcome of his pain and shame. The poet of the *Odyssey* hints in that direction when he breaks the unanimity of the divine reaction and lets Poseidon speak to Hephaestus. Poseidon does not laugh (8.344); he has a serious discussion with Hephaestus concerning the release of the adulterers. In fact, it is this serious discussion that ends the episode on the husband's bed and not the laughter of the gods.

In sum, in both the *Iliad* and the *Odyssey* Hephaestus is portrayed as a god endowed with human characteristics. Afflicted in body and limited in movement, suffering pain and humiliation, and constricted by human institutions such as marriage and divorce, he is unique among the Olympians in his humanized characterization. This uniqueness is used for tragic effect, for this humanized god serves as a figure whose depth is otherwise unavailable to immortals, one of whose main characteristics is a loftiness that is essentially indifferent. Moreover, it is this loftiness that often enables them to deride and mock the agonies of mortals.[67] In the *Iliad,* Hephaestus' tragic awareness finds its most brilliant expression in his creation of the shield of Achilles, where his engravings reveal his humane perspective on the human lot. In the *Odyssey,* his betrayal serves as an emblem of the miseries of mortals and as a reminder of the ineradicable chasm between humans and gods. Despite differences between the epics, the portrayal of this exceptional god serves a twofold function in both cases as a means of representing a tragic perception of the human condition, which is marked by pain and suffering, and to endow this perception with compassion and humaneness that lead their audiences to a profound metaphysical recognition of their own tragic position in the world.

7

The *Iliad,* the *Odyssey,* and the Dual Model of the Tragic

Now, after our circuitous journey into the epic lands of the *Iliad* and the *Odyssey,* we can portray the dual model of the tragic. To reprise what was claimed in the introduction and developed throughout the book, the basic duality of this model of the tragic refers to a movement on the axis of time between two poles of contrasting states of luck, good and ill. The tragic is a reflection of this movement regardless of its points of departure and termination. In both vectors the movement includes immense suffering and culminates in recognition (physical, psychological, or metaphysical).[1]

Although my reading of the epics affirms that the tragic can be applied either to mortals or to immortals, the world of mortals and their notion of irretrievable time is the core of the tragic model. This is why the poet, in utilizing Hephaestus as a tragic figure, accentuates the god's human characteristics and endows his character with mortal perceptions of time and space. The tragic reflects an essential helplessness of the agent, a helplessness that is deeply rooted in his or her limitedness. The gods, who live for an unlimited period of time, are basically indifferent to temporal afflictions since they have more than enough time to forget. From a divine perspective, all is temporary, even affliction. To recapitulate, the tragic axis of mortal time is marked by disastrous suffering regardless of the existence of good luck on its other pole. Tragic works of art merely accelerate human movement on this axis in order to emphasize the malevolent context in which humans are condemned to live.[2]

Obviously, this is a lesson most people wish either not to learn or, having learned it despite themselves, to forget as soon as possible. For, at least initially, it seems that there is little advantage in acquiring this kind of apprehension or in cultivating an awareness of helplessness embedded in the excruciating nature of the human condition. Yet the insistence of tragic works on remembrance is precisely in response to the human proclivity for forgetfulness. In this aspect the *Odyssey* is exemplary. Various scenes represent the difficult human struggle with the wish for oblivious immersion, a wish shared by the epic's eponymous hero, the emblem of craving for home in order to resume a former life. The *Odyssey* also illuminates the close association between the wish to obliterate the memory of suffering and the yearning to detach oneself from everything that is human: country, household, friends, family, and finally life itself.

The arduousness of the lesson lies mainly in the knife of metaphysical recognition and its double edge, the cognitive and the emotional. On the cognitive blade, the tragic lies in that which is basically incomprehensible within human understanding. This is incontestably one of the most difficult lessons the faculty of reason must be taught, for it is the lesson of its own limitations. Worse still, these limitations profoundly shape one of its most important tasks, namely, comprehension of the nature of the universe and the scope of an individual's ability to affect it. But the cognitive aspect of metaphysical recognition is the easier acquisition of the two. What is acutely difficult to internalize is the emotional aspect of metaphysical recognition, that is, acceptance of life's constituent element of irreversible loss, for which there is no compensation and often little consolation. While cognitive recognition is a necessary condition for the possibility of emotional recognition, the cognitive is not, in itself, a sufficient condition for the emotional to come into being. A special and exacting effort is required for achievement of this recognition, as evidenced in the changes Achilles endures in the last book of the *Iliad,* as well as in Odysseus' long journey, in which he reformulates his value system. The usefulness of this lesson may seem dubious in light of its close association with helplessness. I will address this question in a moment, but first I wish to return to a point mentioned earlier, the indifference of the model to the vector of the movement between good and ill luck.

For, indeed, as my discussion of the *Iliad* and the *Odyssey* has shown, the essence of the tragic lies in one's relation to time, a relation branded with unavoidable ill synchronization or its lack (regarding *kairos*). The tragic pattern I have mapped in the *Iliad* is the incarnation of this principle, for it not only repeatedly represents the missed opportunity of *kairos*, but it also demonstrates how the inability to perceive and accept this as an opportunity forever lost is in itself a foundation for missing another, albeit different, *kairos*. In like manner, Odysseus' misunderstanding of changing times and codes, so horrifyingly realized in the Cyclops scene, is another example of a temporal miss that breeds consequences no less harrowing than those in the *Iliad*.[3] Both the *Iliad* and the *Odyssey* insist on the fact that, although the human being finally learns to acknowledge his error, it happens very late and only after terrible and irredeemable loss. As I have just claimed, the difference between these two epics, which manifest the dual model, reflects the nature of this belatedness. Tragic learning is always very late: if you are on the Iliadic (that is to say, the bad) pole of luck, this learning is already too late for practical application, and if you are on the Odyssean, (that is to say, the best) pole of luck, it is merely almost too late. This sorry truth is formulated in Achilles' tale of Zeus' two jars, and it is ingeniously realized in the *Odyssey* through the motif of the late homecoming of the suffering hero. It is now clear why the poet, always attuned to the function of time in his epic, has chosen to kill the dog Argus a moment after he meets his master. The notion of the "almost too late" is condensed there, for the disheartening situation of the dog mirrors the grave consequences of the master's long absence and, more important, also hints at that which is lost to time. The dog's death bars any possibility of consolation for the last and very long period of suffering in its life. In that respect, the animal resembles the hero's mother, who died before this late homecoming, and reflects the lot of the other characters: the wretched father who had to live so long in squalor and misery, the lonely wife who persevered despite immense obstacles during her husband's absence, and the son who had to mature without the guidance of a loving father.

What should be reemphasized in this context is the unavoidable nature of the ill synchronization, namely, of the ineludible missing of opportunity or loss (as regards *kairos*), for it is impossible for one to be constantly, unceasingly, and unremittingly attuned to the vicissitudes of time. Note that even the astute Odysseus did not succeed in that. The example of Odysseus is especially *ad rem* here not only because of his exceptional cognitive and emotional capabilities but also due to the specific nature of his error. Odysseus' misreading of time has nothing to do with divine intervention, but it is no less inevitable.

One might initially assume that the lack of practical applicability of experience is the opposite of the didactic. For what is the use of learning something that cannot be used to any end and, worse still, increases one's suffering and diminishes one's ability to confront the constant challenges of daily life. Nietzsche was no doubt right to associate the tragic (in its realization in drama) with the unbearable essence of human existence so fused with inexplicable and enormous affliction. This is what he says about it in *The Birth of Tragedy*

Sobald aber jene alltägliche Wirklichkeit wieder ins Bewusstsein tritt, wird sie mit Ekel als solche empfunden; [. . .] In diesem Sinne hat der dionysische Mensch Aehnlichkeit mit Hamlet; beide haben einmal einen wahren Blick in das Wesen der Dinge gethan, sie haben *erkannt,* und es ekelt sie zu handeln. [. . .] Die Erkenntniss tödtet das Handeln, zum Handeln gehört das Umschleiertseinßdurch die Illusion—das ist die Hamletlehre [. . .]. In der Bewusstheit der einmal geschauten Wahrheit sieht jetzt der Mensch überall nur das Entsetzliche oder Absurde des Seins.[4]

[Yet the moment this everyday reality reenters consciousness, it is felt as such with revulsion: [. . .] In this sense the Dionysiac man is similar to Hamlet: Both have once had a true glimpse into the essence of things, they have acquired recognition *(sie haben* erkannt*), and this fills them with revulsion as regards action. [. . .] The recognition kills the action, for being veiled by illusion is a part of action. This is the lesson of Hamlet [. . .]. Having the full knowledge of this truth once it has been perceived, the man sees now everywhere merely the horror or the absurd of being.]*

How, then, can we reconcile the elements of this seeming oxymoron of tragic understanding and its "impractical didacticism"? The key to this problem has already been noted in my discussion of Hector's flight and its association with the absurd in chapter 4. In terms of the nature of reality, there is no way to make this tragic wisdom practical. Knowing does add to one's suffering without offering any remedy. Moreover, such knowledge undermines all systems of value and/or meaning by exposing the shaky fundament of human perception and its relative futility. The Nietzschean conception of truth does have the power to overwhelm any value by its assertion of meaninglessness, as could have happened to Hector on recognizing Athena's malevolence and its implications regarding divine intervention, and this when he was in such desperate need of help in combat. Yet it is exactly this harrowing recognition that makes the resurfacing of Hector's valor so compelling and telling, for it indicates the practical aspect of tragic wisdom. True, it is impossible to change the fact of essential helplessness in the face of the dominance of hostile powers. But it is possible, on the paradoxical basis of this absence, to reconstruct a value system that, in its turn, endows life with meaning. This is what both Hector and Odysseus do in their refashioning of the notion of heroism. And this is not all. The practicality of tragic understanding finds its expression in another, and no less important, aspect of human life, the strengthening of humane sensibility.

It is not without cause that the humaneness of the epics is formulated by a god (Hephaestus), by a son of a goddess (Achilles), and by a man of unsurpassed intellectual capacities (Odysseus). All share an exceptional status that lends weight to their insights, and all lead their audience to the same conclusion: the basic dismal human condition, which consists of inevitable suffering and terrible loss, is shared by every human being as such. This is true for all, friend and enemy both. This is what Achilles sees in Priam, and this is what Odysseus sees not only in his former enemies, the Trojans, but also in his enemies at home when they are deservedly dead (22.411–16).[5] This humane lesson is what the tragic in its varied realizations can teach, and it is this lesson that is so magnificently formulated by the poet or poets of these two masterpieces of the tragic, the *Iliad* and the *Odyssey*.

Notes

INTRODUCTION

1. Thus, Stephen Halliwell, *The Aesthetics of Mimesis: Ancient Texts and Modern Problems* (Princeton and Oxford: Princeton University Press, 2002), 100: "[T]he 'emotionalism' of tragic audiences in Athens falls far short of evidence for a full-blown conception of 'the tragic' [. . .] and if we look further for traces of such a conception in the evidence for Athenian responses to tragedy either before or indeed anywhere outside Plato, it remains surprisingly hard to find much of salience."

2. For example, Scholium to Aeschylus' *Prometheus Bound* line 550, to Aristophanes' *Women in the Thesmophoria* line 5, and to Aristophanes' *Plutus* line 39.

3. For example, Scholium to Aristophanes' *Clouds* line 540.

4. Referring to a sword in Scholium to Aeschylus' *Eumenides* line 64 and to garments in Scholia to Aristophanes' *Acharnians* line 418.

5. For example, Scholia to Sophocles' *Ajax* lines 1123 and 1409; Scholium to Euripides' *Hippolytus* line 672; Scholium to Euripides' *The Women of Troy* line 1129. Aristotle's *Poetics* utilizes the word *tragikon* (τραγικόν) in order to denote the right effect of tragedy. The tragedies of Euripides "give the most tragic impression" (1453a27–28), which is why their author seems to be "the most tragic" (*tragikôtatos*) among the poets (1453a29). If a tragedy describes a character intending to act with full knowledge and then, on the brink of action, fails to do so, "this is repulsive (*miaron*) and not tragic (*tragikon*)" (1453b38–39). In composing reversals and simple actions poets usually utilize the astonishing, "for it is tragic (*tragikon*) and arouses human sympathy" ([*philanthrôpon*] 1456a21).

6. Halliwell, *Aesthetics of Mimesis*, 103.

7. See ibid., 103 note 10.

8. Ibid., 98–99.

9. This recurs in contemporary discussions of the tragic; Terry Eagleton, *Sweet Violence: The Idea of the Tragic* (Malden and Oxford: Blackwell, 2003), is a recent example. For the importance of distinguishing between tragedy and the tragic, see Glenn W. Most, "Generating Genres: The Idea of the Tragic," in *Matrices of Genre: Authors, Canons, and Society*, ed. Mary Depew and Dirk Obbink, 22 (Cambridge: Harvard University Press, 2000).

10. Eagleton (*Sweet Violence*, 82), who has marked this phenomenon, resumes his discussion of the topic claiming that "Perhaps happy and unhappy endings are beside the point because what matters is mutability rather than any specific kind of conclusion. The sheer fact of an ending, in the sense that this is all of the action that we spectators will witness, highlights the transience of both happiness and unhappiness and brings to mind the condition to which both will eventually lead, namely death" (84). Yet Eagleton's articulation of the ineluctable teleology of "the" end, death, cancels the inherent duality that he himself formulates. If all action ultimately leads to one and the same end, and if this end is the most important thing, then the transient character of all that precedes death loses much of its significance.

11. Aristotle, of course, would have been averse to an interpretation that so accentuates the random and fortuitous nature of his poles; see Samuel Henry Butcher, *Aristotle's Theory of Poetry and Fine Arts*[4] (New York: Dover, 1951 [1911]), 180–82, for the Aristotelian perception of poetry as the antipode of the accidental and for art in general as the antithesis of chance. See also I. M. Glanville, "Note on ΠΕΡΙΠΕΤΕΙΑ," *CQ* 41 (1947): 74, for the sharp contrast between reversal (*peripeteia*) and chance. For a thorough discussion of Aristotle's conception of *tuche* and its various ramifications, see Martha C. Nussbaum, *The Fragility of Goodness: Luck and Ethics in Greek Tragedy and Philosophy* (Cambridge: Cambridge University Press, 1986), 318–42; for a discussion of Aristotle's usage of *eutuchia* and *dustuchia*, see Stephen Halliwell, *Aristotle's Poetics* (Chicago: University of Chicago Press, 1998 [1986]), 204 note 3 and 205–6 with notes 4 and 5. On *tuche* as not necessarily random, since "it does not exclude the possibility of a concealed order or pattern of events, only the immediate human ability to perceive one," see Halliwell, *Aristotle's Poetics*, 230. See also Elizabeth S. Belfiore, *Tragic Pleasures: Aristotle on Plot and Emotion* (Princeton: Princeton University Press, 1992), 100; Dorothea Frede, "Necessity, Chance, and 'What Happens for the Most Part' in Aristotle's *Poetics*," in *Essays on Aristotle's Poetics*, ed. Amélie Oksenberg Rorty, 202 (Princeton: Princeton University Press, 1992); and Nussbaum, *Fragility of Goodness*, 89. My model is merely suggested by Aristotelian terminology rather than reflecting it.

12. This notion is expressed in Camus' treatise *Le Mythe de Sisyphe*. See Jacqueline Lévi-Valensi, *Albert Camus Œuvres Complètes I: 1931–1944* (Paris: Bibliothèque de la Pléiade, 2006, 308), in a passage where Camus claims that "happiness, too, in its way, lacks reason, since it is inevitable" ("le bonheur aussi, à sa manière, est sans raison, puisqu'il est inévitable"). It is in this context that he comments on the tragic nature of those Greek tragedies that end happily and on Odysseus as a tragic hero. The pertinence of Camus' book to my conception of the tragic is discussed in chapter 4.

13. Thus Emily R. Wilson, *Mocked with Death: Tragic Overliving from Sophocles to Milton* (Baltimore and London: Johns Hopkins University Press, 2004), 7: "[T]ragic time is always out of joint. [. . .] Time is resisted or goes wrong, lives end too soon or too late, the temporal order of human generations is confused by incest or familial murder, and time brings only staleness or repetition or death."

14. On this point, see Patrice Guillamaud, "L'essence du kairos," *REA* 90 (1988): 360. The fullest discussion of the importance of *kairos* to ancient rhetoric is still Augusto Ros-

tagni, "Un nuovo capitolo nella storia della retorica e della sofistica," *Studi italiani di filologica classica,* n.s. 2 (1922). For a recent discussion, see James L. Kinneavy, "*Kairos* in Classical and Modern Rhetorical Theory," in *Rhetoric and Kairos: Essays in History, Theory, and Praxis,* ed. Phillip Sipiora and James S. Baumlin, 58–76 (Albany: State University of New York Press, 2002). On the importance of *kairos* to Isocrates' educational system, see Phillip Sipiora, "Introduction: The Ancient Concept of *Kairos*," in *Rhetoric and Kairos: Essays in History, Theory, and Praxis,* ed. Phillip Sipiora and James S. Baumlin, 7–15 (Albany: State University of New York Press, 2002).

15. John E. Smith, "Time, Times, and the 'Right Time': *Chronos* and *Kairos.*" *Monist* 53 (1969): 1.

16. Ibid., 6, emphasis in the original.

17. I refrain from using this Aristotelian term because of its possibly misleading hue of something that can be avoided. It cannot, which is why it is tragic.

18. Unamuno's anecdote and comment are relevant here: "A pedant who beheld Solon weeping for the death of a son said to him: 'Why do you weep thus, if weeping avails nothing?' And the sage answered him, 'Precisely for that reason—because it does not avail.' It is manifest that weeping avails something, even if only alleviation of distress; but the deep sense of Solon's reply to the impertinent questioner is plainly seen." Miguel de Unamuno, *The Tragic Sense of Life,* trans. J. E. Crawford Flitch (London: Macmillan, 1921 [1912]), 35.

19. Halliwell (*Aesthetics of Mimesis,* 99), who refutes the claim that "while ancient Greece created the first and most concentrated tradition of dramatic tragedy, it lacked anything that can be classified as an explicit notion of the tragic," suggests "ascribing to Plato the first conscious delineation of something we can coherently identify as 'the tragic.'" He does, however, qualify this somewhat, noting that "the first, at any rate, outside tragic poetry itself, though that, of course, is a complex reservation, depending as it does on an answer to the very question of whether tragedy itself is necessarily a vessel of the tragic."

20. What is actually absent from the epics is the noun. Its adjectival forms, *kairios* and its derivatives, do appear in the *Iliad* (6.185, 8.84, 8.326) where they denote "a *vital* or *lethal* place in the body" (William H. Race, "The Word Καιρός in Greek Drama," *TAPA* 111 [1981]: 197). See also Pierre Chantraine, *Dictionnaire étymologique de la langue grecque* (Paris: Klincksieck, 1968). The noun, however, is pervasive in Greek tragedy, which attests to the fact that the importance of such a notion to the tragic vision of the epics could not have been missed by their ardent followers, who utilized it incessantly in their dramas. Race opens his discussion of *kairos* in Greek drama with the claim that "from Hesiod well into the fourth century, καιρός [*kairos*] was one of several important *normative* words, often with little or no temporal connotation, whose basic sense is propriety. [. . .] In general, I have found that translators and commentators have overemphasized the temporal aspect" (197–98). Yet his thorough analysis of the different occurrences of the word and its cognates in tragedy does include cases in which the temporal aspect is prominent (211–13), and, what is more, he concludes his essay by postulating that "the temporal sense often enters the question because we naturally think of 'times,' 'occasions,' and 'moments,' when we are dealing with given circumstances or situations that change in time, and it is a short step from 'appropriate to the given situation' to 'correct at the moment' to 'timely'"(213), thus reaffirming the importance of the timely element in *kairos.*

21. For an interesting discussion of these aspects from a Marxist perspective, see Peter W. Rose, *Sons of the Gods, Children of Earth: Ideology and Literary Form in Ancient Greece*

(Ithaca and London: Cornell University Press, 1992), 94, which regards the *Iliad* as the reflection of a time in which "[t]he most significant political phenomenon [. . .] is the displacement of the institution of monarchy by oligarchy, collectively exercised control by the heads of large estates." Accordingly, the conflict in the Greek army at the core of the *Iliad* is seen as a realization of "the transition from meritocracy to plutocracy, from inherited demonstrable excellence to inherited wealth and status" (94) and "[t]he plot of the *Odyssey* explicitly juxtaposes inherited monarchy to collective domination by the sons of the rich landowners" (102). Rose claims that such conflicts are the tragic patterns that "lie in the background of the traditional stories" used both by the epic poets and their later followers (77). See also Rainer Friedrich, "Everything to Do with Dionysos?" in *Tragedy and the Tragic: Greek Theatre and Beyond*, ed. M. S. Silk, 275 (Oxford: Clarendon, 1996), for a "political" conception of the tragic.

22. References to and citations of Plato are to John Burnet, ed., *Platonis Opera* (Oxford: Clarendon, 1900–1907). For the *Iliad* and the *Odyssey* as reflecting the tragic in Platonic thought, see Halliwell, *Aesthetics of Mimesis*, 110.

23. All citations and references to Scholia on the *Iliad* are to Hatmut Erbse, *Scholia Graeca in Homeri Iliadem* (Berlin: de Gruyter, 1969–83). For other ancient authors who express the same sentiment, see R. B. Rutherford, "Tragic Form and Feeling in the *Iliad*," *JHS* 102 (1982): 145 note 3.

24. Simon Goldhill gives two thorough analyses of the topic in *Language, Sexuality, Narrative: The Oresteia* (Cambridge: Cambridge University Press, 1984), 183–95; and *Reading Greek Tragedy* (Cambridge: Cambridge University Press, 1986), 138–67. See also Jasper Griffin, *Homer on Life and Death* (Oxford: Clarendon, 1980), 118–19; Cecil John Herington, *Poetry into Drama: Early Tragedy and the Greek Poetic Tradition* (Berkeley: University of California Press, 1985), 213–15; Rutherford, "Tragic Form and Feeling"; and Oliver Taplin, *Homeric Soundings: The Shaping of the Iliad* (Oxford: Clarendon, 1992), 73.

25. Halliwell, *Aesthetics of Mimesis*, 104–17.

26. Ibid., 114–15.

27. Gerald Frank Else, *Aristotle's Poetics: The Argument* (Cambridge: Harvard University Press, 1957), 446.

28. Margalit Finkelberg, "Aristotle and Episodic Tragedy," *Greece and Rome* 53 (2006): 61.

29. See R. B. Rutherford, "From the *Iliad* to the *Odyssey*," *BICS* 38 (1991–93): 38, 41. Interestingly, the conception of the *Odyssey* as an epic alien to the tragic is so strong that even Aristotle can be recruited for support. Thus, Wolfgang Kullmann, in "Gods and Men in the *Iliad* and the *Odyssey*," *HSCP* 89 (1985): 2, claims that "[s]implifying Aristotle, we could say that the *Iliad* is tragic, the *Odyssey* 'not tragic'. This seems to be a basic difference between both epics, as far as human fate is concerned." Kullmann's remarks are especially illuminating and representative, for his discussion as a whole leads to the conclusion that "the poet of the *Iliad* and the poet of the *Odyssey* both, with the utmost consistency, base their works on one single aspect of the divine and relate it to their respective views of man" (19). In other words, both epics can be regarded as a dual model of one phenomenon as long as we do not name it "tragic." The question of *why* the *Odyssey* has been identified so persistently as the foundation text of comedy is beyond the scope of my treatise, which aims at uprooting this common error rather than investigating its origins. I will merely note a possible origin in the epic's conclusion, its seemingly "happy ending" with the reaffirmation of the marriage of Odysseus and Penelope. Oliver Taplin, in "Comedy and the

Tragic," in *Tragedy and the Tragic: Greek Theatre and Beyond,* ed. M. S. Silk, 196 (Oxford: Clarendon, 1996), cites Bernard Shaw's formulation of the difference between tragedy and comedy, where "the popular definition of tragedy is heavy drama in which everyone is killed in the last act, comedy being light drama, in which everyone is married in the last act." Taplin's correct observation that "the happy-versus-unhappy-ending polarity is (of course) far from true of fifth-century drama" is irrelevant to the notion of the comic, for (as he concedes) this polarity "may have become more applicable in later antiquity," thus shaping later conceptions of the *Odyssey* as well.

30. Thus, Stephen Halliwell, undoubtedly one of the most perceptive readers of the *Poetics,* finds such treatment of the *Odyssey* "remarkable" (*Aristotle's Poetics,* 263–64). What is more, although he does note that Aristotle is consistent in regarding this epic as tragedy, Halliwell anticipates future assessments of his own commentary in defining the *Odyssey* as "quasi-tragedy" (264 note 18).

31. Fidel Fajardo-Acosta's *The Hero's Failure in the Tragedy of Odysseus: A Revisionist Analysis* (Lampeter, UK: Edwin Mellen Press, 1990) might be considered an exception to this almost totally pervasive rule. Yet his exaggerated valorization of the values of peace, crested by his claim that in the world of the *Iliad* and the *Odyssey* "[t]rue glory [. . .] does not belong to the boastful, arrogant, and self-glorifying heroes but rather to humble, common, self-effacing, and relatively invisible characters" (18), mars his intuition with oversimplification. Certainly, the *Iliad* is much more than a demonstration of "the emptiness and hollowness of the life of the martial hero, a life devoted to destruction and culminating in self-annihilation" (17). In like manner his conception of the gods as "mere narrative devices, symbolic entities controlled and manipulated by the poetic intelligence" (63) overlooks both the subtle complexity of divine characterization in the poems and the deeply religious aspect of the texts. The assumption that fate is "profoundly moral in character" (57) is, as my argument will illustrate, simply wrong, as is the notion that fate "is not a blind deterministic order; it shares in both the qualities of flexibility and fixity. Fate is a process ultimately dependent on free will. A man's character and choices of particular behavior are the triggers which set in motion the wheels of a positive or a tragic fate" (30). The concept of fate is essentially alien to the notion of free will, while the tragic, as I have postulated and will demonstrate, is not an outcome of choice but rather a manifestation of inevitable human helplessness.

32. See, for example, Halliwell, *Aristotle's Poetics,* 226–29; and Stephen E. White, "Aristotle's Favorite Tragedies," in *Essays on Aristotle's Poetics,* ed. Amélie Oksenberg Rorty, 221–40 (Princeton: Princeton University Press, 1992), with note 1 for references to the discussion.

33. See D. W. Lucas, *Aristotle: Poetics* (Oxford: Clarendon, 1972), in his commentary on 53a25.

34. Contra Halliwell, *Aesthetics of Mimesis,* 102: "But it is legitimate to hold that [Aristotle's] theory of tragedy yields something appreciably different from a pronounced sense of the tragic, not least because Aristotle's model of the mutability of human experience repeatedly accommodates the possibility of movement from adversity to prosperity, as well as the reverse. In this respect the *Poetics* adopts a position that is true to long-established patterns within Attic tragedy." Halliwell sums up by "drawing the crucial conclusion that the evidence of the *Poetics* as a whole, at the level of both documentation and theory, leaves us free to believe without paradox that it was entirely feasible within classical Athenian culture to speak about the nature and experience of tragedy without speaking in terms of the tragic" (102). There is little doubt that the *discourse* about tragedy in Athenian culture did not speak

in terms of the tragic, but this neither excludes the existence of such a notion nor implies its irrelevance to both writers and audiences. On the contrary, it is more likely that, while unformulated, this concept was strong enough to shape these tragic "long-established patterns within Attic tragedy." In fact, it is Halliwell himself, in his discussion of the tragic within Platonic thinking, who suggests the notion of the tragic as a potential existing even before its realization in one genre or another: "Both the appeal and the influence of tragedy reflect propensities of the human soul that are *prior* to, and in some sense waiting for, the creation of tragic art forms. On the Platonic view, 'the tragic' could and would have existed as a response to life even if tragic poetry had never come into being, because such a response is rooted in the intrinsic (if disordered) possibilities of the soul" (112, original emphasis).

35. See Halliwell (ibid., 103), who, following Aristotle, accentuates the importance of suffering in his own perception of the tragic, eventually designates death as "the" tragic component "whose interpretation is central to an evaluative attitude to life itself" (108). However, one should adhere to the fork in the road of Aristotle's *either* destructive *or* painful formulation, where death is merely an instance of the destructive, which itself is a category within the much larger group of agonizing experiences essential to the notion of the tragic.

36. For fully detailed research on the topic of recognition from antiquity to the twentieth century, see Terence Cave, *Recognitions: A Study in Poetics* (Oxford: Clarendon, 1988).

37. For a typology of the different realizations of this kind of recognition, see Aristotle's *Poetics* 1454b19–30.

38. It is this aspect of my model, the essential human helplessness in the face of the malevolent forces that shape his or her life, that most saliently marks the difference between my concept of the tragic and Hegel's idealism. What makes the human lot tragic is precisely the impossibility of resolving the horrifying conflict between an individual's aspiration to happiness and the impervious and obdurate reality that hampers its realization. Hegel's view of the realization of the tragic in tragedy is quite the opposite. As concisely presented by Michelle Gellrich in her *Tragedy and Theory: The Problem of Conflict since Aristotle* (Princeton: Princeton University Press, 1988), Hegel "believes [tragedy] is best suited to reintegrate the broken nature of the Ideal, to cancel division and bring the action back to a condition of repose. Such a dramatic process involves simultaneously an annulment or a dissolution of conflict, a suspension of the values in collision, and a raising of these values to a higher level of consciousness" (32). Gellrich herself, however, is well aware of the blindness inherent in Hegel's idealism and is judiciously critical of his conception of the tragic in general as well as his reading of the seminal play exemplifying his theory, Sophocles' *Antigone*. While for Hegel "the ethical struggles in tragedy are a result of the movement of the Ideal into differentiation and [. . .] this movement must be carried only so far by the playwright that mediation is not threatened" (46), a tragic characteristic of Greek tragedy is a "profoundly explorative and interrogative orientation, which does not validate systematic expectations of order so much as complicate or subvert them" (47–48). This critique is succinctly recapitulated in the following remarks: "By imposing an orderly teleology on the collisions and contradictions of the play, [Hegel] can guarantee a mediation that secures the ultimate unity sought by critics of tragedy from the time of Aristotle. But the insistence on unity leads away from an appreciation of the strategies in tragedy that disrupt our categories of understanding, expose the inconsistencies of moral standards, and undermine the stability of such ideas as 'knowledge' or 'wisdom' by means of which we order our sense of truth" (70).

39. Nita Schechet, *Narrative Fissures* (Cranbury, NJ: Associated University Presses, 2005), 11–12.

40. This position is well formulated in Colin Macleod, "Homer on Poetry and the Poetry of Homer," in *Collected Essays*, (Oxford: Clarendon, 1983), 1: "For myself, I am content to believe that the author of both [the *Iliad* and the *Odyssey*] was the same man; and I do not think there is any real evidence to tell against that assumption. But it is hardly possible to prove it either."

41. In the view of R. B. Rutherford, in "From the *Iliad* to the *Odyssey*," 38–39, "I take it for granted that, with the exception of certain limited sections of the text, each poem is essentially a unified creation by a single mind (which is not to deny that both poems make use of stories and episodes already familiar to their audiences)."

42. "The poet of the *Odyssey* is aware of the *Iliad* and, in important respects, composing in response to it"; Jasper Griffin, "Homer and Excess," in *Homer: Beyond Oral Poetry*, ed. J. M. Bremer, I. J. F. de Jong, and J. Kalf, 101 (Amsterdam: B. R. Grüner, 1987). See also William G. Thalmann, *Conventions of Form and Thought in Early Greek Epic Poetry* (Baltimore and London: Johns Hopkins University Press, 1984), 182; and Rutherford, "From the *Iliad* to the *Odyssey*," which has a thorough discussion of the topic.

43. See Barbara Graziosi, *Inventing Homer: The Early Reception of Epic* (Cambridge: Cambridge University Press, 2002), 88–89. This is the conclusion of her exhaustive and persuasive treatment of the issue in her second chapter, "Homer's Name and His Place of Origin," 51–89. See also Ahuvia Kahane, *Diachronic Dialogues: Authority and Continuity in Homer and the Homeric Tradition* (Oxford: Lexington Books, 2005), 56, which regards the name Homer as signifying "an open, fluid and widely accepted tradition, which can have no one master if it is to be kept truly alive."

44. For suggestive interpretations based on a two-way intertextual relationship between the two epics, see, for example, Pietro Pucci, *Odysseus Polutropos: Intertextual Readings in the Odyssey and the Iliad* (Ithaca and London: Cornell University Press, 1987); and Gregory Nagy, *The Best of the Achaeans: Concepts of the Hero in Ancient Greek Poetry* (Baltimore and London: Johns Hopkins University Press, 1979).

CHAPTER 1

An earlier version of this chapter appeared as "A Tragic Pattern in the *Iliad*," in *Harvard Studies in Classical Philology* 104 (2008).

1. Since the following tragic pattern in the *Iliad* refers exclusively to men, I use the masculine reference throughout.

2. Malcolm Davies, "The Judgment of Paris and Solomon," *CQ* 53 (2003): 32 with notes 1, 2, and 3, refers to the insult implied in the verb *neikesse* (νείϰεσσε) in 24.29, which occurs in the only passage in the *Iliad* that alludes to the Judgement of Paris. He also tracks the motif of the meeting with three goddesses in other Greek myths, as well as in folktales from other parts of the world (34–38). Although Davies notes that "[f]olk-tale 'helpers', especially female helpers, can be ambivalent [. . .] offering advice or aid that seems beneficial in the outset, but is in the long run destined to bring the hero ruin" (36–37), his final assertion that Paris "succumbs and makes the wrong choice" (38) ignores the unique feature of his choice, namely, that whatever he chooses implies, in the very act of choice, a disastrous outcome due to the ensuing insult to the other two goddesses. There are therefore only

wrong choices, which is why this divine intervention is ineluctably tragic, for it breeds inevitable suffering.

3. "Divine frivolity" is Griffin's translation, in *Homer on Life and Death* (199), of Karl Reinhardt's "ein erhabener Unernst" in "Das Parisurteil," in *Tradition und Geist*, 25 (Göttingen: Vandenhoeck and Ruprecht, 1960 [1938]). Although it is possible to claim, with Griffin (*Homer on Life and Death,* 5), that "since Paris is the archetypal Trojan, the sin of Paris is one in which Troy is inextricably implicated," it is still impossible to see this deed as satisfactory causality. However representative of his people Paris is, the chasm between his explicit action and their implicit sin remains unbridgeable, and this chasm is at the core of Troy's tragic doom.

4. Albin Lesky's important 1961 essay "Göttliche und menschliche Motivation im homerischen Epos," *SHAW* 4 (1961): 5–52 , is worth noting in this context. Lesky's detailed and persuasive argumentation unravels the convoluted connections between the human and the divine regarding the causal sequence of events in both the *Iliad* and the *Odyssey.* Although some of Lesky's arguments are congruent with mine, I wish to underline the essential difference between his conception of the epics and my own. According to Lesky's main thesis, human and divine motivations converge into a certain harmonious outcome through which the world gradually becomes more and more intelligible. In contrast, my reading of the *Iliad* emphasizes the unbridgeable gap between the human and the divine, thus demarcating not merely the arbitrariness of the gods' decisions and actions but also the harrowing reality in which mortals are doomed to live.

5. "Achilles is actually not complete until the poem is complete. He is learning all the time"; Cedric H. Whitman, *Homer and the Heroic Tradition* (Cambridge: Harvard University Press, 1958), 188. See also Glenn W. Most, "Anger and Pity in Homer's *Iliad,*" in *Ancient Anger: Perceptions from Homer to Galen,* ed. Susanna Braund and Glenn W. Most, 73–74 (*YCS* 32 [2003]), for Achilles' development along the *Iliad.* Contra James M. Redfield, *Nature and Culture in the Iliad: The Tragedy of Hector*[2] (Durham and London: Duke University Press, 1994), 21–22, endorsing, with slight reservations, Hermann Fränkel, *Early Greek Poetry and Philosophy: A History of Greek Epic, Lyric, and Prose to the Middle of the Fifth Century,* trans. Moses Hadas and James Willis (New York and London: Harcourt Brace Jovanovich, 1973 [1962]), 83: "Man in the *Iliad* remains always himself; he is not shattered by the hardest blows, nor is he capable of development. He reacts to situations sharply, and the mood he then takes on passes with the situation without leaving a trace." This notion, which implies "the idea that Homeric men are simple, without depths, and with everything on the surface" (Griffin, *Homer on Life and Death,* 70, with note 37 for references) is refuted in the same work on pages 50–80.

6. Schechet, *Narrative Fissures,* 45.

7. On the word order and its implications, see Joachim Latacz, René Nünlist, and Magdalene Stoevesandt, *Homers Ilias Gesamtkommentar Band I erster Gesang (A) Faszikel 2: Kommentar* (Munich and Leipzig: K. G. Saur, 2002), in their commentary on 1.1.

8. And see Lesky, "Göttliche und menschliche Motivation im homerischen Epos," 15–16, and Peter Von der Mühll, *Kritisches Hypomnema zur Ilias* (Basel: Verlag Friedrich Reinhardt, 1952), 14.

9. "That these glorious warriors should finish up as rotting carrion is a stark and tragic reversal"; Simon Pulleyn, *Homer: Iliad I* (Oxford: Oxford University Press, 2000) in his commentary on 1.4. On the *prooemium,* see Latacz, Nünlist, and Stoevesandt, *Homers Ilias Gesamtkommentar,* in their commentary on 1.1–12a.

10. "It was *Apollo* who started the dispute; an action that is to be so portentous deserves a divine cause"; G. S. Kirk, *The Iliad: A Commentary*, vol. 1: *Books 1–4* (Cambridge: Cambridge University Press, 1985), in his commentary on 1.9. See also Von der Mühll, *Kritisches Hypomnema zur Ilias*, 15.

11. And see Lesky, "Göttliche und menschliche Motivation im homerischen Epos," 16–17.

12. For the polite imperative and the "muted but audible threat" in ἀζόμενοι, see Pulleyn, *Homer: Iliad I*, in his commentary on 1.20 and 1.21; see also Donna F. Wilson, *Ransom, Revenge, and Heroic Identity in the Iliad* (Cambridge: Cambridge University Press, 2002), 42.

13. Casey Dué's description of Briseis in *Homeric Variations on a Lament by Briseis* (Lanham, MD: Rowman and Littlefield, 2002), 37, is applicable to Chryseis as well: "Two chieftains are fighting over a prize of honor, a spoil of war. That prize happens to be a girl, but, at least initially, she may as well be a tripod or a herd of cattle."

14. γέρας (*geras*) is "a concrete expression of the esteem (τιμή [*timê*]) in which one is held by the community"; Pulleyn, *Homer: Iliad I*, in his commentary on 1.118. See also Latacz, Nünlist, and Stoevesandt, *Homers Ilias Gesamtkommentar*, in their commentary on 1.118–29, accentuating the fact that there is no parallel to such a loss of *geras* to someone else.

15. For a detailed description of all the implications of Achilles' offer, see Wilson, *Ransom, Revenge, and Heroic Identity in the Iliad*, 56–57.

16. On *timê* as "prestige" rather than "honor," see Margalit Finkelberg, "*Timê* and *Aretê* in Homer," *CQ* 48 (1998): 16. The notion of *timê* also alludes to the theme of compensation that is about to play a prominent role in the epic. See Wilson, *Ransom, Revenge, and Heroic Identity in the Iliad*, 20–22, for the vocabulary of compensation themes.

17. αἴτιος (*aitios*) in the *Iliad* does not mean "cause," and "the use of the abstract noun αἰτία (*aitia*) to mean 'cause' *tout court* is a later development," as claimed by Annette Teffeteller, "Homeric Excuses," *CQ* 53 (2003): 17 and note 11. This later development, however, is already implied in the epic, where "αἴτιος (*aitios*) most often occurs in a statement of the form 'x is not αἴτιος" (*aitios*); y is', in which it is denied that a person who might reasonably thought to be responsible for some undesirable act or state of affairs is not so in fact, whereas another is" (17–18). By means of his responsibility for Achilles' situation, Agamemnon is also causally associated with Achilles. On the emphasis given anaphoric negation and the usage of the first person, see Latacz, Nünlist, and Stoevesandt, *Homers Ilias Gesamtkommentar*, in their commentary on 1.152–55.

18. The compensatory function is already noted by Scholium bT in his commentary on 1.184–85: "The threat is similar to the one in 'I will not release her' (in 1.29)"; see also Dué, *Homeric Variations*, 37; and Pulleyn, *Homer: Iliad I*, in his commentary on 1.182–84.

19. For Agamemnon's superiority, see Kirk, *The Iliad: A Commentary*, vol. 1, in his commentary on φέρτερος in 1.186.

20. See Pulleyn, *Homer: Iliad I*, in his commentary on 1.349–57, who judiciously criticizes Kirk, *The Iliad: A Commentary*, vol. 1, in his commentary on 1.348–57, for being "so cool about the possibility of deliberate parallelism." The parallels, however, are not devoid of significant differences, as demonstrated in Robert J. Rabel, *Plot and Point of View in the Iliad* (Ann Arbor: University of Michigan Press, 1997), 47–56.

21. On crying as the expected reaction to one's abraded honor, see Dominique Arnould, *Le Rire et les larmes dans la littérature greque d'Homère à Platon* (Paris: Les Belles Lettres, 1990), 53.

22. On this type of request, which can be classified as of the type *da-quia-dedi* (give because I have given), see Simon Pulleyn, *Prayer in Greek Religion* (Oxford: Clarendon, 1997), 16–18, 57–58.

23. On Agamemnon's responsibility, see Arthur W. H. Adkins, *Merit and Responsibility: A Study in Greek Values* (Chicago and London: University of Chicago Press, 1960), 51 with note 18, and E. R. Dodds, *The Greeks and the Irrational* (Berkeley and Los Angeles: University of California Press, 1951), 3. The distinction of Teffeteller, "Homeric Excuses," 18–19, between moral and practical responsibility is pertinent: "Agamemnon accepts practical responsibility for his action in so far as he does not deny that he did in fact take Achilles' prize, and accordingly he offers Achilles compensation. But he rejects moral responsibility and the blame that attaches to it."

24. "The language [that uses the concept of *atê*] is characteristic of Agamemnon [. . .]. Achilles avoids it, for the same reason that Agamemnon uses it, because it is exculpatory"; J. Bryan Hainsworth, *The Iliad: A Commentary*, vol. 3: *Books 9–12* (Cambridge: Cambridge University Press, 1993), in his commentary on 9.116.

25. "116–117 are an ingenious rearrangement of the elements of 97–98, typical of oral style. The effect is to make Agamemnon bitterly echo Nestor's opening compliments"; ibid., commentary on 9.116.

26. For the adept rhetoric of Odysseus' speech, see ibid., commentary on 9.225–306.

27. On φιλοφροσύνη (*philophrosunê*) see Jasper Griffin, *Homer: Iliad 9* (Oxford: Clarendon Press, 1995), in his commentary on 9.256.

28. "It is at this point that the plot of the *Iliad* changes its direction and its nature. [. . .] Achilles' refusal to accept the compensation, or to suggest terms which he would accept, turns events into a baffling position, in which neither Agamemnon nor Achilles knows what to do next"; ibid., commentary on 9.307–429.

29. In fact, as vindicated by Dué, *Homeric Variations*, 38–47, the abduction of Briseis mirrors not only the abduction of Chryseis but also that of Helen. The two abductions described in the *Iliad* should be therefore interpreted and understood as a reflection of the primal sin of Paris. Accordingly, the outcomes of these deeds are no less catastrophic.

30. On the notion of *charis* in this context, as well as its heroic implications, see Rabel, *Plot and Point of View*, 125 and note 29. See also Bonnie MacLachlan, *The Age of Charis* (Princeton: Princeton University Press, 1993), 13–22. On the connection between *charis* and *timê*, see Taplin, *Homeric Soundings*, 59–60.

31. And see Finkelberg, "*Timê* and *Aretê* in Homer," 16–17.

32. There might be another reason for Briseis' special status in Achilles' eyes, namely, his strong emotions toward her, which are hinted at in 9.342–43. See Whitman, *Homer and the Heroic Tradition*, 186–87; see also Dué, *Homeric Variations*, 60–64, for Aeolic traditions and their possible association with this passage.

33. And see Richard P. Martin, *The Language of Heroes: Speech and Performance in the Iliad* (Ithaca and London: Cornell University Press, 1989), 183, who claims that "Achilles' speech contains an explicitly new ethical bent: it enshrines the only attestation in the *Iliad* of the theme of the 'good man'." See also Maureen J. Alden, *Homer beside Himself* (Oxford: Clarendon, 2000), 204–5.

34. "Contrary to a view prevalent in the last century, ὕβρις [*hubris*] is not an attitude of overweening pride towards gods. It is, rather, any action that lessens the τιμή [*timê*] of another. As such, its victims may be either gods or men"; Pulleyn, *Homer: Iliad I*, in his commentary on 1.203. As noted by Hainsworth, *The Iliad: A Commentary*, vol. 3, in his com-

mentary on 9.368, *hubris* "is not a frequent Iliadic idea"; the word appears only four more times in the *Iliad* against twenty-six times in the *Odyssey.*

35. Even in his short answer to Ajax, Achilles claims he would never forget how Agamemnon treated him as a fugitive or wanderer with no status or prestige (9.648).

36. "θυμαλγέα λώβην [*thumalgea lôbên*] is a new point; it explains, psychologically at any rate, why Agamemnon's offers are ἐχθρά [*echthra* 378]. Up to this point the injury to Achilles has been expressed [. . .] in material terms. Now it is revealed that what really matters is Achilles' mental anguish, something that the Achaean Chiefs had not thought of and cannot reach"; Hainsworth, *The Iliad: A Commentary*, vol. 3, in his commentary on 9.387. See also Christopher Gill, *Personality in Greek Epic, Tragedy, and Philosophy: The Self in Dialogue* (Oxford: Clarendon, 1996), 146; Jasper Griffin, "Homeric Words and Speakers." *JHS* 106 (1986): 43; and Rabel, *Plot and Point of View*, 126 note 32. Donna F. Wilson (*Ransom, Revenge, and Heroic Identity in the Iliad*, 76–94) gives a compelling argument regarding Agamemnon's flawed reliability and Achilles' furious reaction to it. She points out Agamemnon's usage of the notion of *apoina* (9.120) and its semantic associations of redeeming or recovering rather than that of *poinê* and its semantic association of paying back. In so doing "Agamemnon *gives apoina* in order to recover something—namely Achaean lives and perhaps even Achilles himself—but he pointedly does not *give back* Briseis or *pay back time*" (77). Achilles understands this perfectly well, which is why he "accuses Agamemnon of disabling the materially based status system by not distributing spoils fairly; he unmasks and rejects the *apoina* and [. . . demands] *poinê*" (83). Her argument, however, is less convincing regarding the emotional aspect of the term θυμαλγέα λώβην (*thumalgea lôbên* 90–93). Although "Achilles' language in 9.387 is not untraditional" and despite the fact that it "conforms precisely to the syntax and logic of traditional *poinê* themes within the *Iliad* and other archaic poetic traditions" (92), the exceptional status of the expression θυμαλγέα λώβην(*thumalgea lôbên*), referring to the emotional aspect of the insult, cannot be overlooked. Wilson herself concedes that "there is no exact verbal parallel for the phrase 'pay back heart-rending outrage' (ἀπὸ . . . δόμεναι θυμαλγέα λώβην) [*apo . . . domenai thumalgea lôbên . . .*]" (91), and her example from 1.97–98 lacks precisely the phrase θυμαλγέα λώβην (*thumalgea lôbên*).

37. "Nestor can say only that the tale of Troy is a tale of woe [. . .]. This passive view regards heroic achievement and endurance in the light of mere suffering inflicted, and looks back on it with self-pity, not with pride"; Griffin, *Homer on Life and Death*, 101. See also Taplin, *Homeric Soundings*, 111–15.

38. "Achilles' own speech [. . .] is [. . .] passionate, confused, continually turning back on itself [presenting] his own vision with a dreadful candor. And what this candor is concerned with is, precisely, the awful distance between appearance and reality; between what Achilles expected and what he got [. . .] it is about [. . .] a cleavage between seeming and being. The disillusionment consequent on Achilles' awareness of this cleavage, the questions his awareness of it gives rise to, and the results of all this in the events of the war, are possibly the real plot of the second half of the *Iliad*"; Adam M. Parry, "The Language of Achilles," in *The Language of Achilles and Other Papers*, 5–6 (Oxford: Clarendon, 1989 [1956]). Parry's claim that Achilles' tragedy is a sociolinguistic one, namely, that he is both alienated from his own society and has "no language, no terms, in which to express this kind of basic disillusionment with society and the external world" (6), was justly refuted by David B. Claus, "*Aidos* in the Language of Achilles," *TAPA* 105 (1975): 13–28, regarding the linguistic aspect; and Gill, *Personality in Greek Epic*, 135–36, regarding the social aspect.

Martin, *Language of Heroes*, 167–205, gives a thorough analysis of Achilles' style in order to vindicate his claim that "an independently existing 'language of Achilles' in the *Iliad* is an illusion" (171). Yet Parry is definitely right in marking this speech as a significant turning point in Achilles' tragic awareness.

39. On the similiarities between the two stories and Achilles' situation, see Ruth Scodel, "The Autobiography of Phoenix: *Iliad* 9.444–95," *AJP* 103 (1982): 131. On the connection between the tragic and the story of Meleager, see Jennifer R. March, *The Creative Poet*, Bulletin Supplement 49 (London: Institute of Classical Studies, 1987), 34–35.

40. Wolfgang Schadewaldt, *Iliasstudien* (Leipzig: Abhandlungen der philologisch-historischen Klasse der Sächsischen Akademie der Wissenschaften Band XLIII, Nr. VI, 1938), 142, is correct in stressing the prophetic aspect of the story of Meleager, although his interpretation concentrates on concrete occurrences and not on general patterns of events.

41. My interpretation underscores the double loss and therefore the double compensation, but it is also possible to see the episode as creating a parallel between two father-son relationships, that of Peleus and Phoenix and that of Phoenix and Achilles; see Dieter Lohmann, *Die Komposition der Reden in der Ilias* (Berlin: de Gruyter, 1970), 251. On surrogacy and its implications in this passage, see Alden, *Homer beside Himself,* 225–26 and note 125.

42. And see Scodel, "Autobiography of Phoenix," 132–34, for another aspect of Phoenix' subtlety concerning this complex situation.

43. On the repugnant appearance of the *Litai* and their deeply ambiguous nature, see Alden, *Homer beside Himself,* 206 and note 75.

44. "It is worth remembering that although the Λιταί [*Litai*] follow behind Ἄτη [*Atê*], they are not penitents for the damage she has done: they are seeking to apply a cure for it afterwards"; ibid., 200 note 55.

45. Emotional focalization is the psychological prism through which events are perceived and conceived emotively. See Shlomith Rimmon-Kenan, *Narrative Fiction: Contemporary Poetics* (London: Routledge, 1983), 80–81.

46. On the sequence according to which *Atê* is activated, see William F. Wyatt, "Homeric ΄ATH," *AJP* 103 (1982): 255–56. On the rejection of the *litai* of the embassy as the trigger for "a visitation from *Atê* resulting in some unspecified catastrophe" for Achilles, see Alden, *Homer beside Himself,* 202–3. On the analogy between Achilles' rejection of the *litai* from the embassy and Agamemnon's rejection of the *litai* from Chryses, see Alden, *Homer beside Himself,* 207–11.

47. For references to the different versions of the story, see Hainsworth, *The Iliad: A Commentary,* vol. 3, in his commentary on 9.524–605; and Alden, *Homer beside Himself,* 237–41 with notes.

48. "An *analepsis* is a narration of a story-event at a point in the text after later events have been told. The narration returns, as it were, to a past point in the story"; Rimmon-Kenan, *Narrative Fiction,* 46, after Gérard Genette, *Narrative Discourse: An Essay in Method,* trans. Jane E. Lewin (Ithaca and New York: Cornell University Press, 1980 [1972]), 40.

49. For a detailed analogy between Meleager and Achilles, see March, *The Creative Poet,* 30–33; see also Rabel, *Plot and Point of View,* 129 note 37, for other references.

50. For the story of Meleager as an exemplum, see Lohmann, *Die Komposition der Reden,* 270; and March, *The Creative Poet,* 30 and note 6. M. M. Willcock, "Mythological Paradeigma in the *Iliad*," *CQ* 14 (1964): 148–53, gives a detailed analysis of the story as a *paradeigma,* namely, as "a myth introduced for exhortation or consolation" (142). See also Von der Mühll, *Kritisches Hypomnema zur Ilias,* 176; and Alden, *Homer beside Himself,* who

perceives this story as "a negative or dissuasive paradigm" and "a pattern not to follow" (29, 179–290).

51. Note that it is not even clear whether Oeneus "forgot or did not intend" to insult (9.537) when he sinned against the goddess.

52. Apollo is also relevant to the story because it echoes one of the versions of Meleager's death, a version in which it was Apollo who brought the end of the hero; see March, *The Creative Poet*, 39–41; and Alden, *Homer beside Himself*, 237 note 145.

53. On the *Erinus*, see Hainsworth, *The Iliad: A Commentary* vol. 3, in his commentary on 9.568–69.

54. On the motif of conjugal love as "standing in higher esteem than the love of friends and relatives," see Johannes Th. Kakridis, *Homeric Researches* (Lund: C. W. K. Gleerup, 1949), 19.

55. On the importance of the notion of the *daimon* in converging divine intervention and human causality, see Lesky, "Göttliche und menschliche Motivation im homerischen Epos," 23–24.

56. On this point, see Ernst Howald, "Meleager und Achill," *RM* 73 (1924): 407; and Ruth Scodel, "The Word of Achilles," *CP* 84 (1989), 94.

57. In addition, there is also the question of the limits of the poet's license to diverge from the tradition in which he works, according to which Achilles must die in Troy. Yet here, as asserted in J. V. Morrison, "*Kerostasia, the Dictates of Fate, and the Will of Zeus in the Iliad*," *Arethusa* 30 (1997): esp. 283, 285, 288, 293, the poet of the *Iliad* repeatedly hints at his potential for transgressing the limits of his own tradition.

58. The death of Patroclus can also be explained by means of the pattern dictated by *Atê*, according to which "*Atê* has deprived Achilles of his friend Patroclus because he refused to accept Agamemnon's offer [. . .]. It matters little that Achilles is not guilty of an overt and more or less unprovoked offense as Agamemnon was: his unwillingness to accept recompense is treated as being as serious as the original offense itself"; Wyatt, "Homeric 'ATH," 256.

59. Claus, "*Aidos* in the Language of Achilles," 20, seems to be right in claiming a rational motivation for rejecting Agamemnon's presents embedded in the heroic code, according to which the hero must "avoid identification of himself from moment to moment with simple calculations of his worth and position" (21). However, his final conclusion that Achilles is "a rational and compassionate man attempting to operate within a complex system of mannered behavior" (28) is an exaggeration that overlooks the subjective and much stronger aspect of Achilles' decision to reject the presents. On the inability of Achilles to relinquish his anger, see Redfield, *Nature and Culture,* 16.

60. See Richard Janko, *The Iliad: A Commentary,* vol. 4: *Books 13–16* (Cambridge: Cambridge University Press, 1994), in his commentary on 16.1–100 and 16.101–277.

61. As claimed by D. L. Cairns, "Ethics, Ethology, Terminology: Iliadic Anger and the Cross-Cultured Study of Emotion," in *Ancient Anger: Perceptions from Homer to Galen,* ed. Susanna Braund and Glenn W. Most, 26 (*YCS* 32, 2003), Achilles' anger is dispositional, and as such it "always has the potential to erupt into occurrence whenever the individual is reminded of its original cause." Cairns's subtle description of the intricate relationship between anger and rationality is worth quoting in this context: "There is thus a rationality to *cholos;* it responds cognitively to a specific sort of scenario [. . .] at the same time, however, it is clearly not merely a cognitive-evaluative judgment; it is typically attended by a (paradoxically pleasant) desire for retaliation, so there is also a desiderative aspect; equally, though exhibiting rationality, it may evade the control of reason (24.584–85) [. . .]" (26).

62. "This is a moment of recognition: ἄρα with the imperfect shows the surprised recognition of what has always been true"; Scodel, "The Word of Achilles," 91. See also Pierre Chantraine, *Grammaire homérique I–II* (Paris: Klincksieck, 1948–53), 2.192. For the translation, in this case, of ἦν in the present tense, see J. D. Denniston, *The Greek Particles*[2] (Oxford: Clarendon, 1959), 36; and Janko, *The Iliad: A Commentary,* vol. 4, in his commentary on 16.60–61.

63. But Achilles' remarks are still equivocal, for "he omits his former stipulation (9.653) that the ships must be ablaze—another sign of weakening resolve"; Janko, *The Iliad: A Commentary,* vol. 4, in his commentary on 16.61–63.

64. On these impossibilities and Achilles' awareness of them, see ibid., commentary on 16.97–100.

65. This is an innovation of the poet, which "visibly identifies Patroclus as Achilles' substitute," as claimed by Janko in ibid., 310–11.

66. As demonstrated by Nagy (*Best of the Achaeans,* 292 and notes), Patroclus, being Achilles' θεράπων (*therapôn*), is also his surrogate. Yet as such he is doomed to death the moment he transgresses the limits set by his master (293–95). On the motif of the substitute and its function in the oral tradition, see Alfred B. Lord, *The Singer of Tales* (Cambridge: Harvard University Press, 1964), 186–87.

67. And see Richard Seaford, *Reciprocity and Ritual: Homer and Tragedy in the Developing City-State* (Oxford: Clarendon, 1994), 165.

68. Achilles mentions his own approaching death as closely connected with that of Hector (18.88–93), thus alluding to his two options: a short and glorious life if he stays in Troy and a long and inglorious one if he returns, indicated in 9.410–16.

69. In fact, Agamemnon's act is already defined as *atê* in the opening book of the *Iliad* (1.411–12) by Achilles and was gradually conceived as such by Agamemnon even before book nine, as demonstrated in Wyatt, "Homeric ᾽ATH," 249–51.

70. On *atê* as a means of explication, see ibid., 261–62.

71. The *locus classicus* for the definition of *atê* is Dodds, *The Greeks and the Irrational,* 5: "[I]n the *Iliad* [. . .] always, or practically always, *atê* is a state of mind—a temporary clouding or bewildering of the normal consciousness. It is, in fact, a partial and temporary insanity, it is ascribed, not to physiological causes, but to an external 'daemonic' agency." See also Margalit Finkelberg, "Patterns of Human Error in Homer," *JHS* 115 (1995): 21; Hainsworth, *The Iliad: A Commentary* vol. 3, in his commentary on 9.502–12; and Alden, *Homer beside Himself,* 200 note 54.

72. "*Atê* in Homer may thus be summed up as [. . .] an act which with hindsight appears inexplicable and hence attributed to an outside, i.e. superhuman agency"; Mark W. Edwards, *The Iliad: A Commentary,* vol. 5: *Books 17–20* (Cambridge: Cambridge University Press, 1991), in his commentary on 19.85–138. On *atê* as caused by external factor, see Finkelberg, "Patterns of Human Error," 20 and note 21. On Agamemnon's responsibility, see Lesky, "Göttliche und menschliche Motivation im homerischen Epos," 38.

73. On the deep change in Agamemnon as reflected in his speech, see Lesky, "Göttliche und menschliche Motivation im homerischen Epos," 42.

74. "There is no doubt that the Greeks, rightly or wrongly, regarded ἄτη (*atê*) and ἀπάτη (*apatê*) as etymologically related concepts"; R. D. Dawe, "Some Reflections on Ate and Hamartia," *HSCP* 72 (1967): 100.

75. On the *Iliad* as "a purposeful artistic composition, structured throughout by a master poet to achieve a particular effect on the *external* audience/readers," see Christine

Perkell, "Reading the Laments of *Iliad* 24," in *Lament: Studies in the Ancient Mediterranean and Beyond*, ed. Ann Suter, 95 (Oxford: Oxford University Press, forthcoming), emphasis in the original.

76. Note that *atê* is probably associated linguistically with *moira*, as claimed by Wyatt, "Homeric 'ATH," 272.

77. "Throughout these scenes [of killing Hector and mutilating his corpse] Achilles remains, oddly, a kind of victim. The intensity of his suffering is only partly hidden by the brilliance of his act. He achieves in his *aristeia* what for any other hero or for himself at another moment would have been the summit of happiness yet for him now is only an act of mourning"; Redfield, *Nature and Culture*, 107. But see Graham Zanker, *The Heart of Achilles: Characterization and Personal Ethics in the Iliad* (Ann Arbor: University of Michigan Press, 1994), 108–9, for a different view according to which "[w]ith the obsequies for Patroclus, Achilles' passion reaches its turning point. As he begins to face his comrade's death squarely, Achilles is enabled to give the fullest and the most direct expression to his affection and grief [. . .]."

78. On the importance of Priam's ritualistic supplication and the pattern consisting of a sequence of "crises of ritual" that is "set in motion by an unsuccessful ritual [the supplication of Chryses] at the very beginning of the *Iliad* [and] is concluded by a successful ritual [the supplication of Priam] at the very end," see Seaford, *Reciprocity and Ritual*, 66, 69–70.

79. "Achilles must come to accept the unchangeable, to release Hector's body, to let go and to let be"; Michael Lynn-George, "Structures of Care in the *Iliad*" *CQ* 46 (1996): 4.

80. See C. W. Macleod, *Iliad Book XXIV* (Cambridge: Cambridge University Press, 1982), in his commentary on 24.16; and Nicholas Richardson, *The Iliad: A Commentary*, vol. 6: *Books 21–24* (Cambridge: Cambridge University Press, 1993), in his commentary on 24.14–18.

81. The sentence preceding the tale (24.525–26) defines mortals as doomed by the gods to live with grief (ζώειν ἀχνυμένους) while the gods themselves are free of care (ἀκηδέες). "This brief statement is fraught with implications. The gods who determine the human condition of care are 'without care', carefree, indifferent, heedless, without concern or solicitude"; Lynn-George, "Structures of Care," 6. The passage is also marked by its atypical language, as demonstrated by Nicholas Richardson, *The Iliad: A Commentary*, vol. 6, in his commentary on 24.527–33.

82. On pity as the proper feeling of the hero toward his φίλοι (*philoi*), see Jinyo Kim, *The Pity of Achilles: Oral Style and the Unity of the Iliad* (Lanham, MD: Rowman and Littlefield, 2000), 67.

83. And see Macleod, "Homer on Poetry," 14; and Kim, *The Pity of Achilles*, 136.

84. On the connection of this passage with the poetics of the *Iliad* as a whole, see Kevin Crotty, *The Poetics of Supplication: Homer's Iliad and Odyssey* (Ithaca and London: Cornell University Press, 1994), 98–99. On the uselessness of mourning and the necessity of action as an exceptional characteristic of the epics, see Arnould, *Le Rire et les larmes*, 109–10.

85. This is Patroclus' claim in 14.33–35; see Janko, *The Iliad: A Commentary*, vol. 4, in his commentary on these lines for other ancient references to this notion.

86. This change corresponds to his movement from anger to pity, a movement that "can even be roughly measured statistically: 36 percent of all the occurrences of words of anger in the *Iliad* and only 9 percent of those of pity are found in the first five books; 10.5 percent of those of anger and 50 percent of those of pity are found in its last five books"; Most, "Anger and Pity," 51.

87. And see Charles Segal, *The Theme of the Mutilation of the Corpse in the Iliad* (Leiden: Brill, 1971), 65; and Graham Zanker, "Beyond Reciprocity: The Akhilleus-Priam Scene in *Iliad* 24," in *Reciprocity in Ancient Greece,* ed. Christopher Gill, Norman Postlethwaite, and Richard Seaford, 91 (Oxford: Oxford University Press, 1998).

88. On the meal as the culmination of Achilles' humane behavior toward Priam, see Zanker, "Beyond Reciprocity," 85.

89. On Niobe's eating after the death of her children as an ad hoc invention of the poet, see Kakridis, *Homeric Researches,* 98–102; and Willcock, "Mythological Paradeigma," 141–42. On the association of this passage and Achilles' renunciation of anger, see Christine Schmitz, "'Denn auch Niobe . . .'—Die Bedeutung der Niobe-Erzählung in Achills Rede (Ω599–620)," *Hermes* 129 (2001): 149–50.

90. See Segal, *Theme of the Mutilation,* 65–66 with note 3, for other references; and Seaford, *Reciprocity and Ritual,* 159–60.

91. "In book 22, when he deals the fatal wound to a Hector still clad in his armor, Achilles seems virtually to be killing himself—especially since we know from Thetis' prophecy in book 18 that he is in fact sealing his own fate"; Thalmann, *Conventions of Form and Thought,* 49.

92. "The ultimate tragedy of the *Iliad* is that Achilleus in the tradition, having first killed Hector in a war that has become partially meaningless for him, remains at Troy to be killed by Paris after that war has become almost totally meaningless"; Frederick Brenk, "Dear Child: The Speech of Phoenix and the Tragedy of Achilleus in the Ninth Book of the *Iliad,*" *Eranos* 84 (1986): 78.

CHAPTER 2

1. Smith, "Time, Times, and the 'Right Time'," 6.

2. Ibid.

3. But see Peter W. Rose, *Sons of the Gods,* 110–11, for a different interpretation, especially as regards Eumaeus.

4. On ἦος, which is "nowhere attested but to be inferred as the early Ionic form from comparison of Doric ἇς and Ionic ἕως, see the extensive note in Stephanie West, "A Commentary on Homer's *Odyssey,* Books i–iv," in *A Commentary on Homer's Odyssey,* vol. 1: *Introduction and Books i–viii,* ed. Alfred Heubeck, Stephanie West, and J. B. Hainsworth (Oxford: Clarendon , 2001 [1988]), in her commentary on 4.90–91.

5. οὐδ' ἄρ' ἔμελλεν / ἐκτελέειν (10.26–27). The emphasis is due to both the enjambment and the usage of ἄρα (*ara*) with μέλλειν (*mellein*), "denoting that the predestination of an event is realized *ex post facto,*" as claimed by Denniston, *The Greek Particles*², 36.

6. Prolepsis is "a narration of a story-event at a point before earlier events have been mentioned. The narration, as it were, takes an excursion into the future of the story"; Rimmon-Kenan, *Narrative Fiction,* 46, after Genette, *Narrative Discourse,* 40. The above case, according to Irene J. F. de Jong, *A Narratological Commentary on the Odyssey* (Cambridge: Cambridge University Press, 2001), in her commentary on 10.26–27, is "[a] somber prolepsis, containing the typical proleptic μέλλω." On prolepsis see the extensive bibliography in de Jong, *Narratological Commentary,* 16 note 41.

7. See also Mario Untersteiner, "Il concetto di δαίμων in Omero," *Atene e Roma* 41 (1939): 102–3.

8. The notion of *daimon* in the *Odyssey* has a specific denotation and refers to a power that thwarts one's genuine intentions; as formulated in ibid., 100: "Nell'*Odyssea* appare in particolar modo un'opposizione fra δαίμων e la volontà dell'uomo, fra la natura potente e le aspirazioni di un'anima.[. . .]. *Δαίμων* è dunque forza que contradice alla volontà dell'uomo, o, più esattamente, alla forma etica che la volontà dell'uomo si propone. [. . .]" [In the *Odyssey* there is an apparent and particular opposition between *daimôn* and man's will, between the potent nature and the aspirations of a soul. [. . .] *Daimôn* is therefore a power that stands in contrast to the will of man or, more precisely, to the ethical form that the will of man proposes.]

9. "The crew is forced into a situation where they are bound to incur guilt and then are justly punished," notes Alfred Heubeck in "A Commentary on Homer's *Odyssey*, Books ix–xii," in *A Commentary on Homer's Odyssey*, vol. 2: *Books ix–xvi*, ed. Alfred Heubeck and Arie Hoekstra (Oxford: Clarendon, 1989), in his commentary on 12.338.

10. As claimed by J. Bryan Hainsworth, "A Commentary on Homer's *Odyssey*, Books v–viii," in *A Commentary on Homer's Odyssey*, vol. 1: *Introduction and Books i–viii*, ed. Alfred Heubeck, Stephanie West, and J. Bryan Hainsworth (Oxford: Clarendon, 1988), in his commentary on 5.74–76.

11. In ibid., commentary on 5.152, Hainsworth states that Odysseus weeps because "all that life means to a hero, activity, struggle, achievement, has been taken away from him in exchange for internal indolence and pleasure." In addition to the fact that at this stage of his wanderings Odysseus has already renounced these values, at least in their crude Iliadic form, the text gives no support to this interpretation. In contrast, it does refer explicitly to the hero as "bewailing his homecoming" (5.153), an event that will not happen, as the hero knows after his visit to Hades, before an extreme quota of suffering will have been filled. The strife with the suitors—although abundant with activity, struggle, and achievement— is hardly a goal aspired to by the worn-out hero who still has so much to endure.

12. And see de Jong, *Narratological Commentary*, 128–29, delineating how "Hermes' embedded focalization is here marked explicitly."

13. On the motif of the hero who cries alone, see Arnould, *Le Rire et les larmes*, 57.

14. On the problematic of this line, see Heubeck, "A Commentary on Homer's *Odyssey*, Books ix–xii," in his commentary on 10.187–97.

15. "The hero has lost the will to live (498) i.e. he wishes to go to Hades, just at the moment when he is ordered, to his horror, to go to Hades. The irony is quite intentional"; ibid., commentary on 10.496–99.

16. κατεκλάσθη φίλον ἦτορ, the same formula as in 10.496.

17. On the formulas of crying, see Arnould, *Le Rire et les larmes*, 130.

18. The recurring formulas are θαλερὸν κατὰ δάκρυ χέοντες (10.570, 11.466, and its variant θαλερὸν κατὰ δάκρυον εἴβων [11.391]) and δάκρυσα ἰδών (11.55, 11.87, 11.395).

19. For this motif, see Joseph Russo, "A Commentary on Homer's *Odyssey*, Books xvii–xx" in *A Commentary on Homer's Odyssey*, vol. 3: *Books xvii–xxiv*, ed. Joseph Russo, Manuel Fernández-Galiano, and Alfred Heubeck (Oxford: Clarendon 1992), in his commentary on 17.304–5.

20. As noted by Heubeck, "A Commentary on Homer's *Odyssey*, Books ix–xii," in his commentary on 9.82–104, "There is significance in Odysseus' meeting the Lotus-eaters first: the λωτός [*lôtos*] plant, with its magical properties of suppressing the desire to return home, is symbolic of the insecurity of human existence poised precariously between the spheres of empirical reality and mythical unreality. [. . .] The encounter with the Lotus-eaters marks a

decisive turning-point; now Odysseus is in another world but he will not remain subject to it; he will succeed in crossing the fundamental boundary between the two worlds in the reverse direction."

21. On the parallel between the scene of the Lotophagi and that of the Sirens, see Gerald K. Gresseth, "The Homeric Sirens," *TAPA* 101 (1970): 207.

22. "The companions do not understand Odysseus' delay, and so address him as δαιμόνιε [*daimonie*] [. . . and] they think he must be possessed by a δαίμων [*daimôn*]"; Heubeck, "A Commentary on Homer's *Odyssey*, Books ix–xii," in his commentary on 10.472.

23. This aspect reveals the power of the Sirens as extraordinary even in the legendary parts of the world of the *Odyssey*. Unlike other sorceresses or female monsters, the Sirens do not have to hide the ghastly aspects of their shapes or actions in order to achieve their goal. The wild animals on Circe's island, an outcome of her witchcraft, are timid and friendly, like loyal dogs (10.212–19), while the heads of Scylla, an abhorrent monster, produce the sound of little puppies (12.85–92). The Sirens, in contrast, have such power that the moment one hears their voices one is doomed to death. On the Sirens' song as "a supreme— but fatal—variant of the heroic song of singers," see de Jong, *Narratological Commentary*, in her commentary on 12.39–54. On their magic song as "the leitmotif of the whole episode," see Gresseth, "The Homeric Sirens," 205 and note 6.

24. The Iliadic nature of the song of the Sirens can be detected on other levels; see Pietro Pucci, *The Song of the Sirens: Essays on Homer* (Lanham, MD: Rowman and Littlefield, 1998), 1–4.

25. "[The Sirens] appeal to two of the most prominent feelings of the Greeks: the love of music and poetry, and love of information and 'new things.' [. . .] So the temptation is something like that of the fruit of the tree of knowledge in Genesis 3.5"; W. B. Stanford, *The Odyssey of Homer*² (London: Macmillan, 1959), in his commentary on 12.184–91. Gresseth, "The Homeric Sirens," 206, however, is surely right to emphasize the fact that Odysseus could have sought this knowledge in a much less dangerous way than that offered by the Sirens. He also judiciously points out that the Sirens do not offer Odysseus any information regarding his homecoming.

26. That the Sirens' abode symbolizes the land of the dead is persuasively claimed by Gresseth, "The Homeric Sirens," 215–17, who thus explicates the otherwise bizarre double reference to the meadow on their island (this is a conventional part of the pattern describing the land of the dead, 208) and the fact that every Siren portrayed in plastic art, including those who appear in a depiction of this scene from the *Odyssey*, has wings (there are traditions, surely known to the poet of this episode, in which the human soul becomes a bird at death, 215). See also his references to Georg Weicker's *Der Seelenvogel in der alten Literatur und Kunst* (203, with notes 1 and 3, and 215).

27. The adjective ἀργός (*argos*) is a common epithet describing dogs in both the *Iliad* and the *Odyssey* (e.g., *Il.* 18.283 and 578, *Od.* 2.11, 17.62, 20.145). For its two meanings, "bright" (or "white") and "swift," see the extensive note in Russo, "A Commentary on Homer's *Odyssey*, Books xvii–xx," in his commentary on 17.292. Russo, in his commentary on 17.290–97, points out the poet's thoughtful decision to use a dog as the recognizer of the master after twenty years' absence. Odysseus' significant moment of return would have otherwise gone unmarked since he cannot be recognized by a human being without risking revealing his disguise.

28. Note also that the motif of "the dog at the door" is one of the conventions of hospitality scenes in the epics, as claimed by Steve Reece, *The Stranger's Welcome: Oral Theory and*

the Aesthetics of the Homeric Hospitality Scene (Ann Arbor: University of Michigan Press, 1993), 14–15. This formulaic element includes Eumaeus' dogs and their reaction both to Odysseus and to Telemachus, as well as Odysseus' encounter with his old dog, Argus.

29. See the thorough investigation of the iconography on tombstones by Carsten Schneider, "Herr und Hund auf archaischen Grabstelen," *JDAI* 115 (2000), where dogs are represented as an aristocratic animal associated with the leisure class.

30. And note Hainsworth, *The Iliad: A Commentary,* vol. 3, in his commentary on 10.360–64: "Greek draws no linguistic distinction between the hound, a noble creature [. . .] to which heroes in their pride may be compared, and the scavenging mongrel cur implied by the use of κύων (*kuôn*) as a term of abuse or insult."

31. "[I]f it were not for the restraints of civility, man would become to man as predator to prey. But on the battlefield, where all community norms are reversed, the warrior aims to establish exactly this relation with his enemy. As the warrior tends to become a predator, as he mobilizes the dog within him, so also he moves in the direction of eating his enemy"; Redfield, *Nature and Culture,* 198.

32. Ibid., 195.

33. "Telemachus, though still in danger, is seen to belong to Ithaca, to be well known, whereas the man who most properly belongs, as *anax* of the house and *basileus* in the community, the one man, moreover, whom Telemachus requires to remove the danger—this man seems a *xenos,* who was nearly killed by Eumaeus' sentries, the dogs"; Gilbert P. Rose, "Odysseus' Barking Heart," *TAPA* 109 (1979): 217–18.

34. I have found only two exceptions. The first takes place when the swineherd tells the disguised Odysseus that he is sure Odysseus is dead and has been eaten by dogs and birds of prey (14.133–34). The second is when the suitors threaten the swineherd that he will be eaten by his, the swineherd's, dogs (21.363–64). The first evokes the world of the *Iliad,* for it hints at a failed *nostos,* while the second reflects the brutality of the suitors, who are all doomed to death in the forthcoming battle with the master of the house.

35. See Manuel Fernández-Galiano, "A Commentary on Homer's *Odyssey,* Books xxi–xxii," in *A Commentary on Homer's Odyssey,* vol. 3: *Books xvii–xxiv,* ed. Joseph Russo, Manuel Fernández-Galiano, and Alfred Heubeck (Oxford: Clarendon, 1992), in his commentary on 22.474–77.

36. On the basic pattern of all recognition scenes after Odysseus' homecoming, see Chris Emlyn-Jones, "The Reunion of Penelope and Odysseus," *G&R* 31 (1984): 6–7.

37. The scar "is etched onto the hero's body and is physically inseparable from it. Indeed, unlike some other bodily attributes of Odysseus [. . .] the scar is implicitly presented as an indelible mark, that is, as an unchanging sign of Odysseus. [. . .] And, of course, the scar is shown only to those competent interpreters who can understand its meaning"; Kahane, *Diachronic Dialogues,* 103.

38. Erich Auerbach, *Mimesis: The Interpretation of Reality in Western Literature,* trans. Willard R. Trask (Princeton: Princeton University Press, 1953 [1946]), 7. Auerbach's thesis will be discussed further in chapter 5 with reference to the tragic and the absurd.

39. Cave, *Recognitions,* 23, justly stresses the association between recognition and narration in this episode: "The scar, then, is more than a sign by which Odysseus is recognized. It composes his identity by calling up retrospectively a fragment of a narrative, since only narrative can compose identity as continuity once a severance has occurred, and the scar here may well look like a sign of the wound, the hiatus, the severance constituted by Odysseus' wanderings."

40. The expression *eu katelexen* [εὖ κατέλεξεν] 19.464) is "another feature of Odysseus' adult character, [. . .] his skill as a story-teller, almost a poet"; R. B. Rutherford, *Homer: Odyssey Books XIX and XX* (Cambridge: Cambridge University Press, 1992), in his commentary on 19.464.

41. On the parallels between this recognition scene and the one with Odysseus' father, see Alfred Heubeck, "A Commentary on Homer's *Odyssey*, Books xxiii–xxiv," in *A Commentary on Homer's Odyssey*, vol. 3: *Books xvii–xxiv*, ed. Joseph Russo, Manuel Fernández-Galiano, and Alfred Heubeck (Oxford: Clarendon, 1992), in his commentary on 24.331–44 with references.

42. For the archaeological evidence, see Russo, "A Commentary on Homer's *Odyssey*, Books xvii–xx," in his commentary on 19.226–31.

43. Rutherford, *Homer*, in his commentary on 19.226–31. See also Gilbert P. Rose, "Odysseus' Barking Heart," 224–25.

44. For a subtle analysis of the triangle husband-wife-son in this recognition scene, see Wolfgang Schadewaldt, *Neue Kriterien zur Odyssee-Analyse: Die Wiedererkennung des Odysseus und der Penelope* (Heidelberg: Carl Winter Universitätsverlag, 1966 [1959]), 16–19.

45. On significant silences in the *Odyssey*, see Rutherford, *Homer*, 68–69.

46. On the interpretation of καὶ αὐτός as "even if alone," see Heubeck, "A Commentary on Homer's *Odyssey*, Books xxiii–xxiv," in his commentary on 23.168–72.

47. The exact meaning of Penelope's instruction, however, is obscure. See ibid., commentary on 23.177–89.

48. "The sign of the bed is, above all, a memory, a narrative of the past. Access to this narrative, the secret of the bed's making, is strictly limited. It is known to the parties involved in the communicative exchange, Odysseus and Penelope, who are also the only parties to make use of the bed"; Kahane, *Diachronic Dialogues*, 104.

49. For the many criticisms of this seemingly cruel and unnecessary test, see the bibliography quoted by Heubeck, "A Commentary on Homer's *Odyssey*, Books xxiii–xxiv," in his commentary on 24.216–18.

50. Heubeck's subtle analysis of this recognition scene and its aims is germane here: "With well-considered words Odysseus has succeeded in breaking down his father's self-control, but also, at the same time, releasing him from the paralysis of emotion, lethargy, and apathy. [. . .] In helping his father to give expression to his grief Odysseus has prepared the way forward to the moment of recognition. [. . .] His intention is not to put his father to the test, and certainly not to do so with 'teasing', 'mocking', 'humiliating', or 'heartlessly cruel' words. [. . .] On the contrary: Odysseus' words are calculated [. . .] to bring about an inner change in his father, and to make him capable of recognition" ("A Commentary on Homer's *Odyssey*, Books xxiii–xxiv," in his commentary on 24.315–17). See also Stephanie West, "Laertes Revisited," *PCPhS* 215 (1989): 126, who points out parallels of the theme of deception of the father in the Old Testament (Joseph and his father in Genesis 42–45) and in Yugoslavian return songs.

CHAPTER 3

An earlier version of this chapter appeared as "The Pivotal Scene: Narration, Colonial Focalization and Transition in *Odyssey* 9" in *American Journal of Philology* 128 (2007): 301–34.

1. See also Michael Silk, *Homer: The Iliad* (Cambridge: Cambridge University Press,

1987), 96: "[T]he greatest literature is wont to subvert the dominant ideological categories that it purports to, and does indeed also, embody: and thanks to Achilles, the *Iliad* surely does just this." See also the compelling reading of Perkell, according to which the laments of *Iliad* 24 serve as another strategy "by which the poet problematizes the traditional values of heroic epic" ("Reading the Laments of *Iliad* 24," 96). Her reading of the laments of Andromache, Hecuba, and Helen at the epic's end asserts that "these particular laments in this particular closure serve, in an exceptional and authentic way, to endorse a range of moral values alternative to those embodied in the heroic code of glory and, thus, that they function in opposition to the poem's dominant ideology" (107).

2. See the insightful remark of Camus in his fourth notebook: "Calypso offers Ulysses a choice between immortality and the land of his fathers. He rejects immortality. This is, perhaps, the whole sense of the *Odyssey*" (Calypso offre à Ulysse de choisir entre l'immortalité et la terre de sa patrie. Il repousse l'immortalité. C'est peut-être tout le sens de l'Odyssée); Jacqueline Lévi-Valensi, ed., *Albert Camus Œuvres Complètes II: 1944–1948* (Paris: Bibliothèque de la Pléiade, 2006), 945. Camus' *Le Mythe de Sisyphe* is discussed in chapter 4.

3. This notion serves as one of the basic theses of Emily R. Wilson's highly persuasive argumentation. She succinctly formulates her claim in the following: "Tragedy need not be concerned primarily with death; it may, rather, be about the failure to die, and about the sense that life is worse than death. [. . .] Living too long may be as upsetting as dying too soon, or more so, and it is equally 'tragic.' Tragedies need not end badly, and death is not the ultimate tragic experience. [. . .] Tragic overliving often blurs the distinctions between life and death. Excessive life is presented as a kind of living death" (*Mocked with Death*, 4–5).

4. Heubeck, "A Commentary on Homer's *Odyssey*, Books ix–xii," is no doubt right when he claims, in his commentary on 10.50–53, that "the resolve to bear patiently the burden imposed on him (ἔτλην [*etlên*] 53) characterizes the hero, whose outstanding quality of τλημοσύνη [*tlêmosunê*] is increasingly manifested during these adventures. [. . .] It cannot reasonably be said [. . .] that the lines reflect badly on the character of Odysseus." Yet to my mind he is wrong in his assertion that "[t]he decision facing Odysseus here [. . .] is radically different from the Iliadic deliberation scenes presenting ethical choice between two alternatives." In the world of the *Odyssey* the choice between death and suffering *is* an ethical one, which is why this deliberation scene is essentially the same as the ones in the *Iliad*. Compare, in contrast, Eurylochus' advice to the crew to kill the oxen of Apollo, claiming that even if the price for this act is death, it is better to die instantly than to waste away through lasting hunger (12.350–51). Heubeck, in his commentary on 12.350–51, notes that this passage is modeled on *Iliad* 15.511–12, where Ajax exhorts his comrades in arms to fight bravely against Hector. Yet, unlike Odysseus' deliberation, where Iliadic resonances shed heroic light on the protagonist, here the Iliadic echo is mainly ironic. Eurylochus' advice is in fact a coward's advice, for it encourages the crew to yield to their temptation instead of resisting courageously their urge to eat.

5. For Artemis as the bringer of "gentle death" (which is especially appealing in these contexts of extreme suffering), see Russo, "A Commentary on Homer's *Odyssey*, Books xvii–xx," in his commentary on 18.202.

6. M. Mikhail Bakhtin, *The Dialogic Imagination: Four Essays*, ed. Michael Holquist, trans. Caryl Emerson and Michael Holquist (Austin: University of Texas Press, 1981), 324, quoted in Schechet, *Narrative Fissures*, 54.

7. Schechet, *Narrative Fissures*, 55.

8. For other cases of Bakhtinian double discourse in the *Odyssey*, see John Peradotto,

"Bakhtin, Milman Parry, and the Problem of Homeric Originality," in *Bakhtin and the Classics,* ed. R. Bracht Branham, 66–68 (Evanston: Northwestern University Press, 2002).

9. Genette, *Narrative Discourse,* 186, emphasis in the original.

10. Ibid., 189.

11. On the different facets of focalization, see Rimmon-Kenan, *Narrative Fiction,* 77–82.

12. Carol Dougherty, *The Raft of Odysseus: The Ethnographic Imagination of Homer's Odyssey* (Oxford: Oxford University Press, 2001), 128 with note 19.

13. Ibid., 128.

14. See Rimmon-Kenan, *Narrative Fiction,* 95; Irene J. F. de Jong, "The Subjective Style in Odysseus' Wanderings," *CQ* 42 (1992): 3; and de Jong, *Narratological Commentary,* 223–24.

15. Many critics, however, regard the Cyclopes as asocial beings who were simply awakened from their sleep and wished to resume it as soon as possible. See Giacomo Bona, *Studi sull'Odissea* (Torino: G. Giappichelli, 1966), 75–77 and note 27; and Deborah Levine Gera, *Ancient Greek Ideas on Speech, Language, and Civilization* (Oxford: Oxford University Press, 2003), 5–6.

16. See de Jong, *Narratological Commentary,* 224, for examples. For critics that undermine the veracity of anything said by Odysseus in his narrative, see Hugh Parry, "The *Apologos* of Odysseus: Lies, All Lies?" *Phoenix* 48 (1994): 7 note 13.

17. Ove Jörgensen, "Das Auftreten der Götter in den Büchern ι-μ der Odyssee," *Hermes* 39 (1904); Werner Suerbaum, "Die Ich-Erzählungen des Odysseus: Überlegungen zur epischen Technik der *Odyssee,*" *Poetica* 2 (1968) . See also de Jong, "Subjective Style," 1, for other examples; and Hugh Parry, "The *Apologos* of Odysseus." Rainer Friedrich, "The Hybris of Odysseus," *JHS* 111 (1991): 16, judiciously points out that Jörgensen's law is not applicable to Odysseus' knowledge of Zeus' thoughts in 9.553–55.

18. Rimmon-Kenan, *Narrative Fiction,* 100, gives three main sources of unreliability: "the narrator's limited knowledge, his personal involvement, and his problematic value-scheme"; all are applicable to Odysseus. Again, unreliability does not necessarily imply lying, but it does call for a very careful reading of the narrator's words, where a distinction between facts and interpretation should be constantly maintained. See de Jong, "Subjective Style," 2 and note 11.

19. de Jong, *Narratological Commentary,* 226, points out the difference between Odysseus' "narrating focalization, i.e., his focalization at the moment of narration, when he has the benefit of hindsight" and his "experiencing focalization, i.e., his focalization in the past, when he was undergoing the events." Occasionally his adherence to experiencing focalization that leaves out important details reflects his seductive narrative technique since when he reveals these details later "he springs a surprise on his narratees and engages them even more in his story." This is definitely not the case here, where experiencing focalization reflects the narrator's loss of control during his regression to the agonizing experience of the past, as if the act of telling revives the scene with all its confusion and uncertainty.

20. And see Heubeck, "A Commentary on Homer's *Odyssey,* Books ix–xii," in his commentary on 9.39–61.

21. See, for example, *Il.* 5.533–42, 576–89; 11.489–91; 13.361–65, and *Od.* 13.384–88.

22. Note that Odysseus does tell his audience that the rest of the crew called the dead by name as part of the mourning process (9.64–66).

23. See Pucci, *Song of the Sirens,* 152–53.

24. On the paradisiacal nature of the places and their resemblance to Hesiod's Golden Age, see Christopher G. Brown, "In the Cyclops' Cave: Revenge and Justice in *Odyssey* 9," *Mnemosyne* 49 (1996): 16 and note 43; Jenny Stuart Clay, *The Wrath of Athena: Gods and Men in the Odyssey* (Princeton: Princeton University Press, 1983), 126–27; Gera, *Ancient Greek Ideas*, 13–14; Pura Nieto Hernández, "Back in the Cave of the Cyclops," *AJP* 121 (2000): 348; Ruth Scodel, "The Achaean Wall and the Myth of Destruction," *HSCP* 86 (1982): 49; and Pierre Vidal-Naquet, "Land and Sacrifice in the *Odyssey*: A Study of Religious and Mythical Meanings," in *Reading the Odyssey: Selected Interpetive Essays,* ed. Seth L. Schein, 41 (Princeton: Princeton University Press, 1996 [1970]). On the association between new worlds and the Golden Age, see Dougherty, *Raft of Odysseus*, 85–92.

25. This is one of the most common characteristics associated with a Golden Age, as claimed by Sue Blundell, *The Origins of Civilization in Greek and Roman Thought* (London and Sydney: Croom Helm, 1986), 137.

26. And note the depiction of the goats as "not avoiding the path trodden by men" (9.119).

27. As noted by de Jong, *Narratological Commentary,* 234, this passage is the longest "description by negation technique" in the epic.

28. On the centrality of the binary opposition civilized/uncivilized to the episode as a whole, see Clay, *Wrath of Athena,* 113.

29. In general, seafaring is far from a merely positive phenomenon in the ancient world. Christopher G . Brown, "In the Cyclops' Cave," 17 note 4, gives many references to seafaring as "fundamentally unnatural or as prompted by greed or as a desperate response to the harshness of human life." It was also a "τόπος [*topos*] to point out that there was no need for seafaring in the Golden Age."

30. For the centrality of the marvelous to the colonizer's focalization in a much later period, see Stephen Greenblatt, *Marvelous Possessions: The Wonder of the New World* (Oxford: Clarendon, 1991), 52–85, who titled the chapter and the book as a whole "marvelous possessions"; note also the direct connection between the voyages of Odysseus and "aesthetic and philosophical speculations on the relation between heroism and the arousal of wonder through a representation of marvels" 74.

31. "To assume that the Nymphs roused the goats so as to have an abundant hunt may correspond to the pious reflex of Odysseus, who would justify in this way the brutal intervention of man in the idyllic and uncanny island"; Pucci, *Song of the Sirens,* 157 note 57. Contra G. S. Kirk, *Myth: Its Meaning and Functions in Ancient and Other Cultures* (Cambridge: Cambridge University Press; Berkeley: University of California Press, 1970), 165, who endorses the colonial focalization without any reservation, regarding the island as "waiting to be developed by culture," seeing the Cyclopes as "inadequate to carry out this development" and commenting that Odysseus' men "begin the process by killing and cooking some wild goats that the Nymphs put up for them."

32. The formulaic expression Διὸς αἰγιόχοιο (*dios aigiochoio,* "of Zeus who bears the Aegis") reflects focalization, expressing an individual perception by means of a general oral device.

33. As claimed by Reece, *The Stranger's Welcome,* 131, the absence of the owner is remarkable since this is "the only Homeric hospitality scene in which the host is not found at home." Reece also discusses the signification of the uninvited crossing of the threshold (143).

34. *Xenia,* using Gabriel Herman's translation, is "ritualized friendship," which he

defines as "a bond of solidarity manifesting itself in an exchange of goods and services between individuals originating from separate social units"; *Ritualised Friendship and the Greek City* (Cambridge: Cambridge University Press, 1987), 10.

35. As indicated by Reece, *The Stranger's Welcome,* 126, the prominence the theme of *xenia* to the episode is even more remarkable due to its absence from all the other versions of this widely distributed folktale. For the different versions of the story, see Justin Glenn, "The Polyphemus Folktale and Homer's *Kyklôpeia,*" *TAPA* 102 (1971): 133–81; and Gabriel Germain, *Genèse de l'Odyssée: Le Fantastique et le sacré* (Paris: Presses Universitaires de France, 1954), 55–129.

36. "That Odysseus would have been better off had he not acted as he did is not so much an indication of recklessness on his part, but a reflection of the more crucial point that the hero assumes a set of values that does not hold true among the Cyclopes"; Christopher G. Brown, "In the Cyclops' Cave," 25. For critics deeming the entrance to the cave as folly, see Rainer Friedrich, "Heroic Man and *Polymetis:* Odysseus in the *Cyclopeia,*" *GRBS* 28 (1987): 121–22; and Heubeck, "A Commentary on Homer's *Odyssey,* Books ix–xii," in his commentary on 9.228–30.

37. The summary of Germain, *Genèse de l'Odyssée,* 68, is worth quoting in full: "Ils ont ensuite pillé les fromages, puis ils se sont cachés au retour du monstre et n'ont donné signe de vie qu'au moment où celui-ci, ranimant le feu, les a découverts. En un mot, ils se sont conduits en cambrioleurs surpris, très peu héroïques, d'une façon, en tout cas, qui n'a jamais été dans les traditions de l'hospitalité" (Then they plundered the cheese and soon afterward, upon the monster's arrival, they hid themselves, giving no sign of life, until this selfsame monster discovered them when he kindled the fire. In short, far from being heroic, they behaved like burglars taken by surprise, and in any case, they behaved in a manner that had never been part of the tradition of hospitality). Even if, as claimed by Friedrich, "Heroic Man," 128 note 17, the verb *ethusamen* does not signify slaughter of the cattle but merely an offering of dairy products, the behavior of Odysseus and his men is still a deep violation of the rules of *xenia,* as vindicated by Reece, *The Stranger's Welcome,* 132.

38. Contra Dougherty, *Raft of Odysseus,* 124, who claims that "the Cyclopes are completely ignorant of both the potential and the dangers of seafaring."

39. In this context, Robert Mondi's comment in "The Homeric Cyclopes: Folkatle, Tradition, and Theme," *TAPA* 113 (1983): 26, is revealing. After mentioning the Phaeacians' transfer from their former home by the Cyclopes, he goes on to say, referring to the island opposite the land of the Cyclopes, "There is no subtlety here: we are told explicitly that the place would have made a good habitation *for the Cyclopes* [*sic*] if only they had technological skill to build and operate ships." There is no subtlety in Odysseus' words, but the heteroglossic text, which consists of more than one focalization, is extremely subtle. The colonial focalization belongs to Odysseus alone, and the Cyclops' focalization gives another perspective on the story as a whole.

40. Friedrich, "Heroic Man," 126.

41. Stanford, *The Odyssey of Homer*².

42. As noted by Heubeck, "A Commentary on Homer's *Odyssey,* Books ix–xii," in his commentary on 9.39–61.

43. On the negative associations of merchandise in the *Odyssey* as realized in the stereotypic representation of the Phoenicians, see Dougherty, *Raft of Odysseus,* 103, 111–16.

44. Herman, *Ritualised Friendship,* 57.

45. And see ibid., 78–79.

46. On equality as the basis of *xenia*, see ibid., 37; on humiliation in *hiketeia*, see ibid., 56–57; see also Karl Reinhardt, "The Adventures in the *Odyssey*," in *Reading the Odyssey: Selected Interpetive Essays*, ed. Seth L. Schein, 81 (Princeton: Princeton University Press, 1996 [1948]).

47. See Heubeck, "A Commentary on Homer's *Odyssey*, Books ix–xii," in his commentary on 9.283–86.

48. Thus Reece, *The Stranger's Welcome*, 134, who analyses the whole scene, sees this act of the Cyclops as the ultimate outrage against the guests, for "instead of offering them a meal he makes a meal of them." It should be noted, however, that cannibalism is also associated with one of the most positive features of the world of the Cyclops, namely, its resemblance to Hesiod's Golden Age: the ruler of the universe during the Golden Age was Cronus, who ate his own children. See Hernández, "Back in the Cave of the Cyclops," 350–53; and Vidal-Naquet, "Land and Sacrifice," 36.

49. Dougherty, *Raft of Odysseus*, 135–38.

50. Gera, *Ancient Greek Ideas*, 14. Clay, *Wrath of Athena*, 114, notes, "The Cyclopes possess the art of fire-making, but, characteristically, they do not utilize it for cooking, but presumably only for light and warmth." Cooking, which is an essential indication of civilization, is also antiparadisiacal by nature since paradise is characterized by means of harmony between men and beasts. See Gera, *Ancient Greek Ideas*, 57–67, for the association between the Golden Age and vegetarianism.

51. Odysseus' two characteristics, "inquisitiveness and acquisitiveness," so exquisitely formulated by W. B. Stanford in *The Ulysses Theme: A Study in the Adaptability of a Traditional Hero*[2] (Ann Arbor: University of Michigan Press, 1963), 76, are often quoted in this context, as demonstrated by Christopher G. Brown, "In the Cyclops' Cave," 22 and note 61. Friedrich, "Heroic Man," who notes that acquisitiveness is a dubious trait for a heroic man (123), solves the problem by subordinating acquisitiveness to *xenia:* the wish to obtain gifts is a characteristic of the heroic man (124–26). So does Christopher G. Brown, "In the Cyclops' Cave," 23, but Odysseus' confused and even improper behavior still leaves room for doubt whether civilized *xenia* can really explain his entrance into the cave.

52. Schechet, *Narrative Fissures*, 30. An implied reader, unlike the real one, is a construct of the text. See Wolfgang Iser, *The Act of Reading: A Theory of Aesthetic Response* (Baltimore and London: Johns Hopkins University Press, 1978), 34; and Rimmon-Kenan, *Narrative Fiction*, 86.

53. For the "double-voiced discourse," see Bakhtin, *The Dialogic Imagination*, 324.

54. And see Reece, *The Stranger's Welcome*, 142, for a summary of the various reasons why "Odysseus and his men's behavior as guests can scarcely be considered exemplary."

55. "The Cyclopes' lack of maritime experience is underscored by the fact that it is the technology of shipbuilding that overcomes Polyphemus. Polyphemus' walking stick, a stick that is as big as the mast of a twenty-oared cargo ship becomes the instrument of his blinding; [. . .] The narrative thus presents maritime expertise as the appropriate and successful response to the threats posed by the Cyclopes"; Dougherty, *Raft of Odysseus*, 123–24.

56. Note that the olive wood is either an invention of the poet or adopted from a very rare version of the tale (Denys Page, *The Homeric Odyssey* [Oxford: Clarendon, 1955], 9 and note 16). As shown by Glenn, "The Polyphemus Folktale," 164, the most frequent weapon is a spit and not a stake (a fact that serves Anthony Snodgrass, *Homer and the Artists* (Cambridge: Cambridge University Press, [1998], 95, as one of the strongest reasons to reject the assumption that it was the Polyphemus passage that inspired the artists of two famous

kraters where the blinding of a giant is depicted). The change is definitely not without cause, and Page (*Homeric Odyssey*, 11), comments, "If the spit was to be used, the human victims must be cooked, as they so often are in the folk-tales, and as they are in the *Cyclops* of Euripides. Often enough they are cooked alive, and often enough the giant compels the survivors to share his dinner." However, the explanation he gives for the change of weapon, namely, that the cooking of human victims is "a deed of utmost barbarism, outside the law prescribed by tradition to the Odyssean story-teller," is not very convincing in light of the detailed description of the Cyclops' cannibalistic dinner. Glenn's explanation ("The Polyphemus Folktale," 166) is based on artistic calculations: the poet did not wish Odysseus to have a ready-made weapon that would give him an easy solution; instead, he preferred a challenging situation to elicit the skills of his hero. Claude Calame, *The Craft of Poetic Speech in Ancient Greece*, trans. Janice Orion (Ithaca and London: Cornell University Press, 1995 [1986]), 170, emphasizes the uncivilized aspect of the weapon, where the "eating of raw flesh underscores the savagery of the monster who [. . .] does not own any iron instrument, in accordance with the norms of ancient Greek culture." While I recognize that the uncivilized aspect of the Cyclops' way of living is indisputable, I find the savagery of the act of blinding impossible to ignore. As already claimed, the text advocates a reading in which civilization is frequently perceived as associated with savagery rather than being its ultimate opposite.

57. Thus Gera, *Ancient Greek Ideas*, 8, who states that "Both Odysseus' wine and his words are too sophisticated and too potent for the Cyclops, who can barely absorb either."

58. Page, *Homeric Odyssey*, 7; James N. O'Sullivan, "Nature and Culture in *Odyssey* 9," *SO* 65 (1990):12. Note also that the expression used by the Cyclops, "wine that is made of fine grapes" (οἶνον ἐριστάφυλον), is the same one used by Odysseus in his description of the land of the Cyclopes in 9.111, which is evidence of their shared focalization.

59. The wine was given to Odysseus by Maron, the priest of Apollo, as a token of his gratitude for the saving of his life during the battle. Odysseus claims that he and his men saved him "due to their pious dread" (ἁζόμενοι 9.200), and Charles Segal, "Divine Justice in the *Odyssey:* Poseidon, Cyclops, and Helios," *AJP* 113 (1992): 501, considers it to be "the result of a civilized exchange between men: respect for the gods, the inhibition of violence, and the giving guest-gifts." And yet the gift of such a huge quantity (9.204) of such rare and excellent wine (it is called "divine," θεῖον [9.205] and is hidden from most of the household [9.205–7] along with other valuables [9.201–3]), does not exclude the option of bribery. See also F. Ahl and H. M. Roisman, *The Odyssey Re-Formed* (Ithaca and London: Cornell University Press, 1996), 106–7, who consider Maron's wine as a means to inebriate Odysseus and his men and thus "destroy the very people who had plundered his city," a reasonable assumption in light of the fact that "[o]verindulgence in its abundance caused [Odysseus'] men to become drunk, indiscriminate in their slaughter of sheep and cattle, and so lax in their vigilance that the surviving Cicones, the city's inhabitants, were able to return." In sum, Odysseus' motives to present himself as a pious warrior are understandable, but the resisting reader is cued by the text not to take his narration at face value.

60. Note that Odysseus gives this false name only after the Cyclops is totally drunk (9.362), an indication of Odysseus' superb calculation: had the Cyclops been sober, he would probably have noticed the true nature of the name. The next time the Cyclops uses this name is immediately after his blindness (9.408), again hardly an occasion inviting stable thinking. Both cases are not an assertion of the Cyclops' sophistication, but rather noting that he is not merely gullible.

61. Contra Fajardo-Acosta, *The Hero's Failure*, 154, who claims that "Polyphemus, the supposed barbarian and enemy of all law and order, undergoes a character transformation which renders him, at the end of the adventure, into a much more pious and, in a sense, civilized creature than Odysseus."

62. See Pucci, *Song of the Sirens*, 127–28 and note 24. Without diminishing Pucci's complex portrait of the Cyclops, it seems to me that his presentation has its shortcomings. To begin with, Polyphemus is not exactly "stupid and intelligent by turns, as the narrative may require"; second, Odysseus' error in betraying his name is much more than a parallel to the Cyclops' stupidity, if stupidity it is; and, third, the claim that, "like the cultured and civilized, who describe the savage as the antithesis of themselves, so the savage sees the civilized man as the antithesis of his characteristics" presupposes an ahierarchical text, where plurality of voices implies equality of significance. The text, however, does not present Odysseus and the ogre as two equal faces of one and the same coin. Rather, it gives precedence to Odysseus' narrative and focalization without annihilating the Cyclops' angle. Complexity and multifaceted narration do not necessarily negate discrimination between different levels of importance. See also Peter Rose, *Sons of the Gods*, who claims that, while "[i]n the adventure that most obviously pits nature against culture, the encounter with the Cyclops, Odysseus emerges most concretely as the aggressive colonist" (137), "the dominant note is a triumphant ethnocentric celebration not only of the superior technology and character type but also of the cultural institutions that enabled the dramatic expansion of Greek horizons and influence in the eighth century" (138).

63. And see Dougherty, *Raft of Odysseus*, 123 note 2, for further discussion of this aspect of the similes. Quite expectedly, the blinding scene also has elements taken from Iliadic descriptions of a warrior's *aristeia*, as noted by Heubeck, "A Commentary on Homer's *Odyssey*, Books ix–xii," in his commentary on 9.375–94; and Reece, *The Stranger's Welcome*, 139. And yet even here there is ambiguity, for the scene arouses both admiration for Odysseus' courage and horror at his cruelty, as claimed by de Jong, *Narratological Commentary*, 243.

64. And see Heubeck, "A Commentary on Homer's *Odyssey*, Books ix–xii," in his commentary on 9.446–61.

65. See Pucci, *Song of the Sirens*, 127–28.

66. See Page, *Homeric Odyssey*, 5 and note 6. See also Calame, *Craft of Poetic Speech*, 143 and 162–63, who, despite persuasive reservations regarding the methodology that looks for an "original version" of the tale, concedes that the false name belongs to a group of stories that is essentially different from the other versions.

67. Page, *Homeric Odyssey*, 5 and note 8; Glenn, "The Polyphemus Folktale," 162–63.

68. And see Simon Goldhill's notion, in *The Poet's Voice: Essays on Poetics and Greek Literature* (Cambridge: Cambridge University Press, 1991), 36, that "Odysseus is both master of and mastered by his name."

69. See Friedrich, "Heroic Man," 129; and Goldhill, *Poet's Voice*, 35.

70. "Thus, the imperative of the moment is survival. The only alternative to ignominy is to escape from a world in which heroic acts become empty gestures and cannot even secure an honourable death"; Friedrich, "Heroic Man," 129.

71. See ibid., 130–31 with notes 21 and 22; and Christopher G . Brown, "In the Cyclops' Cave," 26 with note 73, for references. For the motif of concealing one's name and giving it after achieving victory in Indo-European legend, see Calvin S. Brown, "Odysseus and Polyphemus: The Name and the Curse," *Comparative Literature* 18 (1966): 198–99.

72. "An epithet almost confined to Odysseus and Achilles"; W. B. Stanford, *The Odyssey of Homer*², in his commentary on 8.3–4.

73. On this last remark, see Norman Austin, "Name Magic in the *Odyssey*," *California Studies in Classical Philology* 5 (1972): 16 note 24, who gives Eustathius' comment on the possible connection between the words *Outis* and *outidanos*.

74. The usage of the curse as the starting point for so many future miseries is probably an innovation of the poet. In the folktale analogues of the Polyphemus legend there is a marvelous object that helps the ogre to find the hero, who eventually succeeds in running away. The curse, which is the epic version of the marvelous object, has consequences more far-reaching than those of the object, and Odysseus cannot simply run away from it. The revelation of the name and the ensuing curse have consequences that exceed the limits of the scene, thus turning it into a seminal episode in Odysseus' lot not only in terms of the narrative, which consists of many scenes directly dependent on this occurrence, as claimed by Calvin S. Brown, "Odysseus and Polyphemus," 201–2, but also in terms of signification, for it is the revelation of the name that endows Odysseus with the tragic dimension of his life.

75. See ibid., 196; and Heubeck, "A Commentary on Homer's *Odyssey*, Books ix–xii," in his commentary on 9.531. See also Alice Webber, "The Hero Tells His Name: Formula and Variation in the Phaeacian Episode of the Odyssey," *TAPA* 119 (1989): 6, for the important difference between self-identification and name giving.

76. According to Finkelberg, "Patterns of Human Error," Odysseus' refusal to listen to his comrades is an essential part of his specific pattern of error, which derives from *atasthalie*. Actions stemming from *atasthalie* are "usually represented as having been committed notwithstanding the fact that the agent was explicitly warned not to take a particular course of action" (18). This pattern of error, the most dominant in the *Odyssey* as whole, is applicable to Odysseus' behavior in the Cyclops scene in its entirety, starting with his decision to stay in the cave despite the warnings of his crew (25). Friedrich's claim, in "Hybris," 25, that this is an act of hubris and not an error is refuted, on different grounds, both by Finkelberg, "Patterns of Human Error," 25 with note 46; and Christopher G. Brown, "In the Cyclops' Cave," 21–22. On the inversion of the rules of *xenia* as regards both the revelation of the name upon departure (and not upon arrival) and the subsequent curse (instead of blessing), see Reece, *The Stranger's Welcome*, 128. See also A. J. Podlecki, "Guest-Gifts and Nobodies in *Odyssey* 9," *Phoenix* 15 (1961): 132.

77. See Pucci, *Song of the Sirens*, 127. On the psychological mechanism of the process where the suppressed heroic self "is bound to return, and does so with a vengence after the escape from the cave," see Friedrich, "Heroic Man," 130.

78. For this point, see John Peradotto, *Man in the Middle Voice: Name and Narration in the Odyssey* (Princeton: Princeton University Press, 1990), 140. See also Christopher G. Brown, "In the Cyclops' Cave," 29, who claims that Odysseus' "Iliadic" conduct "both brings him to the cave in the first place and afterwards incurs the wrath of Poseidon."

79. On the several instances in Odysseus' life where he has to become a "nobody," both before and after the Cyclops scene, see Austin, "Name Magic," 14.

80. And see Friedrich, "Heroic Man," 123 note 7 and 132, for the development of the character of Odysseus through his adventures in order to become the new Odysseus.

81. Lines 9.556–57 are formulaic; they recall the ease of the feast in the island opposite that of the Cyclopes at the beginning of the episode (9.161–62) and are constantly utilized to mark the successful end of other hazardous adventures such as the encounter with Circe

(10.476–77) and the descent to Hades (12.29–30). Line 9.556 reverberates the carefree feast of the gods that terminates the first book of the *Iliad* (1.601).

82. For Odysseus' long process of learning, see R. B. Rutherford, "The Philosophy of the *Odyssey*" *JHS* 106 (1986): 153.

83. Bona, *Studi sull'Odissea,* 46, is no doubt right when he claims that these words, far from signifying the narrator's unreliability, indicate his present awareness of his painful lot; for the close association between Odysseus' remarks in the Cyclops scene and the storm raised by Zeus as a punishment for the eating of the cattle, see Heubeck, "A Commentary on Homer's *Odyssey,* Books ix–xii," in his commentary on 12.385–88.

84. On the acquaintance of the Cyclopes with the nearby island and its identification with the former land of the Phaeacians, see Norman Austin, *Archery at the Dark of the Moon: Poetic Problems in Homer's Odyssey* (Berkeley: University of California Press, 1975), 144–45; and Clay, *Wrath of Athena,* 128 and note 136.

85. In fact, the colonial association between the Phaeacians and the Cyclopes goes even deeper, as demonstrated by Dougherty, *Raft of Odysseus,* 122–42.

86. For the historical remnants in the narrative of the Phaeacians' colonization see Hainsworth, "A Commentary on Homer's *Odyssey,* Books v–viii," in his commentary on 6.4–10. See also Dougherty, *Raft of Odysseus,* 127–30; and Vidal-Naquet, "Land and Sacrifice," 41, 52. For a general treatment of the *Odyssey* and historical colonization, see Irad Malkin, *The Returns of Odysseus: Colonization and Ethnicity* (Berkeley: University of California Press, 1998).

87. On the problem of the odd *asyndeton* (τίς πόθεν εἰς) and the solution, reflected in the above translation, see Webber, "The Hero Tells His Name," 6; on the formula, see page 4.

88. See Bernard Fenik's long discussion of the problem under the title "The Nameless Stranger" in his *Studies in the Odyssey* (Wiesbaden: Franz Steiner Verlag, 1974), 5–60. I do not find Webber's dismissal of the problem convincing ("The Hero Tells His Name," 10). Her claim that Odysseus actually answers Arete's question in his opening remarks (7.241–43), where he "distinguishes between telling his whole story and answering Arete's question," is based on regarding the second and unformulaic question as an explanation of the first and formulaic one, as indicated by her translation: "tell me who you are: that is, where did you get those clothes." There is, however, no indication in the text for her "that is," and the first independent part of the question still begs for an answer. On the suppressed name as a leitmotif in the *Odyssey,* see Peradotto, *Man in the Middle Voice,* 101; on the deferral of the hero's name, see pages 116–17.

89. See Webber, "The Hero Tells His Name," 11.

90. Wilhelm Mattes, *Odysseus bei den Phäaken: Kritisches zur Homeranalyse* (Würzburg: K. Triltsch, 1958), 129–40, is surely right when he points out that Odysseus' inner perception of his identity has dramatically changed due to his suffering and that the reason for his silence in response to Arete's question should be sought in his past. I disagree, however, with Mattes's optimistic vision of Odysseus' ability to regain his former self, as well as with his conception of Odysseus being, in fact, even now the same "old Odysseus." There are things that are irrecoverable, and Odysseus, who recovers from his dismal emotional state only partially, will never again be the same old Odysseus.

91. "The Odysseus, then, who embarks on the Cyclops adventure is the essential Heroic Man. Yet little does he know how incongruous are the heroic spirit and the world he is about to enter"; Friedrich, "Hybris," 22. On the *Odyssey* as an epic formulating not just a

different kind of ethics but a different kind of heroism than that of the *Iliad*, see Margalit Finkelberg, "Odysseus and the Genus 'Hero'," *G&R* 42 (1995): 1–14 , especially 10.

92. Dougherty, *Raft of Odysseus*, 162–64.

93. Ibid., 164–65.

94. Ibid., 265. Dougherty also points to the analogy to the blinding of the Cyclops.

95. Ibid., 169.

96. For these echoes see Heubeck, "A Commentary on Homer's *Odyssey*, Books xxiii–xxiv," in his commentary on book twenty-two lines 3, 6–7, 16, 17, 30, 33, 42, 65, 75, 88, 100, 102, 110, 196–98, 224, 286, and 328–29.

97. See ibid., 356–58.

98. And see Rutherford, "Philosophy," 160 note 79.

99. Contra Fajardo-Acosta, *The Hero's Failure*, 35, who claims that "[t]he predatory, savage identity of the original Odysseus resurfaces with a vengeance during the slaughter of the suitors. All the principles of the poetic craft, all semblance of civilization and rationality disappear from Odysseus to give way to his murderous impulses of revenge and destruction."

100. Contra Fajardo-Acosta's unsubstantiated postulation: "According to the principles of fate, as set down and characterized by the different adventures of Odysseus, the killing of the suitors is a morally abhorrent act which cannot escape the divine retribution. A story which appears to have a happy ending is in reality a tragedy in disguise with a severe punishment awaiting the hero at some unspecified point in the future" (ibid., 36).

101. On the usage of the verb εὐχετάασθαι (*euchetaasthai*) in this context, see Heubeck, "A Commentary on Homer's *Odyssey*, Books xxiii–xxiv," in his commentary on 22.412; On "Odysseus' humane and compassionate speech", see Heubeck, "A Commentary on Homer's *Odyssey*, Books xxiii–xxiv," in his commentary on 22.411–16.

102. Rutherford, "Philosophy," 160–61, emphasis in the original.

CHAPTER 4

1. On the complexity of the critical discourse on characterization, especially in light of the fact that "there is no word in fifth-century Greek which means 'character' as it seems most often used in literary criticism," see Goldhill, "Reading Greek Tragedy," 172–74.

2. This same Agamemnon is himself rebuked on two different occasions for suggesting flight. On the first one it is Diomedes who stands against him in the assembly (9.26–49), and in the second Odysseus opposes his idea to flee Troy (14.64–102).

3. On the notion of *charma* and its implications, see Arnould *Le Rire et les larmes*, 33.

4. "In the entire *Iliad*, in fact, retreat of the Greeks is confined to those scenes [. . .] in which they are forcibly pushed back by the gods"; Bernard Fenik, *Typical Battle Scenes in the Iliad: Studies in the Narrative Techniques of Homeric Battle Description* (Wiesbaden: Franz Steiner Verlag, 1968), 64.

5. Reasonable calculations that qualify the strict code of honor can also be detected in the duel that Hector proposes to the Greeks in order to bring the war to its end. When Menelaus stands up to fight Hector, Agamemnon restrains him, saying that he, Menelaus, is not strong enough, a fact confirmed by the remarks of the narrator (7.103–6). Although Agamemnon concedes that this restraint necessarily causes Menelaus distress, he nevertheless insists on Menelaus giving up fighting (7.110), repeating twice the claim that an unnecessary battle with one stronger than oneself is folly (7.109–10). The fact that his speech is

given in public proves such calculation to be legitimate and therefore not necessarily shameful within the heroic context. Menelaus can be brave, but his power is not great enough to fight Hector. Consequently, there is nothing wrong in avoiding the unnecessary and inevitable death that fighting with Hector implies.

6. On the motif of the withdrawal of the hero, see William C. Scott, *The Oral Nature of the Homeric Simile* (Leiden: Brill, 1974), 41–42.

7. On other occasions the narrator emphasizes the fact that in general Ajax does not yield to such forces. See, for example, 13.321–25 and the usage of the verbs *eixeie* (321) and *chôrêseien* (324). For another compulsory retreat by Ajax, see 11.544–74.

8. Menelaus' decision not to fight in this situation is an exception; for the pattern and its specific realization in this case, see Fenik, *Typical Battle Scenes*, 163–65. On the long ancestry of the lion motif, which probably goes back to Mycenaean times, see Scott, *Oral Nature*, 60 and note 2. Scott remarks, "The lion similes occur, naturally enough, in war contexts usually describing one warrior against a hostile group. Whether the lion is pursued or pursuer depends on the hero's situation in the battle" (61).

9. "[The deliberation] confirms Odysseus' stature. He is not, of course, a match for all the enemy, but he never turns to flight. He remains the chieftain Odysseus against a throng of lesser men. We note that his chances of success carry no weight and are not mentioned. They are irrelevant. No distinctions or mitigating allowances are permitted to blur the absoluteness of his choice"; Bernard Fenik, "Stylization and Variety: Four Monologues in the *Iliad*," in *Homer: Tradition and Invention*, ed. Bernard Fenik, 72 (Leiden: Brill, 1978). See also Arthur W. H. Adkins, "Threatening, Abusing, and Feeling Angry in the Homeric Poems," *JHS* 89 (1969): 15; and M. M. Willcock, ed., *The Iliad of Homer: Books I–XII* (London: Macmillan, 1978), in his commentary on 11.404–10.

10. Stephen Scully, "The Language of Achilles: The ΟΧΘΗΣΑΣ Formulas," *TAPA* 114 (1984): 14.

11. G. S. Kirk, *The Iliad: A Commentary*, vol. 2: *Books 5–8* (Cambridge: Cambridge University Press, 1990), in his commentary on 8.146–50, compares this "heroic shame over prudent retreat" to Hector's words to Andromache at 6.441–43. Andromache's offer, however, in which she proposes that Hector avoid returning to battle, has nothing to do with either retreat or prudence, and it is on this basis that it is rejected by Hector.

12. "ἄρα with the imperfect (here pluperfect) has the effect of 'so it is true after all that, etc.'"; Willcock, *The Iliad of Homer: Books I–XII*, in his commentary on 8.163.

13. "The number three is typical in this sort of situation, of a man trying to assert himself against the will of heaven or the restriction of fate"; ibid., commentary on 8.169–70.

14. See also Fenik, "Stylization," 77–78.

15. Note, in this context, the remark of Seth L. Schein, *The Mortal Hero: An Introduction to Homer's Iliad* (Berkeley: University of California Press, 1984), 180, that "Hector is never compared to a predator, but instead several times is a predator's potential victim."

16. And see Edwards, *The Iliad: A Commentary*, vol. 5, in his commentary on 17.142, for this derision and the implications of its resemblance to Hector's words to Paris at 3.39 and 13.769.

17. See ibid., commentary on 18.306–7.

18. On the problematic of Hector's rejection of Polydamas' council and its conception as part of a tragic conflict, see Abrogast Schmitt, "Wesenszüge der griechischen Tragödie: Schicksal, Schuld, Tragik," in *Tragödie: Idee und Transformation*, ed. Hellmut Flashar, 41–45 (Stuttgart: Teubner, 1997).

19. "[T]his image presents a *tableau* of peace and harmony strikingly in contrast with the grim reality of its context"; Carroll Moulton, *Similes in the Homeric Poems* (Göttingen: Vandenhoeck and Ruprecht, 197), 82.

20. There are, however, exceptions. See M. M. Willcock, ed., *The Iliad of Homer: Books XIII–XXIV* (London: Macmillan, 1984), in his commentary on 22.136–37.

21. Von der Mühll, *Kritisches Hypomnema zur Ilias*, 335.

22. Fenik, "Stylization," 83.

23. For this group, see Fenik, *Typical Battle Scenes*, 97–98.

24. Ibid., 83–84.

25. Ibid., 83.

26. Ibid., 85.

27. Ibid., 83.

28. The same unexplained lenience toward Hector's flight can be found in Scully, "Language of Achilles," 15, who, following Fenik, compares Agenor's soliloquy to that of Hector and claims in two consecutive sentences that "[l]ike Agenor, Hector decides to stand firm against Achilles' attack; but after his resolve, he suddenly loses courage and runs. Agenor's soliloquy clearly anticipates this one and seems to underline the magnitude of Hector's [. . .]." If Agenor's soliloquy contributes to the characterization of Hector by means of analogy, then it is on a shared foundation of cowardice rather the nonexistent magnitude of the frightened hero.

29. Auerbach, *Mimesis*, 7.

30. Ibid., 6–7.

31. Ibid., 8–11.

32. Ibid., 11–12.

33. On these similes, see Hermann Fränkel, *Die homerischen Gleichnisse* (Göttingen: Vanderhoeck and Ruprecht, 1921), 78–81.

34. In Rimmon-Kenan's terminology, "permanent gaps" are those that "remain open even after the text has come to an end" (*Narrative Fiction*, 128). Schechet's narratological method describes analysis through this kind of fissure as follows: "The method here is similar to working a puzzle. The puzzle pieces located within the frame both disclose the information they contain and outline the adjacent missing pieces" (66).

35. All citations from *Le Mythe de Sisyphe* are from the edition of Lévi-Valensi, *Albert Camus Œuvres Complètes I*. On the provenance of the notion of the absurd and Camus' originality in using it, see pages xxxiii–xxxiv. It is interesting to note that Aristotle's comment on the episode hints at another parallel between Hector's flight and absurd thinking. In chapter 24 of the *Poetics*, during the comparison between epic and tragedy, Aristotle notes that "the chasing of Hector in the *Iliad*, if presented on the stage, would be ridiculous due to the contrast between Achilles who shakes his head and his men who stand still" (24.1460a14–16). A similar distorted and incomprehensible mimicry is utilized by Camus in one of the most famous passages in his book where he discusses the relationship between mechanical gestures and the absurd: "Dans certaines heures de lucidité, l'aspect mécanique de leurs [les hommes] gestes, leur pantomime privée de sens rend stupide tout ce qui les entoure. Un homme parle au téléphone derrière une cloison vitrée; on ne l'entend pas, mais on voit sa mimique sans portée; on se demande pourquoi il vit. [. . .] C'est encore l'absurde" (229). [In certain hours of lucidity the mechanical aspect of [men's] gestures, their pantomime devoid of sense, renders with stupidity everything that surrounds them. A man speaks on the telephone behind a glass partition. It is impossible to hear him, but one sees

his mimicry without impact: one asks oneself why he lives. [. . .] [T]his is also the absurd.] See also the example in the notebooks where a wife merely sees the gestures of her husband beyond a glass without being able to hear him (Lévi-Valensi, *Albert Camus Œuvres Complètes II,* 879).

36. On the possible association of the absurd with the tragic, see Stephen Halliwell, "Greek Laughter and the Problem of the Absurd," *Arion* 13, no. 2 (2005): 123. Halliwell's article, however, concentrates on the expression of the absurd in ancient Greek thought not by means of the tragic but rather through its opposite, what he terms as "existential laughter," which is "laughter (whether literal or metaphysical) that embodies an attitude not to specific situations but to life, even the cosmos, as a whole" (122).

37. "At the end [. . .] we reach a lucid understanding and a clear perception of human reality as split between a yearning for the absolute and a longing for transcendent unity on the one hand, and an awareness of the limitations and finality of human ability on the other. This, precisely, is the concept of the absurd"; Avi Sagi, "Is the Absurd the Problem or the Solution? *The Myth of Sisyphus* Reconsidered," *Philosophy Today* 38 (1994): 283.

38. In his notebook (Lévi-Valensi, *Albert Camus Œuvres Complètes II,* 871) Camus insists on the fact that "the absurd is the opposite of the irrational" (L'absurde [. . .] est le contraire d'un irrationnel). On the notion of the absurd as including rather than excluding sense, see André Comte-Sponville, "L'absurde dans *Le Mythe de Sisyphe*," in *Albert Camus et la philosophie,* ed. Anne-Marie Amiot and Jean-François Mattéi, 161 (Paris: Presses Universitaires de France, 1997): "L'absurdité n'est donc pas l'absence de sens: ces expressions ont bien un sens (c'est même parce qu'elles ont un sens qu'elles peuvent être absurdes)" [Absurd thinking is therefore not the absence of meaning. Its expressions have, without doubt, sense (actually, it is because they have sense that they are capable of being absurd)]. See also Lévi-Valensi, *Albert Camus œuvres complètes I,* xxxi, on the association between absurd recognition and human grandeur and superiority. On Sisyphus as a tragic hero, resembling, among others, Oedipus, see Monique Crochet, *Les Mythes dans l'œuvre de Camus* (Paris: Editions Universitaires, 1973), 67–68. On the tragic aspect of Oedipus as manifested in his recognition of the absurd, see the remarks in Camus' third notebook (Lévi-Valensi, *Albert Camus œuvres complètes II,*" 882). On the notion of the tragic as a unifying aspect of Camus' oeuvre, see Fernande Bartfeld, *L'effet tragique: Essai sur le tragique dans l'œuvre de Camus* (Paris and Geneva: Champion-Slatkin, 1988).

39. In *Le Mythe de Sisyphe* Kierkegaard is an example of a Christian believer who does not merely reveal the absurd but actually lives it (Kierkegaard "fait mieux que de découvrir l'absurde, il le vit," 236), and Dostoevsky is another in his *The Brothers Karamazov*—a text suffused with the problem of the existence of god, presenting the problem of the absurd. True, this is not an absurd work, "but what contradicts the absurd in this novel is not its Christian character" ("ce qui contredit l'absurde dans cette oeuvre, ce n'est pas son caractère chrétien," 296). "It is possible to be Christian and absurd" ("On peut être chrétien et absurde," 296), "for convictions do not prevent incredulity" ("les convictions n'empêchent pas l'incrédulité," 296). See also Georges Pascal, "Albert Camus ou le philosophe malgré lui," in *Albert Camus et la philosophie,* ed. Anne-Marie Amiot and Jean-François Mattéi, 176 (Paris: Presses Universitaires de France, 1997).

40. And see the entry in his third notebook, in Lévi-Valensi, *Albert Camus Œuvres Complètes II,* 886: "[L]e fond de la noblesse (la vraie, celle du cœur) c'est le mépris, le courage et l'indifférence profonde" [The deepest nobility (the real one, that of the heart) is contempt, courage and profound indifference].

41. The simile is also unusual in its components, for "comparisons which explicitly refer to psychological states are rare in the *Iliad*" (Moulton, *Similes*, 84).

42. Thus Moulton states, "[T]he dream image contrasts with the three pursuit similes which preceded: time is slowed down in the vehicle, and the stasis of the situation in the dream is juxtaposed with the idea of speed, which dominates the other comparisons [. . .] a strange aura of unreality tinges the scene" (ibid., 84). Moulton is disturbed by the fact that "we cannot be sure about what the simile precisely means; for it is not clear in the end who is dreaming. Is it only Achilles or is it both men?"(84). Nevertheless the discussion is concluded by claiming that "what the image may have lost through imprecision is insignificant when compared with its frightening, suggestive power" (84). The simile, however, has lost nothing through imprecision. On the contrary, it is exactly this imprecision that creates the uncanny atmosphere so essential to the suggestive power of this "absurd" simile. For other similes describing a state of unresolved or balanced conflict see Fränkel, *Die homerischen Gleichnisse*, 58–59.

43. The notion of the circle is stated explicitly in the text, when the poet says that both warriors "were whirling around the city" (22.165).

44. On the motif of the "watching gods," see Griffin, *Homer on Life and Death*, 179–204.

45. It is also a sign of their basic indifferent aloofness, as succinctly articulated by Nicholas Richardson, *The Iliad: A Commentary*, vol. 6, in his commentary on 22.185–87: "The formular character of several parts of this scene in heaven gives it a rather detached and stilted quality, in contrast to the intensity of the surrounding narrative. The gods preserve an elaborate courtesy towards each other, as if excessive involvement with the struggle on earth would be undignified."

46. Richardson (ibid., commentary on 22.214–47) says that "[t]he deception of Hector has always disturbed Homer's readers" and brings as evidence Scholium bT's comment on the impropriety of a deceitful goddess. His claim that in the *Iliad* and the *Odyssey* "gods regularly use deception to bring doom" is no doubt true, yet to my mind it merely accentuates their astounding nature rather than mitigating it. After all, deception is not a *sine qua non* in this context, and the gods' decision to indulge their proclivity for trickery is especially horrific when a mortal's lot is on the scales.

47. On the importance of the absence of hope to the notion of the absurd, see Comte-Sponville, "L'absurde," 163.

CHAPTER 5

An earlier version of this chapter appeared as "*Mise en Abyme* and Tragic Signification in the *Odyssey:* The Three Songs of Demodocus," in *Mnemosyne* 59 (2006): 208–25.

1. On reflexive and self-reflexive writing in ethnographic texts, see Schechet *Narrative Fissures*, 85–104.

2. André Gide, *Journal, 1889–1939* (Paris: Bibliothèque de la Pléiade, 1948), 41; Lucien Dällenbach, *Le Récit spéculaire: Essai sur la mise en abyme* (Paris: Seuil 1977). The topic is still a fruitful one; see Brian McHale, "Cognition *en Abyme:* Models, Manuals, Maps," *Partial Answers* 4 (2006): and ibid, 176 for bibliography.

3. Dällenbach, *Le Récit spéculaire*, 16–17. The concept is not restricted to narrative fiction (16 note 1).

4. This realization is beyond the legitimate limits of Dällenbach's treatise, (ibid., 104–5), but see Lillian Eileen Doherty, *Siren Songs: Gender, Audiences, and Narrators in the Odyssey* (Ann Arbor: University of Michigan Press, 1995), 113. On the general nature of Demodocus' songs as *mise en abyme*, see Thalmann, *Conventions of Form and Thought*, 158, who refers to them as a "play within a play." See also Irene J. F. de Jong, "The Homeric Narrator and His Own *Kleos*," *Mnemosyne* 59 (2006): 194–96, for another parallel between Demodocus and his audience and the narrator and his audience regarding the *kleos* of the singer.

5. See Rutherford, "From the *Iliad* to the *Odyssey*," 48 and note 32, for the widely accepted view that this song alludes to the *Iliad*. My treatment of the issue, however, regards the song as more than just alluding to the other epic.

6. The significations of the term *kleos*, however, are subtler than those denoted by the word *glory* as indicated by Margalit Finkelberg, *The Birth of Literary Fiction in Ancient Greece* (Oxford: Clarendon, 1998), 74–88, especially 76. The topic has been much discussed; see Nagy, *Best of the Achaeans*, 16–17, and his notes in these pages; Goldhill, *Poet's Voice*, 69–72; and Pucci, *Song of the Sirens*, 36–48, 208–14. On *klea andrôn* and its echoes of the *Iliad*, see Oliver Taplin, "The Earliest Quotation of the *Iliad*?" in *"Owls to Athens": Essays on Classical Subjects Presented to Sir Kenneth Dover*, ed. E. M. Craik, 111–12 (Oxford: Clarendon, 1990). On the relation of this expression to poetry, see Andrew Ford, *Homer: The Poetry of the Past* (Ithaca and London: Cornell University Press, 1992), 59; and Rice Mackie, "Song and Storytelling: An Odyssean Perspective," *TAPA* 127 (1997): 79 note 6.

7. In fact, book eight of the *Odyssey* reverberates book eighteen of the *Iliad* in many passages; see A. F. Garvie, *Homer: Odyssey Books VI–VIII* (Cambridge: Cambridge University Press, 1994), in his commentary on lines 22–23, 246–49, 274, 275, 349, 461–62, and 556–63. See also Oliver Taplin, "The Shield of Achilles within the *Iliad*," *G&R* 27 (1980): 4–11, for the connection between the scenes on the shield and scenes from the *Odyssey*.

8. On the exceptionality of this kind of presentation of a song see Scott Richardson, *The Homeric Narrator* (Nashville: Vanderbilt University Press, 1990), 84–85. In addition, the song as a whole is quite probably an innovation of the poet of the *Odyssey* as claimed by Walter Marg, "Das erste Lied des Demodokus," in *Navicula Chiloniensis: Studia Philologica Felici Jacoby Professori Chiloniensi Emerito Octogenario Oblata*, 19–22 (Leiden: Brill, 1956); and Margalit Finkelberg, "The First Song of Demodocus," *Mnemosyne* 40 (1987). See also Nagy, *Best of the Achaeans*, 22–25; and Pucci, "Odysseus Polutropos," 218 note 10.

9. However, he does serve as the leader of the embassy to Apollo's priest in the first book of the *Iliad* (1.311, 430–45).

10. Bruce Karl Braswell, "The Song of Ares and Aphrodite: Theme and Relevance to *Odyssey* 8," *Hermes* 110 (1982): 137 and note 27, concludes his essay with an explicit reference to the second poem as a *mise en abyme*. His discussion, however, limits the device to the eighth book of the *Odyssey* and does not apply it to the poem as a whole.

11. On cunning as a characteristic associating Hephaestus and Odysseus, see Jens-Uwe Schmidt, "Ares und Aphrodite—der göttliche Ehebruch und die theologischen Intentionen des Odysseedichters," *Philologus* 142 (1998): 206–7. Note that the epithet *poluphrôn* (inventive) is used solely for Hephaestus (8.297 and 327) and Odysseus (1.83, 14.424, 20.239, 20.329, 21.204). For the resemblance between the two as regards their exceptional intellectual capacities, see Rick M. Newton, "Odysseus and Hephaestus in the *Odyssey*," *CJ* 83 (1987): 14; and Pucci, "Odysseus Polutropos," 197, 217. For other connections between the two see Newton, "Odysseus," 13 and note 8; and Froma I. Zeitlin, *Playing the Other:*

Gender and Society in Classical Greek Literature (Chicago: University of Chicago Press, 1996), 36–37.

12. And see Garvie, *Homer: Odyssey Books VI–VIII*, in his commentary on 8.278.

13. On the notion of the spider and its strong allusion to Penelope in this context, see ibid., commentary on 8.280.

14. The emphasis given to poets and poetry in the *Odyssey* has been discussed by many critics. See Goldhill, *Poet's Voice*, 57 note 98; and de Jong, *Narratological Commentary*, 191 note 1.

15. With only one exception (*Il.* 11.104), this epithet appears solely in formulas used for either Hephaestus or bards; see Keith Stanley, *The Shield of Homer: Narrative Structure in the Iliad* (Princeton: Princeton University Press, 1993), 311 note 38.

16. On the exceptionality of Hephaistos' lameness, see Marie Delcourt, *Héphaistos ou la légende du magicien* (Paris: Les Belles Lettres, 1982 [1957]), 121.

17. The bifurcation of the internal audience of the epic in order to portray two possible responses to the narrated events recurs in Odysseus' story of his descent to the world of the dead; see Doherty, *Siren Songs*, 90–92, for the phenomenon and its implications. On the profound moral and social ambiguities in all of Demodocus' songs and their important implications for the poem as a whole, see S. Douglas Olson, "*Odyssey* 8: Guide, Force, and the Subversive Poetics of Desire," *Arethusa* 22 (1989): 139.

18. And see Penelope's response to Phemius' song (1.328–44). Strong response to terrible events that are highly connected with the recent history of the addressee is not confined to the world of the *Odyssey*. In a much later period the Athenians were overwhelmed by the dramatic representation of the catastrophe that happened to their beloved ally city, Miletus. They consequently fined the poet Phrynichus for emotional abuse as described in Herodotus 6.21.2. For the delicate balance between distance and involvement in the narrated events, see Macleod, "Homer on Poetry," 3.

19. Contra Christopher G. Brown, "Ares, Aphrodite, and the Laughter of the Gods," *Phoenix* 43 (1989): 290, who claims that "the exchange between Apollo and Hermes is in fact [. . .] a parenthesis" and that since Poseidon does not laugh "the basic seriousness [. . .] in the situation is maintained." Poseidon's reticence is the exception rather than the rule here, and the gods' laughter is indicative of their general attitude toward adultery. Despite the fact that "The *Odyssey* seems to be much more preoccupied with the question of justice than the *Iliad*" (287), Brown's comparison between divine and human morality is misleading. The gods can, and do, afford themselves things that mortals cannot and should not afford themselves. Schmidt, "Ares und Aphrodite," 210–19, offers a more subtle reading of this episode, claiming for a transitory stage between two theological perceptions, an old and immoral one that starts giving place to a new and moral one. The song attests to "Theologie im Umbruch" (theology in the midst of radical change), where both theologies appear side by side, interacting in such a way that "die alten Vorstellungen als Basis oder Anlaß zur Manifestation der neuen Überzeugungen dienen" ("the old conceptions serve as a basis or a cause for the manifestation of new convictions," 217).

20. On the ironic implications of this phrase, see Daniel B. Levine, "*Odyssey* 18: Iros as Paradigm for the Suitors," *CJ* 77 (1982): 203.

21. See Donald Lateiner, *Sardonic Smile: Nonverbal Behavior in Homeric Epic* (Ann Arbor: University of Michigan Press, 1995), 28. On the association between the bursting of laughter in these cases, see Arnould, *Le Rire et les larmes*, 158–59.

22. See Paul Friedländer, "Lachende Götter," in *Studien zur antiken Literatur und*

Kunst, 4–5 (Berlin: de Gruyter, 1969 [1934]). On the epithet, see Bryan J. Hainsworth, "Good and Bad Formulae," in *Homer: Tradition and Invention,* ed. Bernard C. Fenik, 45 (Leiden: Brill, 1978); Garvie, *Homer: Odyssey Books VI–VIII,* in his commentary on 8.361–62; and Silvia Milanezi, "Le Rire d'Hadès," *DHA* 21 (1995): 239 and note 44.

23. The Latin quotation is from D. R. Shackleton Bailey's edition, *Q. Horatius Flaccus: Opera*⁴ (Munich und Leipzig: Teubner, 2001).

24. The connection between the verb *terpein* and Odysseus' weeping reaction is discussed in Zs. Ritoók, "The Views of Early Greek Epic on Poetry and Art," *Mnemosyne* 42 (1989): 336–39; see also Macleod, "Homer on Poetry," 8.

25. On the word *kosmos* as referring to the order of the song, as well as to its close connection with the expression *kata moiran* in the context of Demodocus' songs, see Finkelberg, *Birth of Literary Fiction,* 126–29; see also Ford, *Homer,* 121–24.

26. In fact, it is possible to regard the combination of Demodocus' first and third songs as a *mise en abyme* of the Trojan War as a whole, as claimed by Finkelberg, *Birth of Literary Fiction,* 147.

27. On Odysseus' failure to control Demodocus' song, see E. L. Harrison, "Odysseus and Demodocus: Homer, Odyssey θ 492f," *Hermes* 99 (1971): 379.

28. On *aisa* as a preordained event that is destined to occur, see Bernard Clive Dietrich, *Death, Fate, and the Gods* (London: Athlone Press, 1965), 256–57.

29. See ibid., 272–73.

30. See ibid., 227–28.

31. See de Jong, *Narratological Commentary,* 216 note 26, for references.

32. Similes such as those comparing a woman to a man are termed "reverse similes" by Helene P. Foley, "'Reverse Similes' and Sex Roles in the Odyssey," *Arethusa* 11 (1978): 7. These similes "seem to suggest both a sense of identity between people in different social and sexual roles and a loss of stability, an inversion of the moral" (8). See also Moulton, *Similes,* 130–31.

33. On the eccentricity of Odysseus as a heroic figure, see Stanford, *Ulysses Theme,* 66–80; see also Finkelberg, "Odysseus and the Genus 'Hero'."

34. On the expression θητευέμεν ἄλλῳ (*thêteuemen allô*) as denoting a state worse than that of a slave, see Heubeck, "A Commentary on Homer's *Odyssey,* Books ix–xii," in his commentary on 11.488–503; for the difference between the Achilles of the *Iliad* and that of the *Odyssey* as reflecting different types of the genus "hero," see Finkelberg, "Odysseus and the Genus 'Hero'," 11. See also Thalmann, *Conventions of Form and Thought,* 168; and Griffin, "Homer and Excess," 88.

35. A somewhat problematic epithet to begin with, as noted by Garvie, *Homer: Odyssey Books VI–VIII,* in his commentary on 8.2–3. On the process through which Odysseus goes while hearing this poem and the connection of Odysseus' insight on the human condition with Achilles' deep understanding in the last book of the *Iliad,* see Crotty, *Poetics,* 123–27.

36. On this topic see de Jong, *Narratological Commentary,* 198.

37. "[The Phaeacians'] simple enjoyment of Demodocus' songs about Troy is contrasted with Odysseus' tears, and the implied audience of the epic as a whole is invited to observe this contrast rather than merely to adopt the Phaeacians' response"; Doherty, *Siren Songs,* 90–91.

38. See Hainsworth, "A Commentary on Homer's *Odyssey,* Books v–viii," in his commentary on 8.564–71.

39. See Garvie, *Homer: Odyssey Books VI–VIII,* in his commentary on 8.564–70; and

Gregory Nagy, "Reading Bakhtin Reading the Classics," in *Bakhtin and the Classics,* ed. R. Bracht Branham, 71–96 (Evanston: Northwestern University Press, 2002), 84–85.

40. On the ambivalence concerning the Phaeacians in general, see Garvie, *Homer: Odyssey Books VI–VIII,* 22 note 74.

41. This postulation is also relevant to the level of narration of the *Odyssey* in general and its impact on its audience. The *Odyssey* keeps cultivating its narratees' false expectations and incessantly nourishes them with inaccuracies and ambiguities until finally they (or we) are "put in the same position as characters who assume a future course of events that does not occur, and our similarity of perspective encourages the audience's sympathy with the mortal characters and their limited knowledge"; Scott Richardson, "The Devious Narrator of the *Odyssey,*" *CJ* 101 (2006): 339.

42. The translation is based on the edition of H. Lloyd-Jones and N. G. Wilson, *Sophoclis fabulae* (Oxford: Clarendon, 1990).

CHAPTER 6

An earlier version of this chapter appeared as "Tragic Hephaestus: The Humanized God in the *Iliad* and the *Odyssey,*" in *Phoenix* 40 (2006): 1–20.

1. Her smile is mentioned twice, at 1.595 and 1.596, and this proximity adds emphasis to the repetition. See also Latacz, Nünlist, and Stoevesandt, *Homers Ilias Gesamtkommentar,* for formulaic and stylistic characteristics in their commentary on 1.595 and 596.

2. On the laughing gods, see Friedländer, "Lachende Götter," especially 9.

3. As indicated by Kirk, *The Iliad: A Commentary,* vol. 1, in his commentary on 1.599–600. This act of self-humiliation is, however, far from being a convincing basis for the analogy to the "division of the bread and distribution of the wine enacted by Christ at the Last Supper" made by Fajardo-Acosta, let alone for his claim that "[i]n both cases the act of giving and sharing is an attempt to create a community of human beings united by bonds of mutual service, trust, and affection" (*The Hero's Failure,* 26). The gods are definitely not a community of human beings, and "mutual service, trust, and affection" can be hardly claimed as among their representative characteristics.

4. As noted by Scholium bT to line 584.

5. On shared laughter at an object of derision as a unifying force for the laughing group, see Arnould, *Le Rire et les larmes,* 34.

6. The first critic to perceive that the narration in book eighteen depicts another fall was the scholiast in Scholium A in his commentary on 1.591; see Bruce Karl Braswell, "Mythological Innovation in the *Iliad,*" *CQ* 21 (1971): 20–21, for further discussion.

7. On mention of Eurynome in this context, see ibid., 21 note 2.

8. See Kirk, *The Iliad: A Commentary,* vol. 1, in his commentary on 1.586–94.

9. Zeus as Hephaestus' father is probably an innovation of the poet of the *Iliad;* it is also echoed in the *Odyssey* (8.312). In the common tradition, the traces of which can already be found in Hesiod, Hera is the sole parent of Hephaestus; see Delcourt, *Héphaistos,* 31–33.

10. κήδεα λυγρά 18.430, ἄλγε' 18.431, ἔτλην 18.433, γήραϊ λυγρῶι 18.434, ἀρημένος 18.435, ἄχνυται 18.443, ἀχέων 18.446, ἔφθιεν 18.446, λοιγόν 18.450.

11. Parry's article originally appeared in French in 1928. My references are to its English translation in Milman Parry, *The Making of Homeric Verse: The Collected Papers of Milman Parry* (Oxford: Oxford University Press, 1971), 1–190.

12. For treatments of the noun-epithet formula as a literary phenomenon that transgresses the limits of its conventional metrical function, see Egbert J. Bakker, *Poetry in Speech: Orality and Homeric Discourse* (Ithaca and London: Cornell University Press, 1997), 159 note 9.

13. For the poet's innovative usage of a traditional formula in order to express an idea not provided by this same tradition, see Finkelberg, *Birth of Literary Fiction*, 148–49 and 149 note 40.

14. For the applicability of these formulas to oral technique, see the table in Milman Parry, *Making of Homeric Verse*, 39.

15. See C. J. Ruijgh, "D'Homère aux origines proto-mycéniennes de la tradition épique," in *Homeric Questions*, ed. Jan Paul Crielaard, 75–77 (Amsterdam: J. C. Gieben, 1995). See also Hainsworth, "Good and Bad Formulae," 45, who claims that the formula "ox-eyed mistress Hera" (βοῶπις πότνια Ἥρη) is based on a generic, and therefore old, epithet of Hera and lost ground later to the formula "the white-armed goddess Hera" (θεὰ λευκώλενος Ἥρη): the former occurs eleven times in the epics while the latter appears nineteen times. For a detailed discussion of the cultural origins of "ox-eyed," see Pulleyn, *Homer: Iliad I*, in his commentary on 1.551.

16. It should be emphasized, however, that the conception of the dog in the epics is equivocal: in addition to its negative depiction, it is also portrayed very favorably, as I demonstrate in chapter 2.

17. See Manfred Faust, "Die künstlerische Verwendung von κύων 'Hund' in den homerischen Epen," *Glotta* 48 (1970): 25.

18. See 13.623, 21.394, 21.420, and 22.345.

19. "The dog was in Greece emblematic of shamelessness, because it will do in public what people should not, and look you in the eye as it does so"; Pulleyn, *Homer: Iliad I*, in his commentary on 1.159. See also Faust, "Die künstlerische Verwendung," 26–29. The dog as a symbol of shamelessness is also a recurrent interpretation in the Scholia, for which see Margaret Graver, "Dog-Helen and Homeric Insult," *Classical Antiquity* 14 (1995): 44 note 17.

20. See Carla Mainoldi, *L'image du loup et du chien dans la grèce ancienne* (Paris: Ophrys, 1984), 104–9; and Segal, *Theme of the Mutilation*, 38–41.

21. See section C in the classification of Faust, "Die künstlerische Verwendung," 11–19.

22. See Segal, *Theme of the Mutilation*, 33. See also Scholium bT in the commentary on line 67 for the accentuated humiliation in the passage due to the dogs' behavior.

23. On the resemblance of this passage to Tyrtaeus fr.10.21–30 and the problematic this resemblance entails, see the extensive note in Nicholas Richardson, *The Iliad: A Commentary*, vol. 6, in his commentary on 22.66–76. On dogs and cannibalism, see Graver, "Dog-Helen," 48.

24. For the radical nature of the change, see Bakker, *Poetry in Speech*, 201–4, who treats "ox-eyed" (βοῶπις) as the most essential element of this noun-epithet formula. See also Joan O'Brien, "Homer's Savage Hera," *CJ* 86 (1990): 123–24, for the usage of the regular formula as the poet's transformation of the received myth and cult of Hera as a savage goddess.

25. It is either the sky or Mount Olympus (1.497); see Pulleyn, *Homer: Iliad I*, in his commentary on 1.195 for the different traditions of the gods' dwelling.

26. See Griffin, *Homer on Life and Death*, 184; and Laura Slatkin, *The Power of Thetis: Allusion and Interpretation in the Iliad* (Berkeley: University of California Press, 1991), 108–9.

27. In the *Iliad* Lemnos is a symbol of defeat and exile; see Olson, "*Odyssey 8*," 138 note 11.

28. On binding as the ultimate penalty in the divine realm, see Slatkin, *Power,* 68.

29. For the literary evidence, see Delcourt, *Héphaistos,* 86–87; see also Martin L. West, "The Fragmentary Homeric Hymn to Dionysus," *ZPE* 134 (2001): 3 with notes 6 and 7. For the visual evidence, see Guy Hedreen, "The Return of Hephaistos, Dionysiac Procession Ritual, and Its Creation on a Visual Narrative," *JHS* 124 (2004), especially 40–42, 51–53.

30. See West, "Fragmentary Homeric Hymn," 3–4, for the history of the identification of the fragment containing the myth as a part of the hymn.

31. Unlike Braswell, "Song of Ares and Aphrodite," 136 note 25, who rejects any possibility of the poet of the *Odyssey's* acquaintance with that myth, basing his notion on the very problematic claim that "[t]he story of the binding of Hera by Hephaestus is foreign to the *Iliad* and the *Odyssey* in which both are on very good terms," I do not find this possibility entirely improbable; see West, "Fragmentary Homeric Hymn," 3 note 9. Note also that the phrase "Thetis took him to her bosom" (Θέτις θ' ὑπεδέξατο κόλπωι 18.398) is a recurrence, with a very slight modification of 6.136 (Θέτις δ' ὑπεδέξατο κόλπωι). The latter citation refers to Thetis' protection of Dionysus, while the citation from book eighteen alludes to her protection of Hephaestus; although the events are narrated in two completely different contexts, they do share the portrait of Thetis as a motherly and protective figure in addition to the aquatic location of the incident. No doubt, the connection thus created between the three gods would be even more emphatic if the poet of the *Iliad* were acquainted with the above-mentioned myth.

32. Griffin, *Homer on Life and Death,* 199: "Men are of enough importance to make Zeus incur trouble for their disputes; at the same time they are beneath the serious notice of the gods, who apply to them the words which the haughty Suitors use when their princely banquet is disturbed by the quarrel of the beggars."

33. Taplin, *Homeric Soundings,* 133: "The immortals [. . .] have endless time to be carefree, whatever the passing, temporary disturbances."

34. This special status regarding time and space is also the main characteristic of the shield Hephaestus creates for Achilles; see Michael Lynn-George, *Epos, Word, Narrative, and the Iliad* (Atlantic Highlands, NJ: Humanities Press International, 1988), 178–79.

35. See Slatkin, *Power,* 52, for the radical difference between Thetis' helplessness in the *Iliad* and her traditional role as divine protectress.

36. See Griffin, *Homer on Life and Death,* 195.

37. And see Irene J. F. de Jong's comment in *Narrators and Focalizers: The Presentation of the Story in the Iliad* (Amsterdam: John Benjamins, 1987), 217, that Thetis never mentions her son's name because he is the sole person she thinks about.

38. And see Griffin, *Homer on Life and Death,* 190–91. For Thetis' last scene on Olympus, see O'Brien, "Homer's Savage Hera," 119–20.

39. They also recur in 18.462 and with a slight variation in 18.614.

40. Hephaestus is a master builder of magnificent dwellings and a prime creator of miraculous objects of craftsmanship: the scepter of Zeus that was later given to Agamemnon (2.100–102), Hera's chamber (14.166–67), Hera's throne (14.238–40), the Aegis of Zeus (15.307–10), the porticos of Zeus' abode (20.10–12), and, most of all, the shield of Achilles (18.469–613).

41. The literature on this topic is vast; see, for example, the bibliography in Edwards's introduction to this passage in *The Iliad: A Commentary,* vol. 5, 200–209.

42. Thus, Sandrine Dubel, "L'arme et la lyre: Remarques sur le sens du bouclier d'Achille dans l'Iliade," *Ktema* 20 (1995): 252: "C'est donc parce qu'il est incapable de protéger Achille de la mort qu'Héphaistos forge un θαῦμα destiné à glorifier le héros. Les armes

sont ici explicitement coupées de leur fonction utilitaire [. . .] comme le souligne encore l'absence de tout motif apotropaïque dans l'*ecphrasis* qui suit" [It is in fact because he cannot protect Achilles from death that Hephaestus forges a θαῦμα [marvel] that is destined to glorify the hero. The armor here is explicitly denied its aiding function (. . .) an aspect that is underlined once again by the absence of any apotropaic motif in the subsequent *ekphrasis*].

43. Being "a marvel to the eye" (*thauma idesthai*) is also a characteristic of another of Hephaestus' artistic creations, the tripods that can move of their own accord (18.376–80); see Taplin, "Shield," 3. On the expression "a marvel to the eye," see Ritoók, "Views," 344 and note 40.

44. The notion of the shield as an object mainly aimed at the beholder was pointed out by Lynn-George, *Epos, Word, Narrative*, 190. However, his conception of the shield as a symbol of survival due to its capacity to arouse wonder beyond the death of its bearer seems to me inaccurate. The main function of the shield in the *Iliad* is not to present art as a means of transcending death but rather to indicate more forcefully the terrible implications of death's irreversible finality.

45. "Was Homer so hinstellt, sind die *Grundformen* der Welt und des Lebens. Sie sind geordnet nach dem Prinzip des *Gegensatzes*. Doch ist dieser Gegensatz nicht lediglich Symmetrie und nur formale Antithetik. Er ist innere *Polarität*, in der das Gegensätzliche sich gegenseitig bedingt und hält und je das umfassende Ganze darstellt" [What Homer puts down in this way are the *basic forms* of the world and life. They are ordered according to the principle of *opposition*. This opposition, however, is not merely a symmetry, nor is it just a formal antithesis. It is an inner *polarity* in which each of the opposing parts depends on its opposite, holds it, and represents the comprehensive whole]; Wolfgang Schadewaldt, *Von Homers Welt und Werk* (Leipzig: Koehler and Amelang, 1944), 291.

46. See Edwards, *The Iliad: A Commentary*, vol. 5, in his commentary on 18.498–500; on the function of suspension in this scene, see Lynn-George, *Epos, Word, Narrative*, 182–84.

47. On the complexity of the notion of strife (*neikos*), see Adkins, "Threatening," 10.

48. Alden, *Homer beside Himself*, 54–55, points out the basic resemblance between the two scenes that revolve around strife, but she deems the first one a depiction of an ideal world where the disputants settle their argument by means of the law (57). The shield, however, does not provide sureties for such a notion, and, what is more, its engravings as a whole tend to the opposite conclusion.

49. At least according to the version that appears in the *Odyssey* (11.321–25).

50. For another motivation for the mention of Crete on the shield, see Robert J. Rabel, "The Shield of Achilles and the Death of Hector," *Eranos* 87 (1989): 86–87.

51. See 5.29–36, 430, 764–65, 850–87; 20.69; and 21.391–414.

52. See also Øivind Andersen, "Some Thoughts on the Shield of Achilles," *SO* 51 (1976): 10.

53. As demonstrated by Karl Reinhardt in his seminal research, "Das Parisurteil," the judgment of Paris is the basis of the *Iliad* despite being merely hinted at in the last book of the epic. See also Griffin, *Homer on Life and Death*, 195 and note 49. The decision of the beleaguered army to reject the proposal of compensation in favor of a violent breach of the armistice is also reminiscent of the duel scene between Paris and Menelaus that ended with the arrow of Pandarus (4.122–47). Like the scene on the shield, this act was also instigated by a god (4.85–104). On Pandarus as Athena's means to realize divine decision, see Schmitt, "Wesenszüge der griechischen Tragödie," 12 and note 34; and A. Maria van Erp Taalman Kip, "The Gods of the *Iliad* and the Fate of Troy," *Mnemosyne* 53 (2000): 391.

54. Some critics assume that Aphrodite was promised to Hephaestus as a reward for

the release of his mother. The assumption is based on a vase painting where Aphrodite is the first goddess who meets the procession coming toward her with gestures of dismay; see Martin L. West, "Fragmentary Homeric Hymn," for suggestions about lines 18–22 of the *Hymn to Dionysus* (6), and for a discussion of the visual evidence (7). This assumption strengthens even more the importance of this myth to this episode and its creative adaptation: although two important gods of the original story, Ares and Aphrodite, are still notable in Demodocus' song, their role is essentially transformed in order to create a different kind of signification.

55. Seeing, as claimed earlier, is also crucial to the story of Hephaestus' discovery and punishment of the adulterers, and in this context it seems relevant that before the second song the herald leads the blind bard to the same road that the Phaeacians take in order "to marvel at the games" (8.108), the same games in which Odysseus excels to such an extent that even a blind man could perceive his victory (8.195–96).

56. Hephaestus: βῆ ῥ᾽ ἴμεν (8.273, 277), εἴσατ᾽ ἴμεν (8.283), κιόντα (8.286), ἦλθε (8.300), ὑποστρέψας (8.301), βῆ δ᾽ ἴμεναι (8.303); Ares: βῆ δ᾽ ἴμεναι (8.287), ᾔει (8.290), βεβήκει (8.361); Aphrodite: ἐρχομένη (8.290), ἐείσατο (8.295), βεβήκει (8.361); Ares and Aphrodite: βάντε (8.296), βάντες (8.314).

57. On the meaning of *technê* in this context, see Ritoók, "Views," 344–46.

58. For other connections between Demodocus and Hephaestus, see Pucci, "Odysseus Polutropos," 197.

59. On this mixture and its implications, see also Schadewaldt, *Von Homers Welt und Werk*, 70–71.

60. For the importance of the notion of *charis* in archaic poetry, see MacLachlen, *Age of Charis*, 3–5.

61. While there are testimonies to the connection between Ares and Aphrodite (Walter Burkert, "Das Lied von Ares und Aphrodite: Zum Verhältnis von Odyssee und Ilias," *RhM* 103 [1960]: 133 note 6; Delcourt, *Héphaistos*, 81; Hainsworth, "A Commentary on Homer's *Odyssey*, Books v–viii," commenting on 8.267), we do not have much evidence about the marriage of Hephaestus and Aphrodite other than the passage in the *Odyssey*. See Burkert, "Das Lied von Ares und Aphrodite," 133 note 7.

62. See Scholium A *to Il.* 21.416; and Garvie, *Homer: Odyssey Books VI–VIII*, in his commentary on 8.318–19, for references. See also Zeitlin, *Playing the Other*, 36.

63. It is worth noting, however, that the appearance of Charis in book eighteen of the *Iliad* is problematic regardless of the question of Hephaestus' two wives, for it violates the normal "visit" scene; see Edwards, *The Iliad: A Commentary*, vol. 5, in his commentary on 18.380–81, 382. If Aphrodite's marriage to Hephaestus is an innovation of the poet of the *Odyssey*, then the divorce and remarriage to Charis shed explanatory light on this anomaly as well, for they emphasize the prominence of Charis in Hephaestus' life.

64. Contra Christopher G. Brown, "Ares, Aphrodite," 287–88, who regards the laughter in the first book of the *Iliad* as "good humoured" in contrast to this passage from the *Odyssey* where it is deemed serious and expressing punitive mockery toward the adulterers. Brown's claim that "we see a husband restoring both the integrity of the οἶκος [*oikos*, "household"] and his own honor by a public act of shaming" (291) ignores Hephaestus' essential failure to achieve the reaction he wanted.

65. But see Graver, "Dog-Helen," 53–58, for the different treatment given to the two sisters by the poet.

66. See Friedländer, "Lachende Götter," 4–5. On the epithet, see Hainsworth, "Good

and Bad Formulae," 45, Garvie, *Homer: Odyssey Books VI–VIII,* in his commentary on 8.361–62; and Milanezi, "Le Rire d'Hades," 239 and note 44. On smiling as an index of seduction and duplicity, see Arnould, *Le Rire et les larmes,* 90–92. The epithet reflects another subtle relation between Aphrodite and Hera, who "smiled" (*meidêsen*) at Hephaestus and took the chalice from him "with a smile" (*meidêsasa*) at the end of the opening book of the *Iliad* (1.595–96).

67. In this context it is worth quoting the terse remark of Taalman Kip: "The poet needed the gods to open the way for our pity and our awareness of the human condition. When we try to make them just and moralistic in spite of their creator, we dehumanize his poem" ("Gods of the *Iliad,*" 402).

CHAPTER 7

1. "[T]he possibility of the final movement away from adversity entails in itself a preceding stage of sufficient suffering; the ultimate turn of fortune involves an escape from evils which constitutes a serious impairment of status and prosperity"; Halliwell, "Aristotle's Poetics," 180.

2. Eagleton, *Sweet Violence,* 23–40, devotes an entire chapter to the topic of suffering entitled "The Value of Agony," where he justly repudiates the tendency to see suffering as either ennobling or purposive (29), let alone consoling (33–34), only in order to impregnate suffering with meaning once more: "But there is a difference between the belief that suffering is precious in itself, and the view that, though pain is generally to be avoided as an evil, there are kinds of affliction in which loss and gain go curiously together. It is around this aporetic point, at which dispossession begins to blur into power, blindness into insight and victimage into victory, that a good deal of tragedy turns. So does much revolutionary politics" (36). The last sentence is, of course, the gist of the matter, if not of the whole book, but its questionable association with the tragic is beyond the limits of my discussion. What should be emphasized here is the modulation of suffering into something positive. This contradictory moment, so sagaciously termed "aporetic," leads to an apotheosis that enables Eagleton to evoke both Christianity (39) and the notion of hope that is deeply embedded in his Marxism (39–40). Eagleton's maneuvering is ironically the same as that he dismisses in A. C. Bradley, whose *Shakespearian Tragedy* he summarizes as a "lengthy process of analysis [which] is finally thrown to the winds with a saving allusion to mystery" (136).

3. The resemblance of the *Iliad* and the *Odyssey* in terms of a similar basic pattern was noted by Lord, *The Singer of Tales,* 186, in his attempt to give a thorough description of the oral components shared by both epics. His pattern, however, is evidently nontragic, and its signification is confined to the domain of the technique of the poems' composition. Similarly, see Seaford's claim (*Reciprocity and Ritual,* 71) that "the *Iliad* and the *Odyssey* share a certain pattern, consisting of a 'crisis of ritual,' which is finally resolved by 'an act of vengeance' [. . .] which despite its uncontrolled violence is paradoxically assimilated to culture," that is not necessarily tragic.

4. Friedrich Nietzsche, "Die Geburt der Tragödie," in *Werke III,* 52–53 (Berlin and New York: de Gruyter, 1972 [1872]).

5. See the extensive note of Heubeck, "A Commentary on Homer's *Odyssey,* Books xxiii–xxiv," in his commentary on 22.411–16.

Bibliography

Adkins, Arthur W. H. *Merit and Responsibility: A Study in Greek Values.* Chicago and London: University of Chicago Press, 1960.

Adkins, Arthur W. H. "Threatening, Abusing, and Feeling Angry in the Homeric Poems." *JHS* 89 (1969): 7–21.

Ahl, F., and H. M. Roisman. *The Odyssey Re-Formed.* Ithaca and London: Cornell University Press, 1996.

Alden, Maureen J. *Homer beside Himself.* Oxford: Clarendon, 2000.

Allen, T. W., ed. *Homeri opera².* Oxford: Clarendon, 1917.

Anderson, Øivind. "Some Thoughts on the Shield of Achilles." *SO* 51 (1976): 5–18.

Arnould, Dominique. *Le Rire et les larmes dans la littérature greque d'Homère à Platon.* Paris: Les Belles Lettres, 1990.

Auerbach, Erich. *Mimesis: The Interpretation of Reality in Western Literature,* trans. Willard R. Trask. Princeton: Princeton University Press, 1953 (1946).

Austin, Norman. *Archery at the Dark of the Moon: Poetic Problems in Homer's Odyssey.* Berkeley: University of California Press, 1975.

Austin, Norman. "Name Magic in the *Odyssey.*" *California Studies in Classical Philology* 5 (1972): 1–19.

Bakhtin, M. Mikhail. *The Dialogic Imagination: Four Essays,* ed. Michael Holquist, trans. Caryl Emerson and Michael Holquist. Austin: University of Texas Press, 1981.

Bakker, Egbert J. *Poetry in Speech: Orality and Homeric Discourse.* Ithaca and London: Cornell University Press, 1997.

Bartfeld, Fernande. *L'effet tragique: Essai sur le tragique dans l'œuvre de Camus.* Paris and Geneva: Champion-Slatkin, 1988.

Belfiore, Elizabeth S. *Tragic Pleasures: Aristotle on Plot and Emotion.* Princeton: Princeton University Press, 1992.

Blundell, Sue. *The Origins of Civilization in Greek and Roman Thought.* London and Sydney: Croom Helm, 1986.

Bona, Giacomo. *Studi sull'Odissea.* Torino: G. Giappichelli, 1966.

Braswell, Bruce Karl. "Mythological Innovation in the *Iliad.*" *CQ* 21 (1971): 16–26.

Braswell, Bruce Karl. "The Song of Ares and Aphrodite: Theme and Relevance to *Odyssey* 8." *Hermes* 110 (1982): 129–37.

Brenk, Frederick E. "Dear Child: The Speech of Phoenix and the Tragedy of Achilleus in the Ninth Book of the *Iliad.*" *Eranos* 84 (1986): 77–86.

Brown, Calvin S. "Odysseus and Polyphemus: The Name and the Curse." *Comparative Literature* 18 (1966): 193–202.

Brown, Christopher G. "Ares, Aphrodite, and the Laughter of the Gods." *Phoenix* 43 (1989): 283–93.

Brown, Christopher G. "In the Cyclops' Cave: Revenge and Justice in *Odyssey* 9." *Mnemosyne* 49 (1996): 1–29.

Burkert, Walter. "Das Lied von Ares und Aphrodite: Zum Verhältnis von Odyssee und Ilias." *RhM* 103 (1960): 130–44.

Burnet, John, ed. *Platonis Opera.* Oxford: Clarendon, 1900–1907.

Butcher, Samuel Henry. *Aristotle's Theory of Poetry and Fine Arts⁴.* Introduction by John Gassner. New York: Dover, 1951 (1911).

Cairns, D. L. "Ethics, Ethology, Terminology: Iliadic Anger and the Cross-Cultured Study of Emotion." In *Ancient Anger: Perceptions from Homer to Galen,* ed. Susanna Braund and Glenn W. Most, special issue, *YCS* 32 (2003): 11–49.

Calame, Claude. *The Craft of Poetic Speech in Ancient Greece,* trans. Janice Orion. Ithaca and London: Cornell University Press, 1995 (1986).

Cave, Terence. *Recognitions: A Study in Poetics.* Oxford: Clarendon, 1988.

Chantraine, Pierre. *Dictionnaire étymologique de la langue grecque.* Paris: Klincksieck, 1968.

Chantraine, Pierre. *Grammaire homérique I–II.* Paris: Klincksieck, 1948–53.

Claus, David B. "*Aidos* in the Language of Achilles." *TAPA* 105 (1975): 13–28.

Clay, Jenny Strauss. *The Wrath of Athena: Gods and Men in the Odyssey.* Princeton: Princeton University Press, 1983.

Comte-Sponville, André. "L'absurde dans *Le Mythe de Sisyphe.*" In *Albert Camus et la philosophie,* ed. Anne-Marie Amiot and Jean-François Mattéi, 159–71. Paris: Presses Universitaires de France, 1997.

Crochet, Monique. *Les Mythes dans l'œuvre de Camus.* Paris: Editions Universitaires, 1973.

Crotty, Kevin. *The Poetics of Supplication: Homer's Iliad and Odyssey.* Ithaca and London: Cornell University Press, 1994.

Dällenbach, Lucien. *Le Récit spéculaire: Essai sur la mise en abyme.* Paris: Seuil, 1977.

Davies, Malcolm. "The Judgment of Paris and Solomon." *CQ* 53 (2003): 32–43.

Dawe, R. D. "Some Reflections on Ate and Hamartia." *HSCP* 72 (1967): 84–123.

de Jong, Irene J. F. "The Homeric Narrator and His Own *Kleos.*" *Mnemosyne* 59 (2006): 188–207.

de Jong, Irene J. F. *A Narratological Commentary on the Odyssey.* Cambridge: Cambridge University Press, 2001.

de Jong, Irene J. F. *Narrators and Focalizers: The Presentation of the Story in the Iliad.* Amsterdam: John Benjamins, 1987.

de Jong, Irene J. F. "The Subjective Style in Odysseus' Wanderings." *CQ* 42 (1992): 1–11.

Delcourt, Marie. *Héphaistos ou la légende du magicien.* Paris: Les Belles Lettres, 1982 (1957).

Denniston, J. D. *The Greek Particles*[2]. Oxford: Clarendon, 1959.

Dietrich, Bernard Clive. *Death, Fate, and the Gods*. London: Athlone Press, 1965.

Dodds, E. R. *The Greeks and the Irrational*. Berkeley and Los Angeles: University of California Press, 1951.

Doherty, Lillian Eileen. *Siren Songs: Gender, Audiences, and Narrators in the Odyssey*, Ann Arbor: University of Michigan Press, 1995.

Dougherty, Carol. *The Raft of Odysseus: The Ethnographic Imagination of Homer's Odyssey*. Oxford: Oxford University Press, 2001.

Dubel, Sandrine. "L'arme et la lyre: Remarques sur le sens du bouclier d'Achille dans l'Iliade." *Ktema* 20 (1995): 245–57.

Dué, Casey. *Homeric Variations on a Lament by Briseis*. Lanham, MD: Rowman and Littlefield, 2002.

Eagleton, Terry. *Sweet Violence: The Idea of the Tragic*. Malden and Oxford: Blackwell, 2003.

Edwards, Mark W. *The Iliad: A Commentary*. Vol. 5: *Books 17–20*. Cambridge: Cambridge University Press, 1991.

Else, Gerald Frank. *Aristotle's Poetics: The Argument*. Cambridge: Harvard University Press, 1957.

Emlyn-Jones, Chris. "The Reunion of Penelope and Odysseus." *G&R* 31 (1984): 1–18.

Erbse, Hatmut. *Scholia Graeca in Homeri Iliadem*. Berlin: de Gruyter, 1969–83.

Fajardo-Acosta, Fidel. *The Hero's Failure in the Tragedy of Odysseus: A Revisionist Analysis*. Lampeter, Great Britain: Edwin Mellen Press, 1990.

Faust, Manfred. "Die künstlerische Verwendung von κύων 'Hund' in den homerischen Epen." *Glotta* 48 (1970): 8–31.

Fenik, Bernard. *Studies in the Odyssey*. Wiesbaden: Franz Steiner Verlag, 1974.

Fenik, Bernard. "Stylization and Variety: Four Monologues in the *Iliad*." In *Homer: Tradition and Invention*, ed. Bernard Fenik, 68–90. Leiden: Brill, 1978.

Fenik, Bernard. *Typical Battle Scenes in the Iliad: Studies in the Narrative Techniques of Homeric Battle Description*. Wiesbaden: Franz Steiner Verlag, 1968.

Fernández-Galiano, Manuel. "A Commentary on Homer's *Odyssey* Books xxi–xxii." In *A Commentary on Homer's Odyssey*. Vol. 3: *Books xvii–xxiv*, ed. Joseph Russo, Manuel Fernández-Galiano, and Alfred Heubeck, 131–310. Oxford: Clarendon, 1992.

Finkelberg, Margalit. "Aristotle and Episodic Tragedy." *Greece and Rome* 53 (2006): 59–72.

Finkelberg, Margalit. *The Birth of Literary Fiction in Ancient Greece*. Oxford: Clarendon, 1998.

Finkelberg, Margalit. "The First Song of Demodocus." *Mnemosyne* 40 (1987): 128–32.

Finkelberg, Margalit. "Odysseus and the Genus 'Hero'." *G&R* 42 (1995): 1–14.

Finkelberg, Margalit. "Patterns of Human Error in Homer." *JHS* 115 (1995): 15–28.

Finkelberg, Margalit. "*Timê* and *Aretê* in Homer." *CQ* 48 (1998): 14–28.

Foley, Helene P. "'Reverse Similes' and Sex Roles in the Odyssey." *Arethusa* 11 (1978): 7–26.

Ford, Andrew. *Homer: The Poetry of the Past*. Ithaca and London: Cornell University Press, 1992.

Fränkel, Hermann. *Die homerischen Gleichnisse*. Göttingen: Vanderhoeck and Ruprecht, 1921.

Fränkel, Hermann. *Early Greek Poetry and Philosophy: A History of Greek Epic, Lyric, and Prose to the Middle of the Fifth Century*, trans. Moses Hadas and James Willis. New York and London: Harcourt Brace Jovanovich, 1973 (1962).

Frede, Dorothea. "Necessity, Chance, and 'What Happens for the Most Part' in Aristotle's *Poetics.*" In *Essays on Aristotle's Poetics,* ed. Amélie Oksenberg Rorty, 197–219. Princeton: Princeton University Press, 1992.

Friedländer, Paul. "Lachende Götter." In *Studien zur antiken Literatur und Kunst,* 3–18. Berlin: de Gruyter, 1969 (1934).

Friedrich, Rainer. "Everything to Do with Dionysos?" In *Tragedy and the Tragic: Greek Theatre and Beyond,* ed. M. S. Silk, 257–83. Oxford: Clarendon, 1996.

Friedrich, Rainer. "Heroic Man and *Polymetis:* Odysseus in the *Cyclopeia.*" *GRBS* 28 (1987): 121–33.

Friedrich, Rainer. "The Hybris of Odysseus." *JHS* 111 (1991): 16–28.

Garvie, A. F. *Homer: Odyssey Books VI–VIII.* Cambridge: Cambridge University Press, 1994.

Gellrich, Michelle. *Tragedy and Theory: The Problem of Conflict since Aristotle.* Princeton: Princeton University Press, 1988.

Genette, Gérard. *Narrative Discourse: An Essay in Method,* trans. Jane E. Lewin. Ithaca and New York: Cornell University Press, 1980 (1972).

Gera, Deborah Levine. *Ancient Greek Ideas on Speech, Language, and Civilization.* Oxford: Oxford University Press, 2003.

Germain, Gabriel. *Genèse de l'Odyssée: Le Fantastique et le sacré.* Paris: Presses Universitaires de France, 1954.

Gide, André. *Journal, 1889–1939.* Paris: Bibliothèque de la Pléiade, 1948.

Gill, Christopher. *Personality in Greek Epic, Tragedy, and Philosophy: The Self in Dialogue.* Oxford: Clarendon, 1996.

Glanville, I. M. "Note on ΠΕΡΙΠΕΤΕΙΑ." *CQ* 41 (1947): 73–78.

Glenn, Justin. "The Polyphemus Folktale and Homer's *Kyklôpeia.*" *TAPA* 102 (1971): 133–81.

Goldhill, Simon. *Language, Sexuality, Narrative: The Oresteia.* Cambridge: Cambridge University Press, 1984.

Goldhill, Simon. *The Poet's Voice: Essays on Poetics and Greek Literature.* Cambridge: Cambridge University Press, 1991.

Goldhill, Simon. *Reading Greek Tragedy.* Cambridge: Cambridge University Press, 1986.

Graver, Margaret. "Dog-Helen and Homeric Insult." *Classical Antiquity* 14 (1995): 41–61.

Graziosi, Barbara. *Inventing Homer: The Early Reception of Epic.* Cambridge: Cambridge University Press, 2002.

Greenblatt, Stephen. *Marvelous Possessions: The Wonder of the New World.* Oxford: Clarendon, 1991.

Gresseth, Gerald K. "The Homeric Sirens." *TAPA* 101 (1970): 203–18.

Griffin, Jasper. "Homer and Excess." In *Homer: Beyond Oral Poetry,* ed. J. M. Bremer, I. J. F. de Jong, and J. Kalf, 85–104. Amsterdam: B. R. Grüner, 1987.

Griffin, Jasper. *Homer: Iliad 9.* Oxford: Clarendon, 1995.

Griffin, Jasper. *Homer on Life and Death.* Oxford: Clarendon, 1980.

Griffin, Jasper. "Homeric Words and Speakers." *JHS* 106 (1986): 36–57.

Guillamaud, Patrice. "L'essence du kairos." *REA* 90 (1988): 359–71.

Hainsworth, J. Bryan. "A Commentary on Homer's *Odyssey* Books v–viii." In *A Commentary on Homer's Odyssey.* Vol. 1: *Introduction and Books i–viii,* ed. Alfred Heubeck, Stephanie West, and J. Bryan Hainsworth, 249–385. Oxford: Clarendon, 1988.

Hainsworth, J. Bryan. "Good and Bad Formulae." In *Homer Tradition and Invention,* ed. Bernard C. Fenik, 41–50. Leiden: Brill, 1978.

Hainsworth, J. Bryan. *The Iliad: A Commentary.* Vol. 3: *Books 9–12.* Cambridge: Cambridge University Press, 1993.

Halliwell, Stephen. *The Aesthetics of Mimesis: Ancient Texts and Modern Problems.* Princeton and Oxford: Princeton University Press, 2002.

Halliwell, Stephen. *Aristotle's Poetics.* Chicago: University of Chicago Press, 1998 (1986).

Halliwell, Stephen. "Greek Laughter and the Problem of the Absurd." *Arion* 13, no. 2 (2005): 121–46.

Harrison, E. L. "Odysseus and Demodocus: Homer, Odyssey θ 492f." *Hermes* 99 (1971): 378–79.

Hedreen, Guy. "The Return of Hephaistos: Dionysiac Procession Ritual and Its Creation on a Visual Narrative." *JHS* 124 (2004): 38–64.

Herington, Cecil John. *Poetry into Drama: Early Tragedy and the Greek Poetic Tradition.* Berkeley: University of California Press, 1985.

Herman, Gabriel. *Ritualised Friendship and the Greek City.* Cambridge: Cambridge University Press, 1987.

Hernández, Pura Nieto. "Back in the Cave of the Cyclops." *AJP* 121 (2000): 345–66.

Heubeck, Alfred. "A Commentary on Homer's *Odyssey* Books ix–xii." In *A Commentary on Homer's Odyssey.* Vol. 2: *Books ix–xvi,* ed. Alfred Heubeck and Arie Hoekstra, 3–143. Oxford: Clarendon, 1989.

Heubeck, Alfred. "A Commentary on Homer's *Odyssey* Books xxiii–xxiv." In *A Commentary on Homer's Odyssey.* Vol. 3: *Books xvii–xxiv,* ed. Joseph Russo, Manuel Fernández-Galiano, and Alfred Heubeck, 313–418. Oxford: Clarendon, 1992.

Howald, Ernst. "Meleager und Achill." *RM* 73 (1924): 403–25.

Iser, Wolfgang. *The Act of Reading: A Theory of Aesthetic Response.* Baltimore and London: Johns Hopkins University Press, 1978.

Janko, Richard. *The Iliad: A Commentary.* Vol. 4: *Books 13–16.* Cambridge: Cambridge University Press, 1994.

Jörgensen, Ove. "Das Auftreten der Götter in den Büchern ι–μ der Odyssee." *Hermes* 39 (1904): 357–82.

Kahane, Ahuvia. *Diachronic Dialogues: Authority and Continuity in Homer and the Homeric Tradition.* Oxford: Lexington Books, 2005.

Kakridis, Johannes Th. *Homeric Researches.* Lund: C. W. K. Gleerup, 1949.

Kim, Jinyo. *The Pity of Achilles: Oral Style and the Unity of the Iliad.* Lanham, MD: Rowman and Littlefield, 2000.

Kinneavy, James L. "*Kairos* in Classical and Modern Rhetorical Theory." In *Rhetoric and Kairos: Essays in History, Theory, and Praxis,* ed. Phillip Sipiora and James S. Baumlin, 58–76. Albany: State University of New York Press, 2002.

Kirk, G. S. *The Iliad: A Commentary.* Vol. 1: *Books 1–4.* Cambridge: Cambridge University Press, 1985.

Kirk, G. S. *The Iliad: A Commentary.* Vol. 2: *Books 5–8.* Cambridge: Cambridge University Press, 1990.

Kirk, G. S. *Myth: Its Meaning and Functions in Ancient and Other Cultures.* Cambridge: Cambridge University Press; Berkeley: University of California Press, 1970.

Kullmann, Wolfgang. "Gods and Men in the *Iliad* and the *Odyssey.*" *HSCP* 89 (1985): 1–23.

Latacz, Joachim, René Nünlist, and Magdalene Stoevesandt. *Homers Ilias Gesamtkommentar Band I erster Gesang (A) Faszikel 2: Kommentar.* Munich and Leipzig: K. G. Saur, 2002.

Lateiner, Donald. *Sardonic Smile: Nonverbal Behavior in Homeric Epic.* Ann Arbor: University of Michigan Press, 1995.

Lesky, Albin. "Göttliche und menschliche Motivation im homerischen Epos." *SHAW* 4 (1961): 5–52.

Lévi-Valensi, Jacqueline, ed. *Albert Camus Œuvres Complètes I: 1931–1944.* Paris: Bibliothèque de la Pléiade, 2006.

Lévi-Valensi, Jacqueline, ed. *Albert Camus Œuvres Complètes II: 1944–1948.* Paris: Bibliothèque de la Pléiade, 2006.

Levine, Daniel B. "*Odyssey* 18: Iros as Paradigm for the Suitors." *CJ* 77 (1982): 200–204.

Lloyd-Jones, H., and N. G. Wilson, eds. *Sophoclis fabulae.* Oxford: Clarendon, 1990.

Lohmann, Dieter. *Die Komposition der Reden in der Ilias.* Berlin: de Gruyter, 1970.

Lord, Alfred B. *The Singer of Tales.* Cambridge: Harvard University Press, 1960.

Lucas, D. W. *Aristotle: Poetics.* Oxford: Clarendon, 1972.

Lynn-George, Michael. *Epos, Word, Narrative, and the Iliad.* Atlantic Highlands, NJ: Humanities Press International, 1988.

Lynn-George, Michael. "Structures of Care in the *Iliad.*" *CQ* 46 (1996): 1–26.

Mackie, Rice. "Song and Storytelling: An Odyssean Perspective." *TAPA* 127 (1997): 77–95.

MacLachlen, Bonnie. *The Age of Charis.* Princeton: Princeton University Press, 1993.

Macleod, C. W. "Homer on Poetry and the Poetry of Homer." In *Collected Essays,* 1–15. Oxford: Clarendon, 1983.

Macleod, C. W. *Iliad, Book XXIV.* Cambridge: Cambridge University Press, 1982.

Mainoldi, Carla. *L'image du loup et du chien dans la Grèce ancienne.* Paris: Ophrys, 1984.

Malkin, Irad. *The Returns of Odysseus: Colonization and Ethnicity.* Berkeley: University of California Press, 1998.

March, Jennifer R. *The Creative Poet.* Bulletin Supplement 49. London: Institute of Classical Studies, 1987.

Marg, Walter. "Das erste Lied des Demodokus." In *Navicula Chiloniensis: Studia Philologica Felici Jacoby Professori Chiloniensi Emerito Octogenario Oblata,* 16–29. Leiden: Brill, 1956.

Martin, Richard P. *The Language of Heroes: Speech and Performance in the Iliad.* Ithaca and London: Cornell University Press, 1989.

Mattes, Wilhelm. *Odysseus bei den Phäaken: Kritisches zur Homeranalyse.* Würzburg: K. Triltsch, 1958.

McHale, Brian. "Cognition *en Abyme:* Models, Manuals, Maps." *Partial Answers* 4 (2006): 175–89.

Milanezi, Silvia. "Le Rire d'Hadès." *DHA* 21 (1995): 231–45.

Mondi, Robert. "The Homeric Cyclopes: Folktale, Tradition, and Theme." *TAPA* 113 (1983): 17–38.

Morrison, J. V. "*Kerostasia,* the Dictates of Fate, and the Will of Zeus in the *Iliad.*" *Arethusa* 30 (1997): 273–96.

Most, Glenn W. "Anger and Pity in Homer's *Iliad.*" In *Ancient Anger: Perceptions from Homer to Galen,* ed. Susanna Braund and Glenn W. Most, special issue, *YCS* 32 (2003): 50–75.

Most, Glenn W. "Generating Genres: The Idea of the Ttragic." In *Matrices of Genre: Authors, Canons, and Society,* ed. Mary Depew and Dirk Obbink, 15–35. Cambridge: Harvard University Press, 2000.

Moulton, Carroll. *Similes in the Homeric Poems.* Göttingen: Vandenhoeck and Ruprecht, 1977.

Nagy, Gregory. *The Best of the Achaeans: Concepts of the Hero in Ancient Greek Poetry.* Baltimore and London: Johns Hopkins University Press, 1979.

Nagy, Gregory. "Reading Bakhtin Reading the Classics." In *Bakhtin and the Classics,* ed. R. Bracht Branham, 71–96. Evanston: Northwestern University Press, 2002.

Newton, Rick M. "Odysseus and Hephaestus in the *Odyssey.*" *CJ* 83 (1987): 12–20.

Nietzsche, Friedrich. "Die Geburt der Tragödie." In *Werke III,* 5–152. Berlin and New York: de Gruyter, 1972 (1872).

Nussbaum, Martha C. *The Fragility of Goodness: Luck and Ethics in Greek Tragedy and Philosophy.* Cambridge: Cambridge University Press, 1986.

O'Brien, Joan. "Homer's Savage Hera." *CJ* 86 (1990): 105–25.

O'Sullivan, James N. "Nature and Culture in *Odyssey* 9." *SO* 65 (1990): 7–17.

Olson, S. Douglas. "*Odyssey* 8: Guide, Force, and the Subversive Poetics of Desire." *Arethusa* 22 (1989): 135–44.

Page, Denys. *The Homeric Odyssey.* Oxford: Clarendon, 1955.

Parry, Adam M. "The Language of Achilles." In *The Language of Achilles and Other Papers,* 1–7. Oxford: Clarendon, 1989 (1956).

Parry, Hugh. "The *Apologos* of Odysseus: Lies, All Lies?" *Phoenix* 48 (1994): 1–20.

Parry, Milman. *The Making of Homeric Verse: The Collected Papers of Milman Parry.* Oxford: Oxford University Press, 1971.

Pascal, Georges. "Albert Camus ou le philosophe malgré lui." In *Albert Camus et la philosophie,* ed. Anne-Marie Amiot and Jean-François Mattéi, 173–88. Paris: Presses Universitaires de France, 1997.

Peradotto, John. "Bakhtin, Milman Parry, and the Problem of Homeric Originality." In *Bakhtin and the Classics,* ed. R. Bracht Branham, 60–70. Evanston: Northwestern University Press, 2002.

Peradotto, John. *Man in the Middle Voice: Name and Narration in the Odyssey.* Princeton: Princeton University Press, 1990.

Perkell, Christine. "Reading the Laments of *Iliad* 24." In *Lament: Studies in the Ancient Mediterranean and Beyond,* ed. Ann Suter, 93–117. Oxford: Oxford University Press, forthcoming.

Podlecki, A. J. "Guest-Gifts and Nobodies in *Odyssey* 9." *Phoenix* 15 (1961): 125–33.

Pucci, Pietro. *Odysseus Polutropos: Intertextual Readings in the Odyssey and the Iliad.* Ithaca and London: Cornell University Press, 1987.

Pucci, Pietro. *The Song of the Sirens: Essays on Homer.* Lanham, MD: Rowman and Littlefield, 1998.

Pulleyn, Simon. *Homer: Iliad I.* Oxford: Oxford University Press, 2000.

Pulleyn, Simon. *Prayer in Greek Religion.* Oxford: Clarendon, 1997.

Rabel, Robert J. *Plot and Point of View in the Iliad.* Ann Arbor: University of Michigan Press, 1997.

Rabel, Robert J. "The Shield of Achilles and the Death of Hector." *Eranos* 87 (1989): 81–90.

Race, William H. "The Word Καιρός in Greek Drama." *TAPA* 111 (1981): 197–213.

Redfield, James M. *Nature and Culture in the Iliad: The Tragedy of Hector².* Durham and London: Duke University Press, 1994.

Reece, Steve. *The Stranger's Welcome: Oral Theory and the Aesthetics of the Homeric Hospitality Scene.* Ann Arbor: University of Michigan Press, 1993.

Reinhardt, Karl. "The Adventures in the *Odyssey.*" In *Reading the Odyssey: Selected Interpetive Essays,* ed. Seth L. Schein, 63–132. Princeton: Princeton University Press, 1996 (1948).

Reinhardt, Karl. "Das Parisurteil." In *Tradition und Geist,* 16–36. Göttingen: Vandenhoeck and Ruprecht, 1960 (1938).

Richardson, Nicholas. *The Iliad: A Commentary.* Vol. 6: *Books 21–24.* Cambridge: Cambridge University Press, 1993.

Richardson, Scott. "The Devious Narrator of the *Odyssey.*" *CJ* 101 (2006): 337–59.

Richardson, Scott. *The Homeric Narrator.* Nashville: Vanderbilt University Press, 1990.

Rimmon-Kenan, Shlomith. *Narrative Fiction: Contemporary Poetics.* London: Routledge, 1983.

Ritoók, Zs. "The Views of Early Greek Epic on Poetry and Art." *Mnemosyne* 42 (1989): 331–48.

Rose, Gilbert P. "Odysseus' Barking Heart." *TAPA* 109 (1979): 215–30.

Rose, Peter W. *Sons of the Gods, Children of Earth: Ideology and Literary Form in Ancient Greece.* Ithaca and London: Cornell University Press, 1992.

Rostagni, Augusto. "Un nuovo capitolo nella storia della retorica e della sofistica." *Studi italiani di filologica classica,* n.s. 2 (1922): 148–201.

Ruijgh, C. J. "D'Homère aux origines proto-mycéniennes de la tradition épique." In *Homeric Questions,* ed. Jan Paul Crielaard, 1–97. Amsterdam: J. C. Gieben, 1995.

Russo, Joseph. "A Commentary on Homer's *Odyssey* Books xvii–xx." In *A Commentary on Homer's Odyssey.* Vol. 3: *Books xvii–xxiv,* ed. Joseph Russo, Manuel Fernández-Galiano, and Alfred Heubeck, 3–127. Oxford: Clarendon, 1992.

Rutherford, R. B. *Homer: Odyssey Books XIX and XX.* Cambridge: Cambridge University Press, 1992.

Rutherford, R. B. "From the *Iliad* to the *Odyssey.*" *BICS* 38 (1991–93): 37–55.

Rutherford, R. B. "The Philosophy of the *Odyssey.*" *JHS* 106 (1986): 145–62.

Rutherford, R. B. "Tragic Form and Feeling in the *Iliad.*" *JHS* 102 (1982): 145–60.

Sagi, Avi. "Is the Absurd the Problem or the Solution? *The Myth of Sisyphus* Reconsidered." *Philosophy Today* 38 (1994): 278–84.

Schadewaldt, Wolfgang. *Iliasstudien.* Leipzig: Abhandlungen der philologisch-historischen Klasse der Sächsischen Akademie der Wissenschaften Band XLIII, Nr. VI, 1938.

Schadewaldt, Wolfgang. *Neue Kriterien zur Odyssee-Analyse: Die Wiedererkennung des Odysseus und der Penelope.* Heidelberg: Carl Winter Universitätsverlag, 1966 (1959).

Schadewaldt, Wolfgang. *Von Homers Welt und Werk.* Leipzig: Koehler and Amelang, 1944.

Schechet, Nita. *Narrative Fissures.* Cranbury, NJ: Associated University Presses, 2005.

Schein, Seth L. *The Mortal Hero: An Introduction to Homer's Iliad.* Berkeley: University of California Press, 1984.

Schmidt, Jens-Uwe. "Ares und Aphrodite—der göttliche Ehebruch und die theologischen Intentionen des Odysseedichters." *Philologus* 142 (1998): 195–219.

Schmitt, Arbogast. "Wesenszüge der griechischen Tragödie: Schicksal, Schuld, Tragik." In *Tragödie: Idee und Transformation,* ed. Hellmut Flashar, 5–49. Stuttgart: Teubner, 1997.

Schmitz, Christine. "'Denn auch Niobe . . .'—Die Bedeutung der Niobe-Erzählung in Achills Rede (Ω599–620)." *Hermes* 129 (2001): 145–57.

Schneider, Carsten. "Herr und Hund auf archaischen Grabstelen." *JDAI* 115 (2000): 1–36.

Scodel, Ruth. "The Achaean Wall and the Myth of Destruction." *HSCP* 86 (1982): 33–50.

Scodel, Ruth. "The Autobiography of Phoenix: *Iliad* 9.444–95." *AJP* 103 (1982): 128–36.

Scodel, Ruth. "The Word of Achilles." *CP* 84 (1989): 91–99.

Scott, William C. *The Oral Nature of the Homeric Simile*. Leiden: Brill, 1974.

Scully, Stephen. "The Language of Achilles: The ΟΧΘΗΣΑΣ Formulas." *TAPA* 114 (1984): 11–27.

Seaford, Richard. *Reciprocity and Ritual: Homer and Tragedy in the Developing City-State*. Oxford: Clarendon, 1994.

Segal, Charles. "Divine Justice in the *Odyssey:* Poseidon, Cyclops, and Helios." *AJP* 113 (1992): 489–518.

Segal, Charles. *The Theme of the Mutilation of the Corpse in the Iliad*. Leiden: Brill, 1971.

Shackleton Bailey, D. R., ed. *Q. Horatius Flaccus: Opera*⁴. Munich and Leipzig: Teubner, 2001.

Silk, Michael. *Homer:* The Iliad. Cambridge: Cambridge University Press, 1987.

Sipiora, Phillip. "Introduction; The Ancient Concept of *Kairos*." In *Rhetoric and Kairos: Essays in History, Theory, and Praxis,* ed. Phillip Sipiora and James S. Baumlin, 1–22. Albany: State University of New York Press, 2002.

Slatkin, Laura. *The Power of Thetis: Allusion and Interpretation in the Iliad*. Berkeley: University of California Press, 1991.

Smith, John E. "Time, Times, and the 'Right Time': *Chronos* and *Kairos*." *Monist* 53 (1969): 1–13.

Snodgrass, Anthony. *Homer and the Artists*. Cambridge: Cambridge University Press, 1998.

Stanford, W. B. *The Odyssey of Homer*². London: Macmillan, 1959.

Stanford, W. B. *The Ulysses Theme: A Study in the Adaptability of a Traditional Hero*². Ann Arbor: University of Michigan Press, 1963.

Stanley, Keith. *The Shield of Homer: Narrative Structure in the Iliad*. Princeton: Princeton University Press, 1993.

Suerbaum, Werner. "Die Ich-Erzählungen des Odysseus: Überlegungen zur epischen Technik der *Odyssee*." *Poetica* 2 (1968): 150–77.

Taalman Kip, A. Maria van Erp. "The Gods of the *Iliad* and the Fate of Troy." *Mnemosyne* 53 (2000): 385–402.

Taplin, Oliver. "Comedy and the Tragic." In *Tragedy and the Tragic: Greek Theatre and Beyond,* ed. M. S. Silk, 188–202. Oxford: Clarendon, 1996.

Taplin, Oliver. "The Earliest Quotation of the *Iliad*?" In *"Owls to Athens": Essays on Classical Subjects Presented to Sir Kenneth Dover,* ed. E. M. Craik, 109–12. Oxford: Clarendon, 1990.

Taplin, Oliver. *Homeric Soundings: The Shaping of the Iliad*. Oxford: Clarendon, 1992.

Taplin, Oliver. "The Shield of Achilles within the *Iliad*." *G&R* 27 (1980): 1–21.

Teffeteller, Annette. "Homeric Excuses." *CQ* 53 (2003): 13–31.

Thalmann, William G. *Conventions of Form and Thought in Early Greek Epic Poetry*. Baltimore and London: Johns Hopkins University Press, 1984.

Unamuno, Miguel de. *The Tragic Sense of Life,* trans. J. E. Crawford Flitch. London: Macmillan, 1921 (1912).

Untersteiner, Mario. "Il concetto di δαίμων in Omero." *Atene e Roma* 41 (1939): 95–134.

Vidal-Naquet, Pierre. "Land and Sacrifice in the *Odyssey:* A Study of Religious and Mythical Meanings." In *Reading the Odyssey: Selected Interpetive Essays,* ed. Seth L. Schein, 33–55. Princeton: Princeton University Press, 1996 (1970).

Von der Mühll, Peter. *Kritisches Hypomnema zur Ilias*. Basel: Verlag Friedrich Reinhardt, 1952.

Webber, Alice. "The Hero Tells His Name: Formula and Variation in the Phaeacian Episode of the Odyssey." *TAPA* 119 (1989): 1–13.

West, Martin L. "The Fragmentary Homeric Hymn to Dionysus." *ZPE* 134 (2001): 1–11.

West, Martin L., ed. *Homerus: Ilias.* Stuttgart: Teubner, 1998–2000.

West, Stephanie. "A Commentary on Homer's *Odyssey* Books i–iv." In *A Commentary on Homer's Odyssey.* Vol. 1: *Introduction and Books i–viii,* ed. Alfred Heubeck, Stephanie West, and J. B. Hainsworth, 51–245. Oxford: Clarendon, 2001 (1988).

West, Stephanie. "Laertes Revisited." *PCPhS* 215 (1989): 113–43.

White, Stephen E. "Aristotle's Favorite Tragedies." In *Essays on Aristotle's* Poetics, ed. Amélie Oksenberg Rorty, 221–40. Princeton: Princeton University Press, 1992.

Whitman, Cedric H. *Homer and the Heroic Tradition.* Cambridge: Harvard University Press, 1958.

Willcock, M. M. "Mythological Paradeigma in the *Iliad.*" *CQ* 14 (1964): 141–54.

Willcock, M. M., ed. *The Iliad of Homer: Books I–XII.* London: Macmillan, 1978.

Willcock, M. M., ed. *The Iliad of Homer: Books XIII–XXIV.* London: Macmillan, 1984.

Wilson, Donna F. *Ransom, Revenge, and Heroic Identity in the Iliad.* Cambridge: Cambridge University Press, 2002.

Wilson, Emily R. *Mocked with Death: Tragic Overliving from Sophocles to Milton.* Baltimore and London: Johns Hopkins University Press, 2004.

Wyatt, William F. "Homeric ʼATH." *AJP* 103 (1982): 247–76.

Zanker, Graham. "Beyond Reciprocity: The Akhilleus-Priam Scene in *Iliad* 24." In *Reciprocity in Ancient Greece,* ed. Christopher Gill, Norman Postlethwaite, and Richard Seaford, 73–92. Oxford: Oxford University Press, 1998.

Zanker, Graham. *The Heart of Achilles: Characterization and Personal Ethics in the Iliad.* Ann Arbor: University of Michigan Press, 1994.

Zeitlin, Froma I. *Playing the Other: Gender and Society in Classical Greek Literature.* Chicago: University of Chicago Press, 1996.

General Index

Index to the *Iliad* and the *Odyssey*